Effective Teaching

THE NATIONAL SOCIETY
FOR THE STUDY OF EDUCATION

Series on Contemporary Educational Issues
Kenneth J. Rehage, Series Editor

The 1991 Titles

Effective Teaching: Current Research, Hersholt C. Waxman and Herbert J. Walberg, editors

Better Schooling for the Children of Poverty: Alternatives to Conventional Wisdom, Michael S. Knapp and Patrick Shields, editors

The National Society for the Study of Education also publishes Yearbooks which are distributed by the University of Chicago Press. Inquiries regarding all publications of the Society, as well as inquiries about membership in the Society, may be addressed to the Secretary-Treasurer, 5835 Kimbark Avenue, Chicago, IL 60637. Membership in the Society is open to any who wish to receive its publications.

Effective Teaching: Current Research

Edited by

Hersholt C. Waxman
University of Houston

Herbert J. Walberg
University of Illinois at Chicago

McCutchan Publishing Corporation
P.O. Box 774, 2940 San Pablo Ave., Berkeley, CA 94702

ISBN 0–8211–2269–X
Library of Congress Catalog Card Number 91–60679

Copyright © 1991 by McCutchan Publishing Corporation

Printed in the United States of America

Contents

Contributors

Christopher M. Clark, Michigan State University
Saundra Dunn, Michigan State University
Carolyn M. Evertson, Vanderbilt University
Barry J. Fraser, Curtin University of Technology
H. Jerome Freiberg, University of Houston
N. L. Gage, Stanford University
Adam Gamoran, University of Wisconsin, Madison
Pamela Grossman, University of Washington
David W. Johnson, University of Minnesota
Roger T. Johnson, University of Minnesota
Stephanie L. Knight, Texas A & M University
Margaret C. Needels, California State University, Hayward
Martin Nystrand, University of Wisconsin
Allan C. Ornstein, Loyola University of Chicago
Jane Stallings, Texas A & M University
Sam Stringfield, Johns Hopkins University
Charles Teddlie, Louisiana State University
Kenneth Tobin, Florida State University
Herbert J. Walberg, University of Illinois at Chicago
Margaret C. Wang, Temple University
Hersholt C. Waxman, University of Houston
Regina Weade, University of Florida
Phillip H. Winne, Simon Fraser University

Preface

Nearly a decade ago, we analyzed nineteen publications that reviewed the effect of teaching methods on what students learn. We reported our findings in an article entitled "The Relation of Teaching and Learning: A Review of Reviews of the Process-Product Paradigm."[1] At that time we acknowledged that some of the research was disappointing. The reviews had a "great number of serious flaws in search and selection procedures, validity assessments and summarization of empirical results" (p. 118). We concluded, nonetheless, that the results in the primary studies were sufficient to have produced "a substantial body of reasonably consistent, hard-won knowledge about the associations of teaching processes and student learning" (p. 118).

Now, nearly a decade later, we see considerable progress in the field of research on effective teaching. Far more results have accumulated, they have been systematically integrated and criticized, and new ways of studying teaching have evolved. The present volume highlights some of this current research on effective teaching.

Part One, "Conceptual Critiques and Reviews of Research," begins with a chapter by Margaret Needels and N. L. Gage, who

---

[1]Published in *Contemporary Education* 1 (1982): 103–120.

review the criticisms of research on the effects of teaching on learning and categorize them into five areas: conceptualization, methodology, productivity, interpretation, and application. They make an important distinction between the *essence* of process-product research on teaching (i.e., the search for relations between teaching process and student product variables) and the *accidents* of this research (i.e., incidental features that may or may not be present in any study without altering its process-product character). They provide an agenda for process-product research on teaching that calls for improved theory based on cognitive conceptions of learning, on more complete conceptualization, and on studies conducted on all of the various combinations of school subjects, grade levels, cultural groups, teaching methods, and types of educational outcomes.

Herbert Walberg summarizes in Chapter Two research syntheses that have been conducted in the areas of teaching and instruction. He begins with the effects of the psychological elements of teaching and discusses methods and patterns of teaching. After examining systems of instruction that require special planning, student grouping, and materials, he describes effects that are unique to reading, writing, science, and mathematics. He concludes by considering results concerning special students and techniques, and the effects of training on teachers.

In the next chapter Allan Ornstein highlights the importance of theory in guiding practice. He discusses the distinction between teaching as a science and teaching as an art, describes a set of teacher-student variables, and points out how researchers can study multiple relationships among these variables. He examines how teaching style influences research on teacher effectiveness. Finally, he considers the purposes as well as some of the dangers of research on teacher effectiveness.

Margaret Wang and Herbert Walberg report in Chapter Four the results of a survey of professional opinion about teaching and other practices and policies that make for effective education. Approximately one thousand professionals representing eight different groups responded to the survey, which was developed to investigate questions about consensus on variables considered important for learning. The findings from this study suggest a number of variables judged by practitioners to be of high importance in planning teaching and learning environments.

Part Two, "Classroom Observations of Teaching," comprises three chapters dealing with ways in which classroom observation may be used to improve teaching. In the first of these, Jane Stallings and H. Jerome Freiberg describe the development of a comprehensive observation system, the Stallings Observation System (SOS), and they report the results of several studies in which the SOS was used to promote teachers' use of effective teaching strategies. They also describe how a project, "Learning to Teach in Inner-City Schools," has incorporated classroom observation as part of the student teaching experience for those planning to teach in inner-city schools.

In Chapter Six, Carolyn Evertson and Regina Weade consider research from sociolinguistic and ethnographic perspectives. They illustrate how typical methods of classroom observation can be used with alternative sociolinguistic methods in order to examine the ways students and teachers jointly construct meanings in their classroom work. They demonstrate that the ways teachers orchestrate lessons signal instructional participation, present academic information, and influence student engagement and learning.

In Chapter Seven, Sam Stringfield and Charles Teddlie consider effective teaching from the perspective of research on school effects. They summarize some of the findings from pre-1985 school-effects research, pointing out that none of the studies provided classroom-level data. They describe the results of three recent school-effects studies that included observation. Their chapter concludes with a discussion of the implications of their work in which they highlight the processes that distinguish highly effective and ineffective schools.

Part Three, "Research on Teachers," begins with a chapter by Christopher Clark and Saundra Dunn, who summarize current research on teachers' planning, intentions, and routines. They consider theoretical issues related to teachers' planning, and they note some of the recent research in the areas of knowledge transformation, routines, changes in routine over time, and the role of published curriculum materials. They conclude by discussing teachers' planning in the context of other studies of teaching.

Pamela Grossman summarizes in Chapter Nine research on teachers' subject matter knowledge and the representation of content in teaching, pointing out how teachers' own background knowledge in a subject affects how they present the nature of knowing within a subject. She describes how teachers' pedagogical content knowledge affects classroom instruction, and she concludes by discussing the implications of research on teachers' knowledge for curricular changes in schools.

In Chapter Ten, Kenneth Tobin and Barry Fraser look at effective teaching by examining research on expert teachers. Their project, "Exemplary Practice in Science and Mathematics Education," was based on the assumption that much could be learned from case studies of the best science teachers. Their major findings are that exemplary teachers use management strategies that facilitate student engagement and encourage students to participate in learning activities, employ methods designed to increase students' understanding of science and mathematics, and maintain a favorable classroom learning environment. They describe an exemplary teacher and note the importance of epistemologies, beliefs, and values in describing teaching and learning practices.

Part Four, "Cognition, Engagement, Cooperation, and Motivation," contains chapters on each of these topics. Stephanie Knight and Hersholt Waxman focus on classroom instruction from the perspective of student cognition. They summarize the results of studies that examine the relations among students' perceptions of their cognitive strategies, of their teachers' behaviors related to these strategies, of their classroom environment, and of their academic achievement. Such research, they say, can provide both direct and indirect ways to improve classroom instruction.

Martin Nystrand and Adam Gamoran examine in Chapter Twelve students' engagement in the instructional activities of eighth- and ninth-grade English classes. They distinguish "procedural engagement" (i.e., students and teachers merely going through the motions of schooling) from "substantive engagement" (i.e., a sustained commitment to and involvement with academic work). They use examples from transcripts of classroom lessons to illustrate how "high-quality classroom discourse" is substantively engaging. They conclude with a discussion of the implications of their research for the teaching of literature and writing.

In Chapter Thirteen, David Johnson and Roger Johnson describe some of the essential components of effective cooperative learning: positive interdependence, face-to-face promotive interaction, individual accountability, interpersonal and small-group skills, and group processing. After reviewing major types of cooperative learning, they conclude by discussing approaches to implementing cooperative learning in schools and classrooms.

In the final chapter, Philip Winne provides guidelines for planning and providing instruction that develops positive motivation in classrooms. He describes a cognitive model of motivation and five kinds of motivational knowledge: attribution, efficacy, incentive, outcomes, and utility. He points out the relations among cognition, motivation, and affect and between teaching and motivation.

In inviting the chapter authors to contribute to this book, we expressed our intention to avoid duplicating recent voluminous works on research on teaching such as the *Handbook of Research on Teaching* published by the American Educational Research Association. We explained that we aimed not for complete coverage but an exemplary collection of current research with implications for the practice of teaching and the education of teachers.

Our intention was to represent a variety of points of view and methods of research encompassing, for example, both quantitative and qualitative approaches, which sometimes go their separate ways. On the other hand, we asked the authors to focus on substantive results, not details of research methodology that can be cited in previous publications.

We hoped the chapters would represent new theory and ideas, new methods for conducting research, and new problems uncovered. We also hoped to represent a variety of younger and senior scholars that might attract students and teachers to join their inquiries. If some of our readers join their endeavors, we will count the effort worthwhile.

Hersholt C. Waxman
Herbert J. Walberg

Part I

Conceptual Critiques and Reviews of Research

1

Essence and Accident in Process-Product Research on Teaching

Margaret C. Needels and N. L. Gage

Essential attributes are (1) such as belong to their subject as elements in its essential nature (e.g., line thus belongs to triangle, point to line . . .); (2) such that, while they belong to certain subjects, the subjects to which they belong are contained in the attribute's own defining formula. . . .

Extending this classification to all other attributes, I distinguish those that answer the above description as belonging essentially to their respective subjects; whereas attributes related in neither of these two ways to their subjects I call accidents or "coincidents," e.g., musical or white is a "coincident" of animal. [Aristotle, *Posterior Analytics*, Book I, Section 4]

Many societies set up schools, select and educate candidates for teaching, hire teachers, and send children to these teachers to receive a formal education. This education aims to help the children learn what the society considers good for its citizens and itself.

Although seemingly simple, this wonderful arrangement quickly runs into problems, including those concerning how teachers should

---

This chapter summarizes and updates a recent article by Gage and Needels (1989). The updating comprises new experiments and other literature, discussions of when process-product research should not be conducted and of how its results should not be used, and lessons from medical "patient-outcome" research.

3

be educated. Over the centuries, teacher education has rested on accumulated experience, common sense, and philosophical wisdom. Only in recent decades has anyone tried to apply scientific method— that great source of theoretical understanding and practical technology— to the question of how teachers should be educated.

Process-product research on teaching—that is, the search for relations between teaching processes and what students learn—began in earnest about 1960. Before that, research on teaching seldom examined processes in detail or products in the form of student achievement. Since its inception, many summaries and reviews of process-product research have appeared (see, e.g., Brophy and Good, 1986). In proportion to the magnitude, complexity, and importance of its concerns, process-product research on teaching may be regarded as having barely gotten started. Nonetheless, various critics, because they have discerned what they consider to be a host of shortcomings of process-product research, would not lament its demise. This chapter reviews and evaluates their criticisms, discusses the distinction between essence and accident in process-product research, and offers an agenda for such research.

We have categorized the criticisms as they relate to the conceptualization, methodology, productivity, and interpretation of such research. The conceptual criticisms bear on the philosophical and substantive commitments underlying process-product research. The methodological criticisms concern its designs and the methods of gathering and analyzing data. The productivity criticisms question the theoretical and practical yield of process-product research, and the criticisms of interpretation refer to the actual and potential interpretations of the research and uses of the research findings in teacher education. Although this categorization provides a useful organizational scheme, it also results in some questionable classifications of the criticisms. We shall try to face such issues as we go along.

One recurrent theme in our consideration of the criticisms is the ancient distinction (Aristotle, *Posterior Analytics*) between essence and accident. The distinction is crucial here. The essence of process-product research is the search for relations between process and product variables. Other features of such research are incidental. A flaw in the essence would be fatal to the enterprise. Flaws in the incidental features are in principle remediable.

CRITICISMS OF CONCEPTUALIZATION

The conceptual criticisms range widely over the intentional nature of teaching and the normative character of education. One criticism, argued by Macmillan and Garrison (1988, p. 75), is that in the process-product tradition, the unit of observation is a "behavior" of the teacher precisely and technically defined so as to require little or no inference to the teacher's intentions or to the context of the behavior that might give it a broader meaning. The criticism that process-product research does not consider the teachers' *self-reported* intentions is valid; such research falls under the rubric of research on teacher cognitions (reviewed by Clark and Peterson, 1986). The criticism focusing on the teacher's observed behavior concerns the degree to which context is considered in describing teacher behavior, and that criticism is not valid. These critics assume that the observers focus on a single, isolated behavior without concern for the preceding or subsequent behaviors, which provide context and meaning. Most research on human behavior is indeed concerned with the meaning of the behavior being investigated. The "low-inference" process variables used in some process-product research are not "no-inference" variables; they do entail inferences as to the meaning of the behaviors.

A process-product researcher in the classroom infers meaning from events concurrent with and close to a given behavior. Suppose a teacher utters words grammatically identifiable as a question. The researcher must infer the intent of the question, that is, whether it was intended to serve as a management tactic, a check on the student's understanding, a probe of the student's reasoning, or praise. By considering the behavior surrounding the question, the researcher can infer the meaning of the teacher's question. Typically, researchers do so; they do not record mere behavior without interpreting intention.

Another criticism is that process-product research designs disregard the time of day, school term, and subject matter. Thus Shulman (1986) wrote,

Data from early in an observational hour are combined with data from later on the same occasion. Data from fall may be combined with data from spring. Data from a unit on natural selection combines with data from a unit on the circulation of the blood. All these are seen as instances of teaching, an activity that transcends both individual teachers and specific situations." [P. 10]

Aggregation of some kind is indeed necessary in any research on teaching that seeks transsituational relationships, that is, relations of teaching behaviors to events outside their immediate context. But some process-product researchers have aggregated behaviors in more specific ways: they have, for example, studied process-product relationships within a given occasion, time of year, or unit of content (e.g., Crosson and Olson, 1969; Gage et al., 1971; Needels, 1989). The breadth of aggregation shapes the nature of the research problem, and no given breadth is intrinsic to a process-product approach. Relationships based on very small aggregations of process events can have great theoretical and practical value. Larger aggregations—across months and subject matters, for example—may also yield important relationships. Neither kind of aggregation is precluded by the process-product approach.

Critics also argue that the search for process-product relationships may disregard grade level, subject matter, or student characteristics. Such disregard would mean that investigators hypothesize the same process-product relationships in, for example, teaching first-grade reading with students from poor families and teaching tenth-grade geometry with students from middle-income families. But making such generalizations is not always the intent of researchers following the process-product approach. Gage (1979) analyzed the issue of generality of dimensions of teaching in this sense and considered the issue an empirical one. Some process-product relationships may turn out to have wide generality, while others may prove to be specific to particular grade levels, subject matters, and kinds of students.

Several critics (Tom, 1980; Garrison and Macmillan, 1984; Erickson, 1986) argue that because teaching is goal-directed and normative, it is unamenable to empirical investigation. This argument rests on the assertion that for any science seeking to develop laws, the existence and behavior of the objects of investigation (here, process-product relationships) must be consistent and stable, and human affairs do not have such stability and consistency. Thus, "social science" is an oxymoron. We have three responses to this criticism.

First, the critics seem to have difficulty distinguishing between statements properly based on intuition and those needing empirical evidence. The instability of the social world, including teaching, is a matter of degree, determined empirically. It may be that the world of teaching will become radically more unstable than has thus far proven to be the case. Cuban (1984) and Mehan (1979), among others, found teaching patterns unchanged over the past century. Only if instability increased greatly would the possibility of fairly stable and useful scientific knowledge about teaching be ruled out.

Second, process-product research does not assume regularities in the social world. Rather, it seeks to determine the degree to which regularities exist. Process-product investigators do not search for immutable laws of teaching—that is, relationships that will hold forever everywhere. Rather, they seek relationships whose stability and generality are themselves subject to empirical investigation.

And third, the normative nature of education does not place it beyond scientific investigation. Other human enterprises (such as medicine and engineering) also are heavily laden with normative concerns. Yet they have obviously benefited from scientific effort. Medical researchers do "treatment-outcome research" (Dubois and Brook, 1988; Wennberg, 1989), an approach sharing many of the attributes of process-product research on teaching. Those medical investigators attempt to identify relationships between the kind of treatment given a patient and the patient's subsequent health. Although it has a scientific basis, such medical research is not free of the normative complexities of medical practice (for example, the physician's competence in carrying out a particular treatment, the patient's consideration of risk when selecting a treatment, the patient's overall health, the monetary cost and availability of the treatment). These examples of normative concerns in medicine have their counterparts in process-product research on teaching.

Process-product research is also criticized for assuming one-way causal connections between teaching and learning—that is, assuming that what a teacher does affects what students learn (Erickson, 1986; Tom, 1984). This criticism rests on a false assumption, because process-product researchers recognize that many factors in the students' lives in addition to teaching affect learning. Recognizing the distinction between alterable and unalterable variables (Bloom, 1980), process-product researchers regard teaching as the locus of many alterable variables, which contrast with such unalterable factors as the student's genetic endowment and previous achievement. Process-product researchers have long recognized this distinction and have designed studies where unalterable variables have been controlled either statistically or through random assignment of teachers and their classes to different treatments.

This criticism is also concerned with the reciprocality of influence between teacher and pupils. Examples of such reciprocality are instances where pupil recalcitrance distracts teachers, and the resultant inappropriate teaching exacerbates pupil recalcitrance. Or students' correct responses help the teacher move ahead, and in turn the teacher's clarity fosters students' correct responses. Process-product researchers typically recognize this reciprocality. They focus on teachers' influence, however, because teachers have more power to improve what goes on.

Some critics (e.g., Erickson, 1986) have argued that the goals of prediction and control are not attainable in systems where cause is mediated by systems of symbols. According to this interpretive view, a teacher's actions may mean one thing for the teacher, another for student 1, another for student 2, and so on. Thus, any attempt to make causal connections between what a teacher does and what students learn can not succeed. Here, the critics are confused about whether the issue is philosophical or empirical. We need not conclude from the fact that pupils *may* differ radically in how they interpret a teacher's action that they *must* differ in that way. Let the empirical evidence resolve this issue.

The last conceptual criticism we address states that process-product research is atheoretical. We have responded to this criticism at some length elsewhere (see Gage and Needels, 1989, pp. 262–265). In that article we discuss the six kinds of theory identified by Snow (1973): formative hypotheses, elementisms, descriptive theories and taxonomies, conceptual theories and constructs, axiomatic theories, and broken axiomatic theories. We present evidence there to support our argument that process-product research has contributed to several of these kinds of theory and also to theory in the sense of an organized body of knowledge.

CRITICISMS OF METHODOLOGY

Process-product research has been criticized for seeking implausible relationships between teaching behavior occurring in one subject matter domain at one point in time and student achievement in another subject matter at a relatively distant point in time (Berliner, 1979). The issue here concerns the generalizability of teaching actions across time and subject matters: Can the teacher's actions observed and recorded in November, February, and April be considered representative of the teacher's actions during the months in which the teacher was not observed? Are similar teaching actions observed when an elementary school teacher teaches reading and mathematics? Are some teaching actions stable across the school year and subject matters while other actions are not stable? Empirical investigations of the stability of teaching actions contribute answers to these questions.

In any case, extrapolations across subject matters and months of the school year are *not* inherent in process-product studies of classroom teaching. Process-product studies have been conducted within specific subject matters (e.g., Anderson, Evertson, and Brophy, 1979; Good and Grouws, 1979; Needels, 1989; Rowe, 1974; Stallings, Needels, and Stayrook, 1979) and within small periods of time (e.g., Huh, 1986; Needels, 1989; Rosenshine, 1968).

The use of predetermined coding categories has been criticized. Erickson (1986) wrote that this method "gives no clear detailed evidence about the specific classroom processes that are claimed to lead to desired outcomes" (p. 133). It is true that the predetermined categories do not give as rich an account as ethnography can provide, for they constitute an abstraction from the welter of events, similar to that required in any scientific undertaking. The predetermined categories are usually based on prior unstructured observations that have identified teaching variables that may be related to certain student outcomes. This progression from descriptive to correlational research was discussed by Gage (1978) as one in which the process-product researcher conducts unstructured observations, develops categories from these observational data, and uses these categories in subsequent studies. Spindler and Spindler (1982) alluded to this process when they described the use of an observation system they had developed for their ethnographic research: "The statistical treatment of the I.A.I. [Instrumental Activities Inventory] provides a framework within which certain phases of the ethnographic study proceed, but the ethnographic study determines what will be in the instrument" (p. 42).

Reducing classroom events to a system of categories so devoid of detail that no interpretation can be made would indeed be a useless exercise. Process-product researchers must know the particular context in which their research is being conducted and interpret the observational data within that context. Nothing about process-

product research precludes making such a contextually bound interpretation while at the same time seeking relationships that may apply
across a variety of similar contexts.

Tom (1984) wrote that process-product research on teaching is
sorely lacking in its ability to account for variables intervening
between process and product. This criticism fails because process-
product research has indeed embraced such intervening factors. Such
variables show up in the structural models of the teaching-learning
process used by various investigators. Cooley and Leinhardt (1976)
used "motivation." McDonald and Elias (1976) used "student in-
attentive behavior." Corno (1979) used "student anxiety." Stayrook
(1982) used "the student's variety of aims." Helmke, Schneider, and
Weinert (1986) used "student engagement."

In another criticism of methodology, Macmillan and Garrison
(1984) wrote that "experimentation to verify the causal connections
between teacher behaviors and student outcomes is possible, but lies
mostly in the future" (p. 17). More than a decade before this criticism
was made, Rosenshine and Furst (1973) discussed the need for
experiments in research on teaching and a desirable progression from
descriptive to correlational to experimental studies. We (Gage and
Needels, 1989) reviewed thirteen experiments that have translated the
findings of previous process-product research into practices recommended for classroom teachers. We refer to these experiments, all of
which met certain criteria, as "experiments of a special kind." Nine of
these studies were cited by Gage (1984); although Macmillan and
Garrison cited Gage (1984), they ignored those nine experiments.
Since our 1989 publication, three additional "experiments of a special
kind" have appeared, and we review them later in this chapter.

The questionable content validity of the tests used as the measure
of product in process-product research has been a common criticism
(Tom, 1984; Erickson, 1986). For the most part, this criticism is
concerned with standardized achievement tests and the degree to
which the content of these tests (a measure of product) is aligned with
the content of instruction (an aspect of process). Although this
criticism is sometimes valid, it applies not only to process-product
research but also to education in general. Current movements are
attempting to develop new tests that assess with greater validity the
kinds of knowledge and understanding that are the goals of instruction (Mitchell, 1989). State departments of education are working
with test experts to develop tests of higher-order thinking and of

content knowledge more closely related to the state's curriculum. As these tests are developed, process-product researchers can, with the sanction of the local educational community, use the tests in their investigations. In the meantime, process-product researchers will need to emulate researchers who have developed tests specific to the content of instruction for their particular study.

CRITICISMS RELATED TO PRODUCTIVITY

The most important basis for evaluation of a research paradigm is its productivity. On this point we agree with Macmillan and Garrison (1984), who cited the philosopher of science Laudan (1978): "The test of the value of a scientific tradition is its progressiveness, defined as its ability to answer the questions or solve the problems that are crucial to its domain of investigation" (Macmillan and Garrison, 1984, p. 16). This criterion should strike researchers as a truism, hardly requiring "a relatively rigorous approach" (Macmillan and Garrison, 1984, p. 16). Criticisms of the productivity of process-product research have been made by Macmillan and Garrison (1984), Sanders (1978), and Tom (1984), among others.

Yet Shulman (1986), who had criticisms of his own, recognized the productivity of process-product research:

> Finally, the approach worked. The studies conducted under its programmatic direction accomplished the sorts of important aims outlined for them. Teachers who consistently were associated with higher achievement gains tended to behave differently from those who were not. The data accumulated across correlational studies and survived experimental field tests. Teachers seemed capable of learning to perform in the manners suggested by the research program and their performances tended to produce higher achievement among their pupils. (P. 11)

Similarly, other reviewers not identified with process-product research held the opinion that the "process-product tradition has generated a corpus of knowledge about classrooms, teachers, and students that describes the reality of classroom instruction and serves as the foundation for teacher preservice and in-service programs" (Pintrich, Cross, Kozma, and McKeachie, 1986, p. 423). The chapter by Stallings and Freiberg in this volume describes in greater detail the role of process-product research in teacher education.

To consider the evidence of the productivity of process-product research in solving its problems, we need first to define the problems at which such research is aimed, that is, the problems of revealing, understanding, and controlling process-product relationships. Consistent process-product relationships have shown up in many correlational studies (Brophy and Good, 1986). We have already examined the problem of understanding in terms of the fruitfulness of process-product research in contributing to theory (Gage and Needels, 1989, pp. 262–265). The problem of control, or (less neutrally) improvement, is tantamount to the problem of improving the attainment of educational goals. Has process-product research yielded bases for such improvement?

Improvement implies causation—to change teaching in such a way as to cause greater achievement of desired ends. In science, one prime way to determine whether a relationship is causal is to conduct an experiment, that is, an investigation in which the "independent" variable is manipulated and the subsequent values of another, or "dependent," variable, are measured. An experiment ascertains whether dependent-variable measures differ according to the differing values or levels of the independent variable. If things (other than the independent variable) that might affect the dependent variable have been controlled, the independent variable is considered to have caused the change in the dependent variable. To control for the other variables, it is highly desirable to assign subjects (examples of subjects in process-product research are teachers and their classes) at random to the various levels of the independent variable.

These methodological principles have long been well established in the behavioral sciences and in research on teaching (Campbell and Stanley, 1963; Cook and Campbell, 1979). The principles derive from the methods of agreement, difference, and concomitant variation proposed by John Stuart Mill. Their advantages lead to what the statisticians Gilbert and Mosteller (1972) called "the urgent need for experimentation."

To assess the improvement value of process-product research, we set forth eight criteria to identify "experiments of a special kind" that were developed to determine whether causal efficacy was reflected in process-product relationships: (1) regular teachers were studied; (2) the regular curriculum was used; (3) the exposure of students to the teachers' influence, or to the "treatment," lasted for at least a whole school term; these experiments thus belied the impression, promulgated by Eisner (1984) and uncritically accepted by Gibboney (1989), that educational experiments involve treatments lasting on the average only an hour; (4) random assignment of teachers or schools was used to form the experimental and control groups; (5) the independent variables were derived, in large part, from the findings of correlational studies of process-product relationships; (6) the teachers were observed; (7) measures of treatment implementation were obtained; and (8) measures of student achievement, attitude, or conduct were obtained.

We reviewed thirteen studies that satisfied these criteria (Gage and Needels, 1989). Since that review, three additional experimental studies have been identified (Fitzpatrick, 1981; Nitsaisook and Anderson, 1989; Van Der Sijde, 1989)—bringing the total number of "experiments of a special kind" to sixteen. Here, we present descriptions of those three additional experiments.

The Fitzpatrick Study

Fitzpatrick (1981) studied eighteen teachers in grades nine through twelve in two suburban high schools in the same midwestern school district. Teachers in one school served as the treatment group, and teachers in the other school served as the control group; thus, the criterion of random assignment was *not* fully satisfied. Ten mathematics classes and eight French and Spanish classes constituted the sample. An equal number of classes in each subject area and grade level were represented in the treatment and control groups. The nine teachers in the treatment group participated in a ninety-minute workshop presented by the researcher during a one-day teachers' institute held the week before the school year began. Teachers in both the mathematics and foreign language departments attended. At this workshop, teachers were given a copy of a training manual prepared by the researcher, and a discussion of the major aspects of the recommended strategies was held. The manual presented thirteen general principles regarding the management and organization of the secondary-school classroom—principles derived from previous correlational research on teaching and research on mastery learning. Two weeks after the first workshop, a thirty-minute follow-up session was held at the school.

Both the treatment group and the control group of teachers were observed by one observer on five occasions over a ten-week period. The first, third, and fifth observation sessions focused on measuring the teachers' implementation of the managerial strategies presented in the treatment program. The second and fourth sessions focused on student academic engaged time. The first observation session was conducted two weeks after the workshop at the treatment school, and the subsequent observations occurred at two-week intervals. Each observation session lasted for one class period. One observer for each subject area observed both the treatment and the control classes. Observers were unaware of which group the teachers belonged to. Two observation instruments were used to measure the teachers' implementation of the treatment: (1) a summary checklist of the teaching practices outlined in the manual given to the teachers in the treatment group; the checklist was completed by the observer at the end of the class period; and (2) an instrument for time-sampling implementation of the treatment program and assessing the amount of teacher-student academic interaction; on this instrument the observer coded the teachers' activity, at one-minute intervals, according to whether it was an academic or a nonacademic interaction with the students.

In addition, an observation form for recording students' academic engaged time was used; this instrument was the same as that used in the Beginning Teacher Evaluation Study (Fisher and Berliner, 1985) and was applied to six randomly chosen students in each class. Each teacher was assigned fifteen implementation scores: (a) a summary score consisting of the percentage of "yes" responses, (b) thirteen principle-implementation scores consisting of the percentage of "yes" responses for each principle, and (c) a teacher-student academic interaction score consisting of the percentage of events coded as teacher-student academic interactions.

Of the thirteen effect sizes we calculated for the thirteen principle-implementation scores, eleven were positive, one was negative, and one was zero. The effect sizes ranged from -0.38 to 0.87, with a median of 0.54. The effect size obtained for the summary checklist score was 0.98, and that for the teacher-student academic interaction was 0.68. The outcome measure in this experiment (student academic engaged time) showed a large positive effect size of 1.31, indicating that teachers who had been educated in the principles were more effective in helping their classes become engaged in academic tasks.

The Nitsaisook-Anderson Study

Nitsaisook and Anderson (1989) experimented with ninety-seven fifth-grade teachers and their 2,430 students in Thailand, focusing on the teaching and learning of mathematics. The teachers were drawn from ten teachers-college areas and divided at random (on one side or the other of a vertical line on a map of each of the ten areas), so as "to minimize the likelihood that the control group teachers would be contaminated by the experimental treatment" (p. 289). Most of the students came from low-income families. The forty-nine experimental teachers participated in a six-day in-service teacher education program on classroom organization and management, lesson development, and teacher questioning and feedback; the program was based on the results of a previous two and one-half year correlational study in Thailand and similar studies conducted in the United States. Observations of the ninety-seven teachers were made by six staff members from each of the ten teachers colleges; of these, two used rating scales, two recorded frequencies and time estimates, and two wrote narrative descriptions. The observers were trained in a first session lasting for four eight-hour days. "Observers were unaware of whether the classroom being observed was experimental or control" (p. 292). Interobserver agreement "indices of .90 or higher were common" (p. 292).

Results indicated that the experimental teachers were rated higher on classroom climate and management of teaching materials, but the experimental and control teachers and their classes did not differ significantly in the management of student behavior, reactions to inappropriate behavior, transitions, and the amounts of misbehavior and of disruptive behaviors. The experimental teachers, as was intended by the in-service program, used mental computation much more (in 94 percent of the lessons as against 4 percent in the control group) and assigned homework much more often (72 percent versus 33 percent). Differences of 20 percent or more for reviewing previous content, the use of teacher-directed practice, and the use of independent practice were noted. The amount of time the experimental teachers allotted to various activities was closer to that recommended for most activities. In short, the teaching practices of the experimental and control teachers differed substantially and in the directions intended by the in-service teacher education program, which was based on prior research.

Finally, the classes of the experimental teachers had significantly higher mean scores on the achievement tests for each of the eight units taught; effect sizes ranged from 0.16 to 0.44, with a median of 0.285. On the omnibus achievement test given at the end of the study, the effect size was 0.48. On the attitude-toward-mathematics scale given at the end of the study, the effect size was very small.

The Van der Sijde Study

Van der Sijde (1989) studied thirty-three teachers of eighth-grade mathematics in schools close to one or the other of three universities in the Netherlands. In September, teachers were assigned at random to one of four conditions. Condition 1 teachers (n=13) participated in a one-day training course at the university. Shortly after the training, student achievement and attitude premeasures were administered to these teachers' students. Trained observers then observed eight to ten lessons during a three-month period (September to December). Achievement and attitude measures were administered again in January and April to obtain postmeasures. Condition 2 teachers (n=8) were treated as in Condition 1, except that they received the training in January, that is, *after* the observation, rather than before. The testing schedule (September, January, April) followed was the same as that used in Condition 1. Condition 3 teachers (n=6) and Condition 4 teachers (n=6) participated only during the December to April period, and achievement tests were administered in their classrooms in December and April. The teachers in Condition 3 received a copy of the training manual by mail but had no training session. Teachers in Condition 4 were the control group and received neither the manual nor the training session.

The training program used ideas from three sources: (1) results of a previous correlational study in the Netherlands, (2) results from others' similar research studies, and (3) instructional theory and research consistent with the first two sources. The observation system used was designed especially to record teachers' implementation of the recommendations contained in the training. Four categories of teacher actions were recorded: (1) direction of gaze; (2) management, (3) instruction, and (4) lesson phases. During a one-period lesson, every five minutes for five minutes, the observer categorized the direction of the teacher's gaze, the lesson phase, the management activity, and the instruction activity. This procedure was followed at five-minute intervals for a total of five five-minute observation periods during the lesson.

The observation data indicated that the training did influence the teachers' instructional practices. Comparing the observation data from Condition 1 (after teachers received the training) with those from Condition 2 (before teachers received the training) yielded an average effect size across all recommendations of 0.33.

Unfortunately, we are unable at present to describe differences in the students' mean achievement test scores because across all four conditions, the mean of students' achievement test scores *declined*! Until the author explains the decline in achievement test scores, these results seem anomalous. Combined scores on a measure of students' self-image for Conditions 1 and 2 showed a significantly greater gain (p <0.05) in self-image than did those for Conditions 3 and 4.

Summary

In summary, the grade level studied in these sixteen "experiments of a special kind" ranged from first grade to college freshman. Nine experiments were conducted in elementary schools; five, in secondary schools; and one, in a college. The subject matter areas included foreign language, mathematics, reading, and social studies. The teacher education programs lasted from two hours to forty-five hours, with a median of six hours. Eight of the experiments based the recommended teaching practices primarily, or almost exclusively, on the findings of prior correlational studies; one experiment relied primarily on the findings of previous short-term experiments lasting typically only a few days or weeks; seven of the experiments derived the teaching practices from a combination of prior correlational findings and writings consistent with those findings. The outcome measures included observations of students' behavior, norm-referenced and criterion-referenced achievement tests, and inventories on student attitude.

The teacher education programs brought about substantial increases— in fifteen of the sixteen experimental groups—in the use of the recommended teaching practices. In the one experiment (Coladarci and Gage, 1984) in which the teacher education program was conducted entirely by mail, no effects on teaching practices or student achievement were found. In thirteen of the experiments, the available data permitted computations of the approximate effect size for student achievement. (Approximate effect size is computed by subtracting the mean of the control-class means from the mean of the experimental-class means and dividing the difference by the standard deviation of either the control-class means or the pooled-group class means.) In all but two of these thirteen experiments, approximate effect sizes were positive. They ranged from slightly negative (-0.25) to large (1.53), with a median of 0.52. An effect size of 0.52 suggests that the median class of the experimental group had a percentile rank of about 70 in the distribution of control-group class means, where the median class of the control group had a percentile rank of 50.

In short, the teacher education programs, based substantially on the results of previous correlational process-product studies, tended to improve mean class achievement by about twenty percentile ranks. In view of the relative brevity of the teacher education programs in these experiments—a brevity usually necessitated by the paucity of time for in-service teacher education—the results are substantial. For this reason, along with our summary of theoretical contributions, we consider critics' allegations of lack of productivity to be unwarranted.

One shortcoming of our collation of the results of these experiments is that we have accepted the authors' statistical analyses and results as reported. It would have been desirable to reanalyze the experiments' data, applying the same procedures to them all on such matters as methods of estimating statistical significance (parametric or nonparametric methods), the treatment of anomalous cases (outliers, withdrawals, etc.), and the computation of effect sizes. Pending such a difficult-to-arrange reanalysis, the positive character of our present summary of these sixteen experiments nonetheless impresses us. We need further experiments along the same lines in the many still unstudied contexts in which knowledge of causal process-product relationships would serve education well.

CRITICISMS OF INTERPRETATION AND APPLICATION

We turn now to criticisms related to interpretation and application of the results of process-product research. Shulman (1986) and

Macmillan and Garrison (1984) are among those who fault the use of meta-analysis in synthesizing process-product research results.

> There is assumed to be an underlying "true score" for the relationship between a given teacher behavior and a pupil outcome measure. There is a parameter or law which can be estimated. The problem is to get beyond the limitations of particular teachers, particular classrooms, particular studies to a more stable generalization. [Shulman, 1986, p. 10]

The statement is correct, except for its references to "true score," "parameter," and "law." These terms suggest an aspiration toward unchangeable and universally applicable findings. Most behavioral scientists have no such aspiration. More modestly, meta-analysis seeks whatever consistencies may be uncovered in the correlations or effect sizes across a set of more or less similar studies. To deny the importance of such evidence is to rely on one set of findings from one study. Most natural and behavioral scientists value highly the confirmatory or disconfirmatory power of replications.

A criticism of the application of process-product research comes from those (e.g., Fenstermacher, 1979; Floden, 1985; Zumwalt, 1982) who allege that process-product researchers convert their correlations directly into rules for teachers' conduct and hand them down to the teachers without regard for the ways in which these rules fit into the teachers' own "subjectively reasonable beliefs" about teaching (Fenstermacher, 1979, p. 169). In considering this criticism, we should first ask, Do process-product researchers regard their findings as "rules," or teaching as a set of competencies, technical skills, or algorithms to be applied "nondeliberatively" and mechanically? We respond with an unequivocal "No!" A look into the training manuals used in the "experiments of a special kind" will support our response. Crawford and colleagues (1978) wrote in their training manual that "although we cannot ask you to use strategies which you strongly oppose, we do hope you can accept most of them as promising components of effective teaching and at least give them a try. Your judgment as to their usefulness and value will be crucial" (p. 239). Brophy and Evertson (1976) wrote that "effective teachers not only must be able to do a lot of things, they must also be able to recognize which of the many things they know how to do applies at any given moment" (p. 139). Berliner (1987) expressed the views of process-product researchers:

Communicating research findings by means of rules brings little, if any, advantage to practitioners and makes most researchers angry. It takes research findings out of context, and it also ignores the limits to generalization that concern researchers. . . . Persons expected to change their behavior on the basis of rules imposed by others are denied a portion of their freedom to think and act independently. . . . Developing rules is not a style of communicating knowledge that we can approve. [P. 29]

Moreover, experience with translating research findings into recommendations of teaching practices (Mohlman, Coladarci, and Gage, 1982; Stallings, Needels, and Stayrook, 1979) indicates that teachers *decide for themselves* whether research findings will apply to their classrooms.

Macmillan and Garrison (1988) wrote that "merely to provide 'facts' or 'findings' of nontheoretically driven research is to provide teachers with no help in developing their own theories of the pedagogical situation" (p. 14). They assume that teacher education programs based on process-product findings are simple congeries of facts. That assumption would be contradicted by a perusal of the materials and procedures used in those programs, which typically provide a considerable rationale for their recommendations. Further, the question of whether only "theory-driven" research can help teachers to develop their own theories calls for empirical investigations not even suggested by Macmillan and Garrison (1988). Much everyday observation suggests strongly that people change deeply ingrained habits (such as smoking, or eating meat, fats, and salt) without needing to have their own "theory" interact with a "new theory." Whether "facts" alone (e.g., correlations, effect sizes) can help teachers seems not a "philosophical" issue to be resolved solely on the basis of a kind of logic, but rather an empirical one to be settled through observation and experimentation. Macmillan and Garrison (1988) illustrate a lamentable tendency to resolve educational issues rhetorically and "philosophically" even when those issues call for what only careful empirical research can tell us. A teacher's implicit "theory" that results in the practice of seldom asking higher-order questions can indeed be changed through informing the teacher of the "fact" that higher-order questions tend to improve important kinds of achievement.

ESSENCE VERSUS ACCIDENT

The essence of process-product research on teaching consists in the search for relations between process and product variables. The accidents are those incidental features of such research that may or may not be present in any specific process-product investigation without altering its process-product character.

The distinction between essence and accident has been blurred in the thinking of many critics of process-product research. They have found fault with many incidental characteristics without realizing that they were attacking nothing essential to the enterprise. We shall briefly look at the distinction in two of the areas of criticism we have already considered in this chapter: conceptual and methodological.

Many criticisms in the conceptual area are based on the belief that process-product research must necessarily relate simple teacher behaviors relatively low in intrinsic meaning to student achievement of relatively low-level cognitive objectives (recalled or recognized information). This conception excludes from the process variables any concern with complex teacher actions relatively high in intrinsic meaning. Such a conception of the archetypal process-product study is well-nigh a caricature. Process-product studies have dealt with fairly complex variables. They have studied achievement of high-level cognitive objectives and also of social-emotional objectives, such as attitudes, sensibilities, and appreciations. Nonetheless, even if the caricature were valid, nothing essential to process-product research prevents more adequate realization of the critics' ideals. More complex and subtle ways of describing process variables can be developed and used. For example, examinations of what Shulman (1986) called pedagogical content knowledge (e.g., metaphors for elucidating the Bill of Rights, analogies for clarifying the Pythagorean theorem, convincing examples of inherited and acquired characteristics) can be studied as process variables in relation to students' subsequent understanding.

The methods of describing or measuring process variables are also incidental features of a process-product study. Process variables may be measured through structured live observations of low-inference variables. The process variables may, however, also be described through analysis of audiotapes (Needels, 1989), videotapes (Friedman and Stomper, 1983), questionnaires filled out by teachers (Bennett,

1976), or interviews with teachers (Crocker and Brooker, 1986). How the product variables are measured is also only incidental. Such outcomes have often been measured with standardized achievement tests, but the achievement tests used have sometimes been constructed locally, within the school district in which the study was conducted, to increase the content validity of the test (Needels, 1989). Achievement has also been measured with essay tests (Clark et al., 1979).

The way in which the relation between process and product variables is determined is also only incidental. Although the relationship has often been determined with a correlation coefficient, other ways of determining such relationships are admissible. Many experiments and path analyses have been performed. Intensive case studies, single-subject experiments, and ethnographic analyses (e.g., Au and Jordan, 1980) may also be legitimate ways of ascertaining process-product relationships.

When Should Process-Product Research Not Be Conducted?

We have devoted most of this chapter to a defense of process-product research against the criticisms of that research. This defense should not be regarded as implying that all teaching practices—or all educational practices and policies—require validation through process-product research. Under certain conditions and for certain educational problems, process-product research is uncalled for. Certain values of our society are important enough to stand without scientific investigation of their effectiveness in improving student achievement or attitude. All children should be treated with equal respect and consideration. They should be given equal opportunities to acquire the skills, knowledge, and appreciations vital to living in our society. They should be guaranteed a physically and an emotionally safe environment. They should be given a curriculum where all groups— regardless of economic status, ethnicity, religion, or gender—are treated with equal respect. They should be taught principles of democracy and the responsibilities of a citizen in a democratic society. We need no process-product research to evaluate classrooms where teachers fail to respect these values.

Process-product researchers are, for the most part, interested in investigating process-product relationships in environments where these values of our society are respected and serve as a backdrop. Research descriptive of processes may reveal the degree to which these values are or are not realized in the classroom. Such research can be used to increase educators' awareness of a need for change, without process-product research to support that need. Environments where children are not treated with equal respect, given equal opportunity, or taught the basic democratic principles can be regarded as harmful to children without evidence from process-product research.

When Should Process-Product Findings Not Be Used with Teachers?

When should the findings from process-product research not be used with teachers? The fifteen interpretable "experiments of a special kind" already described showed that teachers used many of the research findings in their teaching and that such use typically improved student achievement, conduct, or attitudes—or all three of these. In their eagerness to improve education, educators might use these findings inappropriately. We have identified two ways in which process-product findings should not be used. First, process-product research findings should not be regarded as a substitute for, rather than merely a component of, the rich content of valid teacher education. Teaching is a complex profession enhanced by an understanding of learning processes, cognitive development, motivation, test construction and interpretation, ethnic and other group differences, individual differences, and curriculum development. Process-product research findings offer insight into some important aspects of the practice of teaching but do not encompass all that should be covered in teacher education programs.

Second, process-product findings should not be used to develop instruments (checklists, rating scales, observation schedules) for summary evaluations of teachers. Such a use of process-product research findings could push teaching toward becoming unthinking and mechanical. Teachers would begin to behave in the ways dictated by the evaluation form and give inadequate thought to the appropriateness of their behavior. This use of process-product research might lead to the "set of rules" mentioned by Fenstermacher (1979). Educational administrators, teacher educators, teachers, and researchers need to work together to ensure that the findings of process-product research are used thoughtfully and artistically with due regard for circumstances that may call for exceptions to the trends indicated by the findings.

An Agenda

The many criticisms of process-product research on teaching fail to weaken the record and promise of such research. Knowledge of process-product relationships should be considered central to the understanding and improvement of teaching.

Future research should aim at improving theory based on cognitive conceptions of learning. When we understand the process of learning within a classroom, we can identify the teaching processes that facilitate learning in that kind of environment. A theory of learning in classrooms (e.g., that of Carroll, 1989) would begin to explain why teaching practices of different kinds result in differences in student knowledge and comprehension. Dyson's case studies (1989) of the influence of children's conversations on their learning to write in the classroom illustrate the kind of research that can serve as a basis for subsequent process-product investigations.

Future research should also rest on more complete conceptualizations. Thus, new formulations should include (a) the students' cognitive processes mediating between process and product variables, and (b) the teachers' thought processes associated with particular teaching practices. The study of these processes should be conducted with a variety of methods, including ethnographic case studies. Product variables should be measured with criterion-referenced achievement tests and unobtrusive measures. Relationships between process and product variables should be studied with the whole variety of methods mentioned above.

Process-product studies should be conducted on all of the various combinations of school subjects, grade levels, cultural groups, teaching methods, and types of educational outcomes found in the many settings in which teaching and learning go on. More experiments should be performed to test the causal potential of correlational findings. In just two of these dimensions of setting—grade level and subject matter—the need for further process-product research is glaring. Most process-product research has centered on teaching and achievement in reading and mathematics in the early grades (Brophy and Good, 1986). Yet consider the other major academic subjects taught in elementary and secondary schools: literature, writing, science, social studies, and foreign languages. If we eliminate infrequent combinations of grade level and subject, we still have many important combinations. Most of these combinations remain unexplored; the process-product relations within them are almost unknown. For grade-level and subject matter variations alone, the agenda is long and important.

Is it realistic to envisage such a movement—one entailing many investigations of process-product relationships? Other fields of research concerned with improving the quality of life have done such work. Bacteriology marched along such lines. Following what might be called the "germ-disease paradigm," researchers sought causal connections between specific bacteria and specific diseases. The search required innumerable investigations, which revealed many bacteria-disease connections (Thomas, 1976). Process-product studies of psychotherapy also number many hundreds (Smith, Glass, and Miller, 1980).

As was noted above, process-product research on teaching has its counterpart in patient-outcome research in medicine (Wennberg, 1989). Although medical practice has a scientific basis, it is a normative activity, and a particular treatment will not always be the most effective one to administer for a given illness or accident. Other variables mediate the influence of a given treatment. In their description of patient-outcome research, Dubois and Brook (1988) discussed these complexities and proposed research methods sensitive to them:

> In contrast, the more complex explicit methods better identify the needs of important patient subgroups. They also more consistently demonstrate a relationship between process and outcome. . . . We then propose a system that would have an additional level of complexity. Using Bayesian analysis, an explicit system could use a patient's pertinent symptoms and findings to determine proper care. Unfortunately, this hypothetical system requires more than 10 billion pathways, and would be totally infeasible. We suggest a potential solution that involves pruning our massive logic tree to those elements that truly matter. . . . Further research could answer the following types of questions: Which components of a physician's history [of the patient] and physical examination identify the information that most influences patient care? Which laboratory studies and treatment options influence patient outcomes? [Pp. 63–64]

It will probably be similarly unnecessary to do process-product studies in all the well-nigh infinite number of combinations of grade level, subject matter, student characteristics, cultural contexts, types of objectives, and so on. In medicine reasonable inferences are made, for example, about the applicability to women of the relationship of blood cholesterol level to heart attacks based on research with men. Thus,

the 1984 National Institutes of Health consensus panel . . . considered the extrapolation justified because (1) even though premenopausal women generally have a lower risk of heart attacks, premenopausal women with higher blood cholesterol levels have higher risk—just as men have; (2) the heart attack rate in women rises after menopause to approach that of men, and (3) there is no evidence that the basic biochemistry and biology of the arteries is any different in women. We would have been remiss had we not urged women to lower their cholesterol levels. [Steinberg, 1989]

Using similar reasoning, educators will be able to generalize process-product relationships found in one combination of grade level, subject matter, and the like, to other combinations, without having to wait for studies in the other combinations. The extrapolation can be made when knowledge gives us a basis for assuming the applicability of findings.

Educators and researchers might well heed the other professions dedicated to working with and helping people. Medicine and psychotherapy have a base of knowledge built on laboratory and clinical research. But when the individual physician or psychotherapist works with his or her individual patients, a new layer of complexity is introduced. To identify the most effective treatment (possibly between competing available treatments), research is needed at that level of complexity. The parallel with process-product research on teaching is apparent.

Perhaps those critics who accept the need for research on medical practice but reject the need for process-product research on teaching are guided by a belief that research in the natural sciences is more stable and valid. If so, these critics should note that Hedges (1987) compared the consistency of research findings in particle physics with that of research findings in psychology (gender differences in spatial ability, open education, desegregation-achievement relationships, relationships between student ratings of professors and student course grades). His review of the research in specific areas unique to each of these fields revealed no differences in the consistency of the research findings:

What is surprising is that the research results in the physical sciences are not markedly more consistent than those in the social sciences. The notion that experiments in physics produce strikingly consistent (empirically cumulative) results is simply not supported by these data. Similarly the notion that experiments in the social sciences produce relatively inconsistent (empirically noncumulative) results is not supported by these data either. [P. 450]

Thus, the investigation of process-product relationships should continue. We should not let the complexity of the classroom deter our efforts; rather, we should seek more valid methods for our investigations. And we should remember that, as is true in all research, the answer to any current question will bring with it a host of new questions about the process-product relationships. The new questions will reflect deeper understanding and enhanced capability for improving teaching.

REFERENCES

Anderson, Linda; Evertson, Carolyn M.; and Brophy, Jere E. "An Experimental Study of Effective Teaching in First-Grade Reading Groups," *Elementary School Journal* 79 (1979): 193–223.

Aristotle. *Posterior Analytics.* In *Introduction to Aristotle: Edited, with a General Introduction and Introductions to the Particular Works,* edited by Richard McKeon. New York: Modern Library, Random House, 1947.

Au, Kathryn H., and Jordan, C. "Teaching Reading to Hawaiian Children: Finding a Culturally Appropriate Solution." In *Culture and the Bilingual Classroom,* edited by Henry T. Trueba, Grace P. Guthrie, and Kathryn H. Au. Rowley, Mass.: Newbury House, 1980.

Bennett, Neville, with Jordan, Joyce; Long, George; and Wade, Barbara. *Teaching Styles and Pupil Progress.* Cambridge, Mass.: Harvard University Press, 1976.

Berliner, David C. "Tempus Educare." In *Research on Teaching,* edited by Penelope L. Peterson and Herbert J. Walberg. Berkeley, Calif.: McCutchan, 1979.

Berliner, David C. "Knowledge Is Power." In *Talks to Teachers,* edited by David C. Berliner and Barak Rosenshine. New York: Random House, 1987.

Bloom, Benjamin, S. "The New Direction in Educational Research: Alterable Variables." In MESA Seminar, *The State of Research on Selected Alterable Variables in Education.* Chicago: Department of Education, University of Chicago, 1980.

Brophy, Jere E., and Evertson, Carolyn M. *Learning from Teaching: A Developmental Perspective.* Boston: Allyn and Bacon, 1976.

Brophy, Jere E., and Good, Thomas L. "Teacher Behavior and Student Achievement." In *Handbook of Research on Teaching,* 3d ed., edited by Merlin C. Wittrock. New York: Macmillan, 1986.

Campbell, Donald T., and Stanley, Julian C. "Experimental and Quasi-experimental Designs for Research on Teaching." In *Handbook of Research on Teaching,* edited by

N. L. Gage. Chicago: Rand McNally, 1963.

Carroll, John B. "The Carroll Model: A 25-Year Retrospective and Prospective View," *Educational Researcher* 18, no. 1 (1989): 26–31.

Clark, Christopher M.; Gage, N. L.; Marx, Ronald; Peterson, Penelope L.; Stayrook, Nicholas; and Winne, Philip. "A Factorial Experiment on Teacher Structuring, Soliciting, and Reacting," *Journal of Educational Psychology* 71 (1979): 534–552.

Clark, Christopher M., and Peterson, Penelope L. "Teachers' Thought Processes." In *Handbook of Research on Teaching*, 3d ed., edited by Merlin C. Wittrock. New York: Macmillan, 1986.

Coladarci, Theodore, and Gage, N. L. "Effects of a Minimal Intervention on Teacher Behavior and Student Achievement," *American Educational Research Journal* 21 (1984): 539–555.

Cook, Thomas D., and Campbell, Donald T. *Quasi-experimentation: Design and Analysis Issues for Field Settings*. Chicago: Rand McNally, 1979.

Cooley, William W., and Leinhardt, Gaea. *The Application of a Model for Investigating Classroom Processes*. Pittsburgh: Learning Research and Developmental Center, University of Pittsburgh, 1976.

Corno, Lyn. "A Hierarchical Analysis of Selected Naturally Occurring Aptitude-Treatment Interactions in the Third Grade," *American Educational Research Journal* 16 (1979): 391–409.

Crawford, John; Gage, N. L.; Corno, Lyn; Stayrook, Nicholas; and Mitman, Alexis. *An Experiment on Teacher Effectiveness and Parent Assisted Instruction in the Third Grade*, vols. 1–3. Stanford, Calif.: Program on Teaching Effectiveness, Center for Educational Research, Stanford University, 1978. ERIC ED 160 648.

Crocker, Robert K., and Brooker, Gwen M. "Classroom Control and Student Outcomes in Grades 2 and 5," *American Education Research Journal* 23 (1986): 1–11.

Crosson, V., and Olson, David R. "Encoding Ability in Teacher-Student Communication Games." Paper presented at the Annual Meeting of the American Educational Research Association, Los Angeles, 1969.

Cuban, Larry. *How Teachers Taught: Constancy and Change in American Classrooms 1890–1980*. New York: Longman, 1984.

Dubois, R. W., and Brook, R. H. "Assessing Clinical Decision Making: Is the Ideal System Feasible?" *Inquiry* 28 (1988): 59–84.

Dyson, Anne H. *Multiple Worlds of Child Writers*. New York: Teachers College Press, 1989.

Eisner, Elliot W. "Can Educational Research Inform Educational Practice?" *Phi Delta Kappan* 66 (1984): 447–452.

Erickson, Frederick. "Qualitative Methods in Research on Teaching." In *Handbook of Research on Teaching*, 3d ed., edited by Merlin C. Wittrock. New York: Macmillan, 1986.

Fenstermacher, Gary D. "A Philosophical Reconsideration of Recent Research on Teacher Effectiveness." In *Review of Research in Education*, vol. 6, edited by Lee Shulman. Itasca, Ill.: Peacock, 1979.

Fisher, Charles W., and Berliner, David C., eds. *Perspectives on Instructional Time*. White Plains, N.Y.: Longman, 1985.

Fitzpatrick, Kathleen A. "A Study of the Effect of a Secondary Classroom Management Training Program on Teacher and Student Behavior." Doctoral dissertation, University of Illinois, 1981.

Floden, Robert E. "The Role of Rhetoric in Changing Teachers' Beliefs," *Teaching and Teacher Education* 1 (1985): 19–32.

Friedman, Mordechai, and Stomper, Connie. "The Effectiveness of a Faculty Development Program: A Process-Product Experimental Study," *Review of Higher Education* 7 (1983): 49–65.

Gage, N. L. *The Scientific Basis of the Art of Teaching.* New York: Teachers College Press, 1978.

Gage, N. L. "The Generality of Dimensions of Teaching." In *Research on Teaching*, edited by Penelope L. Peterson and Herbert J. Walberg. Berkeley, Calif.: McCutchan, 1979.

Gage, N. L. "What Do We Know about Teaching Effectiveness?" *Phi Delta Kappan* 66 (1984): 87–93.

Gage, N. L.; Belgard, Maria; Rosenshine, Barak V.; Unruh, W. R.; Dell, Daryl; and Hiller, Jack H. "Explorations of the Teacher's Effectiveness in Lecturing." In *Research into Classroom Processes*, edited by Ian Westbury and Arno A. Bellack. New York: Teachers College Press, 1971.

Gage, N. L., and Needels, Margaret C. "Process-Product Research on Teaching: A Review of Criticisms," *Elementary School Journal* 89 (1989): 253–300.

Garrison, James W., and Macmillan, C. J. B. "A Philosophical Critique of Process-Product Research on Teaching," *Educational Theory* 34 (1984): 255–274.

Gibboney, Richard A. "The Unscientific Character of Educational Research," *Phi Delta Kappan* 71 (1989): 225–227.

Gilbert, John P., and Mosteller, Frederick. "The Urgent Need for Experimentation." In *On Equality of Educational Opportunity*, edited by Frederick Mosteller and Daniel P. Moynihan. New York: Vantage Books, 1972.

Good, Thomas L., and Grouws, Douglas A. "The Missouri Mathematics Effectiveness Project: An Experimental Study in Fourth-Grade Classrooms," *Journal of Educational Psychology* 71 (1979): 355–362.

Hedges, Larry V. "How Hard Is Hard Science, How Soft Is Soft Science? The Empirical Cumulativeness of Research," *American Psychologist* 42 (1987): 443–455.

Helmke, A.; Schneider, W.; and Weinert, F. E. "Quality of Instruction and Classroom Learning Outcomes: The German Contribution to the IEA Classroom Environment Study," *Teaching and Teacher Education* 2 (1986): 1–18.

Huh, Kyung Chul. "The Role of Teacher Logic and Clarity in Student Achievement." Doctoral dissertation, Stanford University, 1986.

Laudan, Larry. *Progress and Its Problems.* Berkeley, Calif.: University of California Press, 1978.

Macmillan, C. J. B., and Garrison, James W. "Using the 'New Philosophy of Science' in Criticizing Current Research Traditions in Education," *Educational Researcher* 13, no. 10 (1984): 15–21.

Macmillan, C. J. B., and Garrison, James W. *A Logical Theory of Teaching: Erotetics and Intentionality.* Boston: Kluwer Academic Publishers, 1988.

McDonald, Frederick J., and Elias, Patricia. *The Effects of Teaching Performance on Pupil Learning*, Beginning Teacher Evaluation Study, Phase II, Final Report, Vol. 1.

Princeton, N.J.: Educational Testing Service, 1976.

Mehan, Hugh. *Learning Lessons.* Cambridge, Mass.: Harvard University Press, 1979.

Mitchell, R. "Beyond the Bubble." Paper presented at the Curriculum/Assessment Alignment Conferences, Sacramento and Long Beach, Calif., 1989.

Mohlman, Georgea G.; Coladarci, Theodore; and Gage, N. L. "Comprehension and Attitude as Predictors of Implementation in Teacher Training," *Journal of Teacher Education* 33 (1982): 31–36.

Needels, Margaret C. "A New Design for Process-Product Research on the Quality of Discourse in Teaching," *American Educational Research Journal* 25 (1989): 503–526.

Nitsaisook, M., and Anderson, Lorin. "An Experimental Investigation of the Effectiveness of Inservice Teacher Education in Thailand," *Teaching and Teacher Education* 5 (1989): 287–302.

Pintrich, Paul R.; Cross, David R.; Kozma, Robert B.; and McKeachie, Wilbert J. "Instructional Psychology," *Annual Review of Psychology* 37 (1986): 611–651.

Rosenshine, Barak. "Behavioral Predictors of Effectiveness in Explaining Social Studies Material." Doctoral dissertation, Stanford University, 1968.

Rosenshine, Barak, and Furst, Norma. "The Use of Direct Observation to Study Teaching." In *Second Handbook of Research on Teaching,* edited by R. M. W. Travers. Chicago: Rand McNally, 1973.

Rowe, Mary B. "Wait-Time and Rewards as Instructional Variables, Their Influence on Language, Logic, and Fate Control, Part 1. Wait-Time," *Journal of Research in Science Teaching* 11 (1974): 81–94.

Sanders, James T. "Teaching Effectiveness: Accepting the Null Hypothesis," *Journal of Educational Thought* 12 (1978): 184–189.

Shulman, Lee S. "Paradigms and Research Programs in the Study of Teaching." In *Handbook of Research on Teaching,* 3d ed., edited by Merlin C. Wittrock. New York: Macmillan, 1986.

Smith, Mary L.; Glass, Gene V; and Miller, Thomas I. *The Benefits of Psychotherapy.* Baltimore: Johns Hopkins University Press, 1980.

Snow, Richard E. "Theory Construction for Research on Teaching." In *Second Handbook of Research on Teaching,* edited by R. M. W. Travers. Chicago: Rand McNally, 1973.

Spindler, George, and Spindler, Louise. "Roger Harder and Schönhausen: From the Familiar to the Strange and Back Again." In *Doing the Ethnography of Schooling,* edited by George Spindler. New York: Holt, Rinehart and Winston, 1982.

Stallings, Jane A.; Needels, Margaret C.; and Stayrook, Nicholas. *How to Change the Process of Teaching Basic Reading Skills at the Secondary School Level.* Menlo Park, Calif.: SRI International, 1979.

Stayrook, Nicholas. "A Comparison of Two Causal Models in Elementary School Reading." Doctoral dissertation, Stanford University, 1982.

Steinberg, D. "Studies Confirm Cholesterol-Heart Attack Link," *New York Times,* editorial page, September 26, 1989.

Thomas, Lewis. "The Future Place of Science in the Art of Healing," *Journal of Medical Education* 51 (1976): 23–29.

Tom, Alan R. "The Reform of Teacher Education through Research: A Futile Quest," *Teachers College Record* 82 (1980): 15–29.

Tom, Alan R. *Teaching as a Moral Craft.* New York: Longman, 1984.

Van Der Sijde, Pieter C. "The Effect of a Brief Teacher Training on Student Achievement," *Teaching and Teacher Education* 5 (1989): 303–314.

Wennberg, John E. *Outcomes Research and the Evaluative Clinical Sciences at Dartmouth.* Hanover, N.H.: Dartmouth Medical School, 1989.

Zumwalt, Karen K. "Research on Teaching: Policy Implications for Teacher Education." In *Policy Making in Education*, 81st Yearbook of the National Society for the Study of Education, Part 1, edited by Ann Lieberman and Milbrey W. McLaughlin. Chicago: University of Chicago Press, 1982.

—— 2 ——

Productive Teaching and Instruction: Assessing the Knowledge Base

Herbert J. Walberg

Over ten years ago several psychologists wrote an article entitled "The Quiet Revolution in Educational Research" (Walberg, Schiller, and Haertel, 1979). Surprisingly, five years later, the results of nearly 3,000 studies could be analyzed and reported (Walberg, 1984). In 1987, an Australian-United States team assessed 134 reviews of 7,827 field studies and several large-scale United States and international surveys of learning (Fraser, Walberg, Welch, and Hattie, 1987). This chapter provides a compact summary of the findings of approximately 8,000 studies on elementary and secondary school students and also assesses still more recent and definitive reviews of research on teaching and instruction.

I begin with the effects of the psychological elements of teaching and then discuss methods and patterns of teaching—all of which can be accomplished by a single teacher without unusual arrangements and equipment. Then I turn to the effects of systems of instruction that require special planning, student grouping, and materials. Next described are effects that are unique to reading, writing, science, and mathematics. The remaining results concern special students and techniques, and the effects of training on teachers.

The tables in this chapter summarize the results for each of fifteen categories of effects. Each table shows the number of studies reviewed and the size of the effect (expressed as the difference between experimental and control groups in units of standard deviation), and also gives a graphic representation of the size of the effect. (For further details and references as to the procedures followed, see Walberg [1986] and Fraser et al. [1987].)

The compilation of effects allows us to compare educational methods with one another—including some effective ones that are no longer popular. We can see that some techniques have enormous effects, while others confer only trivial advantages or even harm learning. To plan and evaluate programs, we can examine the findings in the light of our own experience. In practice, however, we might attain results half or twice as good as the average estimates reported here. Our success will depend on our care in implementing our purposes. The best saw swung as a hammer may do little good.

PSYCHOLOGICAL ELEMENTS OF TEACHING

A little history will help us understand the evolution of psychological research on teaching. Psychologists have often emphasized either thought, feeling, or behavior at the expense of the other two, even though educators require a balance of the three. Today, thinking or cognition is sovereign in psychology, but a half-century ago behaviorists insisted on specific operational definitions—a standard still required.

In particular, Yale psychologists Neal Miller and John Dollard (1941), stimulated by E. L. Thorndike and B. F. Skinner, wrote about cues, response, and positive reinforcement, especially in psychotherapy. Later Dollard and Miller (1950) emphasized three components of teaching—cues, engagement, and reinforcement—similar to input, process, and output in physiology. Their influential conception stimulated research on what teachers do rather than on their age, experience, certification, college degrees, and other characteristics unconnected with what their students learn.

Table 2-1
Effects of Psychological Elements of Teaching

Elements	Number of Studies	Effect Size*	Graphic Representation of Effect Size
Cues	17	1.25	.xxxxxxxxxxxxx
Engagement	22	0.88	.xxxxxxxxx
Corrective feedback	20	0.94	.xxxxxxxxx
Reinforcement	39	1.17	.xxxxxxxxxxxx

*In all tables in this chapter, effect size is expressed as the difference between experimental and control groups in units of standard deviation.

The behavioral model emphasized the quality of instructional cues impinging on the learner, the learner's active engagement in the process, and reinforcement or rewards that encourage continuing effort over time. Benjamin Bloom (1976) recognized, however, that learners may fail the first time or even repeatedly in cycles of cues and effort; if they make no progress, they may practice incorrect behaviors, and they cannot be reinforced. Therefore, he introduced the ideas of feedback to correct errors and frequent testing to check progress. Inspired by John Carroll's (1963) model of school learning, Bloom emphasized learning time, and he also pointed out that some learners require much more time than others.

Table 2-1 shows the effects of certain psychological elements of teaching. Since an effect of 0.2 or 0.3 is worthwhile, the effects of cues, engagement, corrective feedback, and reinforcement that range from 0.88 to 1.25 are huge—they are among the largest estimates in this compilation. The underlying research has been unusually rigorous and well controlled. Even though it was conducted in school classes, the investigators helped to ensure precise timing and deployment of the elements in short-term studies lasting usually less than a month. Similar effects are difficult to sustain for long time periods.

Cues, as operationalized, show what is to be learned and explain how to learn it. Their quality can be seen in the clarity, salience, and meaningfulness of explanations and directions provided by teacher, instructional materials, or both. Ideally, as the learners gain confidence, the salience and numbers of cues can be reduced.

Engagement is the extent to which learners actively and persistently participate until appropriate responses are firmly entrenched in their repertoires. Such participation can be indexed by the extent to which the teacher engages students in overt or covert activity—indicated by absence of irrelevant behavior, concentration on tasks, enthusiastic contributions to group discussion, and lengthy study.

Corrective feedback remedies errors in oral or written responses. Ideally, students waste little time on incorrect responses, and teachers rapidly detect and remedy difficulties by reteaching or using alternate methods. When necessary, teachers also provide additional time for practice.

Reinforcement. The immense effort elicited by athletics, games, and other cooperative and competitive activities illustrates the power of immediate and direct reinforcement, and how some activities are intrinsically rewarding. By comparison, reinforcement in the classroom may seem crass or jejune.

The usual classroom reinforcers are acknowledgement of correctness and social approval in the form of, say, a smile or praise. More unusual reinforcers include contingent activity—allowing, for example, a music lesson or some other enjoyable activity for 90 percent correctness on a math test. Other reinforcers are tokens or check marks accumulated for steps accomplished and later exchanged for tangible reinforcers such as cookies, trinkets, or toys.

In special education programs, students have been reinforced not only for achievement but also for minutes of reading, attempts to learn, and accuracy of performance on tasks in special programs. When the environment can be rigorously controlled, and when teachers are able to gear reinforcement to performance accurately, as in programs for unruly or emotionally disturbed students, the results have been impressive (Mastropieri and Scruggs, 1987). Improved behavior and achievement, however, often fail to extend past the period of reinforcement or beyond the special environment.

Educators ordinarily confine reinforcement to marks, grades, and awards because they must assume that students work for intangible, long-term goals such as pleasing parents, further education, and adult success, and also (we hope) for an ultimate aim of education—the reward of learning itself. Even so, when corrective feedback and reinforcement are clear, rapid, and appropriate, they can powerfully affect learning by signaling what to do next without wasting time. In ordinary classrooms, then, the chief value of reinforcement is in providing information rather than incentive.

METHODS OF TEACHING

The psychological elements undergird many teaching methods and the design of instructional media. When the affective or informational content of cues, engagement, correctives, and reinforcement is improved, these methods have shown a range of effects from small to enormous, although generally not as big as short-term, highly controlled studies of the pure elements. (See Table 2-2.)

Cues

Cues can take many forms, of which the following are examples.

Advance organizers are brief overviews that abstractly relate new concepts or terms to previous learning. They are effective if they bridge new to old learning. Those spoken by the teacher or graphically illustrated in texts work best.

Adjunct questions alert students about key questions to answer—particularly in texts. They work best on questions repeated on post-tests, and moderately well on questions related to the adjuncts. As we might expect, however, adjunct questions distract attention away from incidental material that might otherwise be learned.

Goal setting sets forth objectives, guidelines, methods, or standards for learning. Like adjunct questions, goal setting sacrifices incidental for intended learning.

Learning hierarchies assume that instruction can be made efficient if facts, skills, or ideas that logically or psychologically precede others are presented first. Teaching and instructional media sequenced in this way appear slightly more effective. Learners, however, may adapt themselves to apparently ill-sequenced material; and it may be advantageous to learn to do so, since human life, as Franz Kafka showed, may depart from logical progression.

Pretests are benchmarks for determining how much students learn under various methods of teaching. Psychologists have found, however, that pretests can have positive cuing effects if they show students what will be emphasized by instruction and on posttests.

Several principles follow from these results. To concentrate learning on essential points and to save time, as in training, remove elaborations and extraneous oral and written prose. To focus learners on selected questions or to teach them to find answers in elaborated

Table 2-2
Effects of Methods of Teaching

Method	Number of Studies	Effect Size	Graphic Representation of Effect Size
Advance organizers			
Overall effect	29	0.45	.xxxxx
Bridging			
from previous knowledge	a	0.75	.xxxxxxxxx
from previous material	a	0.71	.xxxxxxx
unspecified bridging	a	−0.02	
Presentation mode			
spoken	a	0.68	.xxxxxxx
written and illustrated	a	0.40	.xxxx
written only	a	0.34	.xxx
Advance organizers in science	16	0.24	.xx
Adjunct questions			
repeated	61	0.96	.xxxxxxxxxx
related	61	0.50	.xxxxx
unrelated	61	−0.13	x.
Goal setting			
on intended outcomes	21	0.40	.xxxx
on unintended outcomes	20	−0.20	xx.
Focusing in science	25	0.48	.xxxxx
Learning hierarchies	15	0.18	.xx
Pretests			
outcome			
cognitive	a	0.43	.xxxx
attitude	a	0.29	.xxx
pretest-posttest			
same	a	0.25	.xxx
different	a	0.11	.x
Behavioral objectives	111	0.12	.x
High expectations	77	0.32	.xxx
Frequent testing			
on quizzes	4	0.49	.xxxxx
on final examinations	30	0.19	.xx
on attitudes	5	0.50	.xxxxx
Increased testing in science	33	0.37	.xxxx
Questioning	14	0.26	.xxx
Questioning in science	11	0.56	.xxxxxx
Wait time in science	2	0.53	.xxxxx
Homework			
with teacher comments	2	0.83	.xxxxxxxx
graded	5	0.78	.xxxxxxxx
assigned	47	0.28	.xxx

Table 2-2 *continued*
Effects of Methods of Teaching

Method	Number of Studies	Effect Size	Graphic Representation of Effect Size
Remediation/Feedback in science	28	0.54	.xxxxx
Feedback	15	0.45	.xxxxx
Praise	14	0.16	.xx

The reviews examined did not include information on the number of studies involved in these comparisons.

prose such as in textbooks, use adjunct questions and goal setting. To encourage acquisition of as much undifferentiated material as possible, as in college lecture courses, assign big blocks of text and test students on randomly selected points. Although the means may seem clear, consensus about educational purposes may be difficult.

Clarity at the start saves time and helps learners to see things the teacher's way; but it deters autonomy and deep, personal insights. For example, at one extreme, Zen masters ask novitiates about the sound of one hand clapping and wait a decade or two for an answer. Hiroshi Azuma and Robert Hess find that Japanese mothers use indirection and vagueness in teaching their young children more than do assertive American mothers; and I have observed Japanese science teachers asking questions and leaving them long unresolved. Does such vagueness cultivate initiative and perseverance?

Engagement

A variety of means can help to increase students' engagement.

High expectations transmit teachers' standards of learning and performance. These may function as both cues and incentives for students to engage actively with extended effort and perseverance.

Frequent tests increase learning by demanding increased effort and feedback. Their effects are larger, however, on performance on quizzes than on final examinations.

Questioning also appears to work by increasing students' engagement and may encourage deeper thinking, as in Plato's accounts of Socrates. Questioning has bigger effects in science than in other subjects. Mary Budd Rowe and Ken Tobin have shown that *wait time*, that is, allowing students several seconds to reflect rather than the usual 0.9 seconds, leads to longer and better answers.

Correctives and Reinforcement

Corrective feedback remedies errors by reteaching, using the same or a different method. It has moderate effects that are somewhat higher in science than in other subjects—perhaps because science requires more conceptual thinking than memorization.

Homework by itself constructively extends engagement or learning time. Correctives and reinforcement in the form of grades and comments on homework raise its effects dramatically.

Praise has a small, positive effect. For young or disturbed children, praise may lack the power of tangible and token reinforcers used in psychological experiments. For students able to see ahead, grades and personal standards may be more powerful reinforcers than momentary encouragement. Praise may be under- or oversupplied; it may appear demeaning or sardonic; and it may pale in comparison with the incentives of U.S. youth culture, such as cars, clothes, dating, and athletics.

None of this is to say that encouragement, incentives, and good classroom morale should be abandoned; honey may be better than vinegar. As cognitive psychologists point out, moreover, the main classroom value of reinforcement may lie in its information for the student about his or her progress rather than in its power to reward.

PATTERNS OF TEACHING

As explained above, methods of teaching enact or combine more fundamental psychological elements. By further extension, patterns of teaching integrate elements and methods of teaching. These more inclusive formulations follow the evolution of psychological research on education. Behavioral research moved in the 1950s from psychological laboratories to classrooms, where short-term, controlled experiments were conducted on one element at a time. And in the 1970s, educational researchers tried to find patterns of effective practices from observations of ordinary teaching.

Thus, behaviorists traded educational realism for theoretical parsimony and scientific rigor; later psychologists preferred realism until

Table 2-3
Effects of Patterns of Teaching

Patterns	Number of Studies	Effect Size	Graphic Representation of Effect Size
Explicit or direct teaching	13	0.55	.xxxxxx
Comprehension teaching	20	0.71	.xxxxxxx

their insights were experimentally confirmed. Fortunately, the results from both approaches appear to converge. It seems possible, moreover, to incorporate the work of cognitive psychologists that took place during the 1980s into an enlarged understanding of teaching.

Table 2-3 summarizes results of studies of two patterns of teaching—explicit teaching and comprehension teaching.

Explicit Teaching

Explicit teaching can be viewed as traditional or conventional whole-group teaching done well. Since most teaching has changed little in the last three-quarters of a century (Hoetker and Ahlbrand, 1969) and may not change substantially in the near future, it is worthwhile knowing how the usual practice can excel. Since it has evolved from ordinary practice, explicit teaching is easy to carry out and does not disrupt conventional institutions and expectations. It can, moreover, incorporate many previously discussed elements and methods.

Systematic research was initiated about 1960 by N. L. Gage, Donald Medley, and others who employed "process-product" investigations of the association between what teachers do and how much their students learn. Jere Brophy, Carolyn Evertson, Thomas Good, and Jane Stallings later contributed substantially to this effort. Walter Doyle, Penelope Peterson, and Lee Shulman put the results in a psychological, particularly cognitive, context. Barak Rosenshine has periodically reviewed the research; Gage and Margaret Needels recently measured the results and sharply pointed out their implications.

These various contributors do not completely agree about the essential components of explicit teaching; and they refer to it by different names, such as explicit, process-product, direct, active, and effective teaching. The researchers, moreover, weigh their own results heavily; but Rosenshine, a long-standing and comprehensive reviewer, has given us an eagle's eye view of the results (see Wittrock, 1986).

In his early reviews of correlation studies, Rosenshine discussed the traits of effective teachers, which include clarity, task orientation, enthusiasm, and flexibility, as well as their tendencies to structure their presentations and occasionally use student ideas. From later observational and control-group research, Rosenshine identified six phased functions of explicit teaching: (1) daily review, homework check, and, if necessary, reteaching; (2) rapid presentation of new content and skills in small steps; (3) guided student practice with close monitoring by teachers; (4) corrective feedback and instructional reinforcement; (5) independent practice in seatwork and homework with a high, more than 90 percent, success rate; and (6) weekly and monthly review.

Comprehension Teaching

The descendants of Aristotle and the Anglo-American tradition of Bacon, Locke, Thorndike, and Skinner objected to philosophical "armchair" opinions—mid-century behaviorists, particularly John Watson, constructively insisted on hard empirical facts about learning. But they also saw the child's mind as a blank tablet, and seemed to encourage active teaching and passive acquisition of isolated facts. Around 1980, cognitive psychologists reacted to such atomism and William James's "bucket" metaphor by reviving research on student-centered learning and "higher mental processes," in the tradition of Plato, Socrates, Kant, Rousseau, Dewey, Freud, and Piaget. At times, however, contemporary interpretation of this tradition has led to vacuity and permissiveness, as in the extremes of the "progressive education" movement of the 1930s.

The Russian psychologist Lev Vygotsky (1978) developed an influential compromise. Emphasizing the two-way nature of teaching, he identified a "zone of proximal development" extending from what learners can do independently to the maximum they can do with the teacher's help. Accordingly, teachers should set up "scaffolding" for building knowledge but remove it when it becomes unnecessary. In mathematics, for example, the teacher can give hints and examples, foster independent use, and then remove support. This approach is similar to the "prompting" and "fading" of the behavioral cues and to common sense; but it sufficed to revive interest in transferring some autonomy to students.

In the 1980s, cognitive research on teaching sought ways to encourage self-monitoring, self-teaching, and "meta-cognition" to foster independence. Skills were important, but the learner's monitoring and management of them had primacy, as the explicit teaching functions of planning, allocating time, and review are partly transferred to learners.

Pearson (1985), for example, outlined three phases of meta-cognitive teaching: (1) modeling, where the teacher exhibits the desired behavior; (2) guided practice, where students perform with help from the teacher; and (3) application, where the student performs independently of the teacher—much like explicit teaching functions. Pallincsar and Brown (1984), moreover, described a program of "reciprocal teaching" to foster comprehension. In that program, students took turns leading dialogues on pertinent features of a text. By assuming the planning and executive control ordinarily exercised by teachers, students learned planning, structuring, and self-management—which is perhaps why tutors learn from teaching, and why we say that if you want to learn something well, teach it.

Comprehension teaching encourages students to measure their progress toward explicit goals. If necessary, they can reallocate time for different activities. In this way, self-awareness, personal control, and positive self-evaluation can be enlarged.

Learner Autonomy in Science

The National Science Foundation sponsored many studies of student inquiry and autonomy which showed that giving students opportunities to manipulate science materials, to contract with teachers about what to learn, to inquire on their own, and to engage in activity-based curricula all have substantial effects, as shown in Table 2-4. Group work and self-direction, however, had smaller positive effects; and pass-fail grading and self-grading had small negative effects. Methods of providing greater learner autonomy may work well in subjects other than science, as in the more radical and general approach discussed next.

Open Education

In the late 1960s, open educators increased autonomy in primary grades by enabling students to join teachers in planning educational

Table 2-4
Effects of Learner Autonomy in Science

Method	Number of Studies	Effect Size	Graphic Representation of Effect Size
Student manipulatives	24	0.56	.xxxxxx
Contracts for learning	12	0.47	.xxxxx
Inquiry-discovery	38	0.41	.xxxx
Activity-based curricula	57	0.35	.xxxx
Self-directed study	27	0.08	.x
Pass-fail or self-grading	13	−0.13	x.

purposes, means, and evaluation. In contrast to teacher- and textbook-centered education, students were given a voice in choosing what to learn—even to the point of writing their own texts to share with one another. Open educators tried to foster cooperation, critical thinking, constructive attitudes, and self-directed life-long learning. Open educators revived the spirit of the New England town meeting—of Thoreau's self-reliance, Emerson's transcendentalism, and Dewey's progressivism. Their ideas also resonate with the late Carl Rogers's "client-centered" psychotherapy that emphasizes the "unconditional worth" of the person. The effects of open education are summarized in Table 2-5.

Giaconia and Hedges's (1982) synthesis of 153 studies showed that open education had worthwhile effects on creativity, independence, cooperation, attitudes toward teachers and schools, mental ability, psychological adjustment, and curiosity. They found that students in open programs were less motivated to grub for grades, but they differed little from other students in actual achievement, self-concept, and anxiety. They also found, however, that open programs that are more effective in producing the nonachievement outcomes—attitudes, creativity, and self-concept—sacrificed some academic achievement on standardized measures. These programs emphasized the role of the child in learning, use of diagnostic rather than norm-referenced evaluation, individualized instruction, and manipulative materials; but they neglected to emphasize three other components thought by some to be essential to open programs—multi-age grouping, open space, and team teaching.

Giaconia and Hedges speculated that children in the most extreme open programs may do somewhat less well on conventional

Table 2-5
Effects of Open Education

Attitude/Achievement	Number of Studies	Effect Size	Graphic Representation of Effect Size
Creativity	22	0.29	.xxx
Independence	22	0.28	.xxx
Cooperativeness	8	0.23	.xx
Attitude toward teachers	17	0.20	.xx
Mental ability	16	0.18	.xx
Adjustment	9	0.17	.xx
Attitude toward school	50	0.17	.xx
Curiosity	7	0.17	.xx
Self-concept	60	0.07	.x
Locus of control	16	0.01	.
Anxiety	19	−0.01	.
Mathematics achievement	57	−0.04	.
Language achievement	33	−0.07	x.
Reading achievement	63	−0.08	x.
Achievement motivation	8	−0.26	xxx.

achievement tests because they have little experience with them. At any rate, it appears that unless they are radically extreme, open classes enhance several nonstandard outcomes without detracting from academic achievement.

EFFECTS OF INSTRUCTIONAL SYSTEMS

All the techniques discussed thus far can be planned and executed by a single teacher with perhaps some extra effort, encouragement, or training but without unusual preparation and materials. In contrast, instructional systems require special arrangements and planning, and they often combine several components of instruction. Moreover, they tend to emphasize adaption of instruction to individual students rather than student adaption to a fixed pattern of teaching such as explicit whole-group instruction. The effects of instructional systems are shown in Table 2-6.

A little history will aid our understanding of current systems.

Programmed instruction, popular in the 1950s, presents a series of "frames," each one of which conveys an item of information and

Table 2-6
Effects of Instructional Systems

System	Number of Studies	Effect Size	Graphic Representation of Effect Size
Programmed instruction			
in science			
branched	5	0.21	.xx
linear	47	0.17	.xx
in mathematics	153	0.10	.x
Individualization			
in science	131	0.17	.xx
in mathematics	153	0.16	.xx
in high schools	51	0.10	.x
Mastery learning			
require mastery before			
next unit	3	0.99	.xxxxxxxxxx
unit mastery level			
91–100	17	0.73	.xxxxxxx
81–90	15	0.51	.xxxxx
70–80	17	0.38	.xxxx
Duration of program			
up to one month	12	0.65	.xxxxxxx
17 or more weeks	6	0.30	.xxx
Level			
college	27	0.58	.xxxxxx
precollege	22	0.49	.xxxxx
Adaptive instruction	37	0.45	.xxxxx

requires a student response. *Linear* programs present a graduated series of frames with knowledge increments so small that learning steps may be nearly errorless and continuously reinforced by progression to the next frame; able students proceed quickly. *Branched* programs direct students back when necessary for reteaching; to the side for correctives; and ahead when they already know parts of the material. The ideas of continuous progress and branching influenced later developers who tried to optimize learning by individualization, mastery learning, and computer-assisted instruction.

Individualization adapts instruction to individual needs by varying speed or branching and by using booklets, worksheets, coaching, and the like. Perhaps because they have been vaguely defined and operationalized, individualized programs have had small effects. Other systems such as mastery learning (discussed below) appear more effective for adapting instruction to the needs of individual learners.

Mastery learning combines the psychological elements of instruction with suitable amounts of time. Formative tests are employed to allocate time and guide reinforcement and corrective feedback. In the most definitive synthesis, Kulik and Kulik (1986) reported substantial effects for mastery learning. Mastery programs that yielded larger effects established a criterion of 95 to 100 percent mastery and required repeated testing to ensure mastery before allowing students to proceed to additional units (which yielded a gigantic effect of one standard deviation). Mastery learning yielded larger effects on less able students, and reduced the disparities in performance to 82 percent of the control groups.

The success of mastery learning is attributable to several features. The Kuliks, for example, found that when control groups were provided feedback from quizzes, the mastery groups' advantage was smaller. Mastery, as Bloom pointed out, takes additional time; the Kuliks found that it required a median of 16 percent (and up to 97 percent) more time than did conventional instruction. The seven mastery studies that provided equal time for mastery and control groups showed a very small advantage for mastery learning, indicated by performance on standardized tests. The advantage, however, was moderate on experimenter-made, criterion-referenced tests for nine equal-time studies. These results illustrate the separate contribution of cues, feedback, and time components of mastery learning.

Mastery learning studies lasting less than a month's duration yielded larger effects than those lasting more than four months. Retention probably declines sharply no matter what the educational method, but the decline can be more confidently noted about mastery, since it has been more extensively investigated.

Bloom and his students have reported larger effects than has Slavin (1987), who reviewed their work. Guskey and Gates (1986), for example, reported an effect of 0.78, estimated from thirty-eight studies of elementary and secondary students. Anderson and Burns (1987), in response to Slavin, pointed out two reasons for larger effects in some studies, especially those under Bloom's supervision. Bloom has been interested more in what is possible than in what is likely; he has sought to find the limits of learning. His students, moreover, have conducted tightly controlled experiments over time periods shorter than a semester or a year.

Adaptive instruction, developed by Margaret Wang and others, combines mastery, cooperative, open, tutoring, computer, and comprehension approaches into a complex system to tailor instruction to individual and small-group needs. It includes managerial steps executed by a master teacher, including planning, time allocation, task delegation to aides and students, and quality control. It is a comprehensive program for the whole school day rather than a single method that requires simple integration into one subject or into a single teacher's repertoire. Its achievement effects are substantial, but its broader effects are probably underestimated, since adaptive instruction aims at diverse ends including student autonomy, intrinsic motivation, and teacher and student choice, which are poorly indicated by the usual outcome measures.

Computer-Assisted Instruction

Ours may be the age of computers, and they have already been shown to have substantial effects on learning. With hardware costs declining and software increasing in sophistication, we may hope that computers will have still more effects on learning as they become better integrated into school programs.

Computers show the greatest advantage for handicapped students—probably because they may be more adaptive to these students' special needs; computers may also be more patient, discreet, nonjudgmental, or even encouraging about students' progress. Perhaps for the same reasons, computers have generally bigger effects in elementary schools than in high schools and colleges. Effects of computer-assisted instruction are shown in Table 2-7.

Another explanation, however, is plausible. Elementary schools provide less tracking and differentiated courses for homogeneous groups. Computers may adapt to larger within-class differences among elementary students by allowing them to proceed at their own pace, without making invidious comparisons between students.

Simulation and games, with or without computer implementation, require active, specific learner responses and may strike a balance between the vicarious book learning and the dynamic, complicated, and competitive "real world." Their interactiveness, speed, intensity, movement, color, and sound add interest and information to academic learning. If games are not geared to an educational purpose, however, they can also waste time—as in arcade games.

Table 2-7
Effects of Computer-Assisted Instruction

Level	Number of Studies	Effect Size	Graphic Representation of Effect Size
Handicapped	26	0.66	.xxxxxxx
Elementary	28	0.47	.xxxxx
Elementary	28	0.45	.xxxxx
Japanese elementary and secondary	4	0.45	.xxxxx
Adult	24	0.42	.xxxx
Secondary, college	11	0.42	.xxxx
Elementary, secondary	33	0.42	.xxxx
Secondary	42	0.42	.xxxx
Elementary and secondary mathematics	46	0.39	.xxxx
Secondary	42	0.32	.xxx
College	101	0.26	.xxx
Simulation and games	93	0.35	.xxxx

Student Grouping

Teaching students what they already know and what they are yet incapable of learning are equally wasteful—they are perhaps even harmful to motivation. For this reason, traditional whole-class teaching of heterogeneous groups can present serious difficulties and inefficiency—often unacknowledged in our egalitarian age. Most educators recognize that it is difficult to teach arithmetic and trigonometry at the same time. (Even some English professors might balk at teaching phonics and deconstructionism simultaneously.) If we want students to learn as much as possible rather than make them all alike, we need to consider how they are grouped, and try to help the full range. Effects of various types of student grouping are shown in Table 2-8.

Acceleration programs identify talented youth (often in mathematics and science) and group them together or with older students. Such programs provide counseling, encouragement, contact with accomplished adults, grade skipping, summer school, and the compression of the standard curriculum into fewer years. The effects are huge in elementary schools, substantial in junior high schools, and

Table 2-8
Effects of Student Grouping

Type of Grouping	Number of Studies	Effect Size	Graphic Representation of Effect Size
Acceleration of talented students			
elementary	3	1.43	.xxxxxxxxxxxxxxx
junior high school	9	0.76	.xxxxxxxx
senior high school	1	0.28	.xxx
Ability grouping in high school			
talented students	14	0.33	.xxx
senior high school	18	0.20	.xx
junior high school	33	0.05	.x
average and deficient students	27	0.02	.
on subject matter attitudes	8	0.37	.xxxx
Ability grouping in elementary school			
cross-grade reading group	14	0.45	.xxxxx
within-class mathematics	5	0.32	.xxx
self-contained classes	14	0.00	.
Tutoring			
in mathematics	153	0.61	.xxxxxx
all courses	65	0.41	.xxxx

moderate in senior high schools. The smaller effects at advanced levels may be attributable to the smaller advantage of acceleration over tracking and differentiated course placement practiced in high schools.

The effects of acceleration on educational attitudes, vocational plans, participation in school activities, popularity, psychological adjustment, and character ratings were mixed and often insignificant. These outcomes may not be systematically affected in either direction.

Ability grouping is based on achievement, intelligence tests, personal insights, and subjective opinions. In high school, ability grouping leaves deficient and average students unaffected but yields big benefits with talented students and on improving students' attitudes toward the subject matter. In elementary schools, the grouping of students with similar reading achievement but from different grades yields substantial effects. Within-class grouping in mathematics yields worthwhile effects, but generalized grouping does not.

Tutoring, because it gears instruction to individual or small-group needs, yields big effects on both tutees and tutors. It yields particularly large effects in mathematics—perhaps because of the subject's well-defined scope and organization.

In whole-group instruction, teachers may ordinarily focus on average or deficient students to ensure that they master the lessons. But when talented students are freed from repetition and slow progression, they can proceed quickly. Grouping may work best when students are accurately grouped according to their specific subject matter needs rather than IQ, demeanor, or other irrelevant characteristics.

Well-defined subject matter and student grouping may be among the chief reasons why Japanese students lead the world in achievement; their curriculum is explicit, rigorous, and nationally uniform. In primary schools, weaker students, with maternal help, study harder and longer to keep up with exacting requirements. Subject matter admission tests are used several times to screen students into lower and upper secondary schools and universities of well-known gradations of rigor and prestige. Each gradation indicates occupational, marital, and other adult prospects; future adult rewards thus reinforce educational effort.

Social Environment

The effects of various types of social environments are shown in Table 2-9. *Cooperative learning* programs delegate some control of the pacing and methods of learning to groups of two to six students who work together (and sometimes compete with other groups within classes). Their success may be attributable to (a) relief from the exclusively teacher-to-student interaction of whole-group teaching, (b) the time freed for interactive engagement of students (highest in two-person teams), and (c) the opportunities for targeted cues, engagement, correctives, and reinforcement. As in comprehension teaching, moreover, the acts of tutoring and teaching may encourage students to think about subject matter organization and productive time allocation.

Many correlational studies suggest that *classroom morale* is associated with achievement gains, greater subject matter interest, and the worthy end of voluntary participation in nonrequired subject-related activities. Morale is assessed by asking students to agree or disagree with such statements as "Most of the students know each other well" and "The class members know the purpose of the lessons."

Table 2-9
Effects of Social Environment

Type of Environment	Number of Studies	Effect Size	Graphic Representation of Effect Size
Cooperative learning	182	0.78	.xxxxxxxx
Classroom morale (correlational)			
cohesiveness	50	0.23	.xx
satisfaction	54	0.22	.xx
material environment	49	0.18	.xx
goal direction	51	0.17	.xx
democracy	50	0.17	.xx
task difficulty	50	0.13	.x
formality	57	0.06	.x
competition	35	0.06	.x
diversity	47	0.02	.
speed	48	−0.02	.
cliqueness	46	−0.12	x.
disorganization	50	−0.13	x.
apathy	48	−0.14	x.
favoritism	46	−0.16	xx.
friction	53	−0.23	xx.

Students who perceive their classroom morale as friendly, satisfying, goal-directed, and challenging and their classroom as having the required materials tend to learn more. Those who perceive student cliques, disorganization, apathy, favoritism, and friction learn less. The research, though plausible, lacks the causal confidence and specificity of control-group experiments on directly alterable methods discussed previously and in following paragraphs.

Reading Effects

Comprehension teaching, because it may extend to several subjects in elementary schools, is discussed above under patterns of teaching. Several other reading effects are substantial. (See Table 2-10.)

Adaptive speed training involves principles similar to those of comprehension training. It shows learners how to vary their pace and depth of reflection according to the difficulty of material and their purposes in reading. It yields big effects on the capacity to shift gears in reading.

Table 2-10
Effects of Reading Methods

Method	Number of Studies	Effect Size	Graphic Representation of Effect Size
Adaptive speed training	28	0.95	.xxxxxxxxxx
Reading methods	97	0.61	.xxxxxx
Adjunct pictures	16	0.22	.xx
Pictures in prose			
transformative	18	1.42	.xxxxxxxxxxxxxx
interpretive	24	0.75	.xxxxxxxx
organizational	21	0.72	.xxxxxxx
representative	79	0.54	.xxxxx
decorative	8	−0.12	x.

Reading methods vary widely, but their largest effects seem to occur when teachers are systematically trained almost irrespective of particularities of method. *Phonics* or "word-attack" approaches, however, have moderate advantage over guessing and "whole-word" approaches in the teaching of beginning reading—perhaps because early misconceptions are avoided. Phonics may also reduce the need for excessive reteaching and correctives.

Pictures in the text can be very helpful, although they increase the cost of books, and occupy space that could otherwise be used for prose. Several types of pictures can be distinguished; in order of their effects they are:

Transformational pictures recode information into concrete memorable form, relate information in a well-organized context, and provide links for systematic retrieval.

Interpretive pictures, like advance organizers, make text comprehensible by relating abstract to concrete terms and the unfamiliar and difficult to previous knowledge.

Organizational pictures, including maps and diagrams, show the coherence of objects or events in space and time.

Representational pictures are photos or other concrete representations of what the prose relates.

Decorative pictures present information incidental to (and possibly irrelevant to or conflicting with) intended learning (researchers might concede that decoration may add interest if not information).

Table 2-11
Effects of Writing Methods

Method	Number of Studies	Effect Size	Graphic Representation of Effect Size
Inquiry	6	0.57	.xxxxxx
Scales	6	0.36	.xxxx
Sentence combining	5	0.35	.xxxx
Models	7	0.22	.xx
Free writing	10	0.16	.xx
Grammar/Mechanics	5	−0.30	xxx.

As Levin, Anglin, and Carney (forthcoming) conclude, pictures can provide vivid imagery and metaphors that facilitate memorization, show what is important to learn, and intensify the effects of oral prose, as in ordinary teaching. Pictures may allow students to bypass the text; but memorable, well-written prose may obviate pictures.

Writing Effects

Well-designed studies of methods of teaching writing contrasted experimental treatments with control groups. In order of the sizes of effects on prose quality (see Table 2-11), the methods were as follows:

Inquiry requires students to find and state specific details that convey personal experience vividly; to examine sets of data to develop and support explanatory generalizations; or to analyze situations that present ethical problems and arguments.

Scales are criteria or specific questions students apply to their own and others' writing to improve it.

Sentence combining shows students how to build complex sentences from simpler ones.

Models are presentations of good pieces of writing for students to follow.

Free writing allows students to write about whatever occurs to them.

Grammar and mechanics includes sentence parsing and analysis of the parts of speech.

Science Effects

Begun about 1960 in response to the Russian space launch, the "new" science curricula, sponsored by the National Science Foundation, yielded substantial effects on learning. The curricula efficiently added value by producing superior learning on tests of their intended outcomes and general subject matter goals. The new curricula also yielded small to substantial effects on often unmeasured outcomes such as creativity, problem solving, science attitudes and skills, logical thinking, and achievement in nonscience subject matter. The effects of various science programs are shown in Table 2-12.

Perhaps these advantages were gained by a collaboration of teachers, psychologists, and scientists to ensure modern content and teaching efficacy. Scientists may have generated enthusiasm for teaching scientific methods, laboratory work, and other course reforms.

The new science curricula worked well in improving achievement and other outcomes. Ironically, they are often forgotten today despite poor U.S. mathematics and science scores by international standards. A discussion of some of these methods follows,

Inquiry teaching, often practiced in Japan, requires students to formulate hypotheses, reason about their creditability, and design experiments to test their validity. Inquiry teaching yields substantial effects—particularly on the understanding of scientific processes.

Audio-tutorials are tape-recorded instructions for using media such as laboratory equipment, manipulatives, and readings for topical lessons or whole courses. This simple approach yields somewhat better results than conventional instruction, allows independent learning, and has the further advantage of individual pacing—allowing students to pursue special topics or take courses on their own.

Original source papers derive from the "Great Books" approach of University of Chicago President Robert Maynard Hutchins and his colleague Mortimore Adler, who saw more value in reading Plato or Newton than predigested textbook accounts. Those who trade depth for breadth believe it is better to know few ideas of transcending importance than many unconnected bits of soon forgotten information. They have shown that such knowledge can be acquired by studying and discussing science papers of historical or scientific significance.

The effects of other science instruction methods are near zero, that

Table 2-12
Effects of Science Programs

Program	Number of Studies	Effect Size	Graphic Representation of Effect Size
New curricula in general	105	0.37	.xxxx
New curricula on tests of			
new content	9	0.39	.xxxx
neutral content	11	0.41	.xxxx
old content	1	−0.13	x.
New curricula on			
creativity	5	0.71	.xxxxxxx
problem solving	4	0.71	.xxxxxxx
scientific understanding	28	0.61	.xxxxxx
spatial relations	2	0.57	.xxxxxx
subject attitude	6	0.51	.xxxxx
science attitude	25	0.50	.xxxxx
general science achievement	111	0.43	.xxxx
science method attitude	10	0.41	.xxxx
mathematics achievement	18	0.40	.xxxx
communication skills	5	0.40	.xxxx
social studies achievement	2	0.25	.xxx
critical thinking	31	0.19	.xx
scientific skills	28	0.17	.xx
logical thinking	14	0.16	.xx
reading achievement	23	0.10	.x
synthesis and analysis	11	0.05	.x
fact recall	8	0.02	.
self-concept	10	−0.08	x.
Inquiry teaching	68	0.43	.xxxx
Audio-tutorial	7	0.17	.xx
Original source papers	13	0.14	.x
Team teaching	41	0.06	.x
Departmentalized elementary			
programs	3	−0.09	x.
Media-based instruction			
television	40	0.06	.x
film	58	−0.07	x.

is, close to the effects of the usual methods of teaching. They include *team teaching, departmentalized elementary programs*, and *media-based instruction*. The results for media-based instruction, however, suggest choices that can be based on cost and convenience. In particular, since live television and canned film can be broadcast, they can provide equally effective education over wide areas (even the world by satellite); and students today, moreover, can interact "on-line" with far-away teachers and fellow students. Some precedents follow:

1. For a decade, the Chicago Community Colleges gave dozens of mainly one-way television courses to hundreds of thousands of students who studied mostly at home but also participated in discussion and testing sessions at several sites in the metropolitan area. The best lecturers, media specialists, and test constructors could be employed; and tapes of the courses could be rebroadcast indefinitely.

2. In several third-world countries gaining in student achievement and enrollments, ministries of education make efficient use of such low-cost but effective "distance education" for remote elementary and secondary schools.

3. The Oklahoma and Minnesota state departments of education apparently lead the nation in providing specialized teachers and two-way courses in advanced science, mathematics, foreign language, and other subjects by broadcasting them to small high schools in rural areas.

Mathematics Effects

In the heyday of its Education Directorate, the National Science Foundation sponsored considerable research not only on science but also on mathematics. Some worthwhile effects were found, as shown in Table 2-13.

Manipulative materials such as Cuisinnaire rods, balance beams, counting sticks, and measuring scales allow students to engage directly in learning rather than to follow passively abstract teacher presentations. Students can handle the material, see the relation of abstract ideas and concrete embodiments, and check hypothesized answers by doing quick empirical tests—without having to wait for quiz results or teacher feedback. The apparent result: enormous effects.

Problem solving in mathematics yields worthwhile effects. It requires comprehension of terms and their application to varied examples. It may motivate students by showing them the application of mathematical ideas to "real-world" questions.

The new mathematics produced beneficial results, although not as

Table 2-13
Effects of Mathematics Methods

Method	Number of Studies	Effect Size	Graphic Representation of Effect Size
Manipulative materials	64	1.04	.xxxxxxxxxx
Problem solving	33	0.35	.xxxx
New mathematics	134	0.24	.xx

big as the new science curricula. Both reforms probably gained their learning advantages partly by testing what they taught.

Special Populations and Techniques

We can gain insights from programs outside the usual scope of elementary and secondary classrooms. (See Table 2-14.)

Early intervention programs include educational, psychological, and therapeutic components for handicapped, at-risk, and disadvantaged children from one month to sixty-six months of age. The immediate and large outcome advantages declined rapidly and disappeared after three years.

Preschool programs also showed initial learning effects that were unsustained. It appears that young children can learn more than is normally assumed; but, like other learners, they can also forget. The key to sustained gains may be sustained programs and effective families—not one-shot approaches.

Handicapped students classified as mentally retarded, emotionally disturbed, and learning disabled have been subjects in research that has several important implications. When they serve as *tutors* of one another and younger students, handicapped students can learn well—a finding similar to those in comprehension monitoring and tutoring studies of nonhandicapped children that show beneficial effects of teaching on tutors. "Handicapped" students, moreover, are often spuriously classified, and we may underestimate their capacities.

Mainstreaming studies show that mildly to moderately handicapped students can prosper in regular classes and thereby avoid the stereotyped, invidious "labeling" often based on misclassifications. *Psycholinguistic training* of special-needs students yields positive effects; it consists of testing and remedying specific deficits in language skills.

Patient education can affect mortality, morbidity, and lengths of

Table 2-14
Effects of Programs for Special Populations

Program	Number of Studies	Effect Size	Graphic Representation of Effect Size
Preschool			
early intervention	326	0.50	.xxxxx
preschool programs	11	0.22	.xx
Handicapped students			
handicapped students as tutors	19	0.48	.xxxxx
psycholinguistic training	34	0.39	.xxxx
mainstreaming	11	0.33	.xxx
perceptual motor training	180	0.08	.x
Superior patient education	70	0.84	.xxxxxxxx
In-service training of M.D.s on			
physician knowledge	41	0.81	.xxxxxxxx
physician performance	41	0.74	.xxxxxxx
patient outcomes	41	0.34	.xxx

illness and hospitalization. In studies of patients' learning about drug use for hypertension, diabetes, and other chronic conditions, one-to-one and group counseling (with or without instructional material) produced the greatest effects—in contrast to leaving instruction to bottle labels or "patient-package inserts." But labels, special containers, memory aids, and behavior modification were successful in minimizing later errors in drug use. The most efficacious educational principles were specification of intentions; relevance to learner needs; personal answers to questions; reinforcement and feedback on progress; facilitation such as unit-dose containers; and instructional and treatment regimens suited to personal convenience, such as prescribing drugs for mealtime administration.

In-service physician training shows large effects on knowledge and on classroom or laboratory performance; but only moderate effects of training can be found for patient outcomes. Knowledge and performance, even in practical training, may help but hardly guarantee successful application in practice. Can an accomplished mathematical problem solver do income tax returns?

At the request of the U.S. Army, the National Academy of Sciences evaluated exotic techniques and *"shortcuts"* for learning and performance enhancement described in popular psychology and presumably being exploited in California and the U.S.S.R. (Druckman

Table 2-15
Effects on Teachers

Program	Number of Studies	Effect Size	Graphic Representation of Effect Size
Microteaching	47	0.55	.xxxxx
In-service teacher education on	91		
teacher achievement	[a]	0.90	.xxxxxxxxx
teacher classroom behavior	[a]	0.60	.xxxxxx
teacher achievement	[a]	0.37	.xxxx

[a] The reviews examined did not include information on the number of studies involved in these comparisons.

and Swets, 1988). Little or no evidence, however, was found for the efficacy of learning during sleep, mental practice of motor skills, "integration" of left and right brain hemispheres, parapsychological techniques, biofeedback, extrasensory perception, mental telepathy, "mind over matter" exercises, and "neurolinguistic programming" (in which instructors identify students' mode of learning and mimic the students' behavior as they teach). The Greeks found no royal road to geometry. Even kings, if they desired mastery, had to sweat over Euclid's elements. Perhaps brain research will eventually yield an elixir or panacea; but, for proof, educators should insist on hard data in scientific journals.

Effects on Teachers

Programs to help teachers in their work have had substantial effects, notwithstanding complaints about teaching practices of in-service sessions. (See Table 2-15.) Do physicians complain about the medical care they get?

Microteaching, developed at Stanford University in the 1960s, is a behavioral approach for preservice and in-service training that has substantial effects. It employs explanation and modeling of selected teaching techniques; televised practice with small groups of students; discussion, correctives, and reinforcement while watching playback; and recycling through subsequent practice and playback sessions with new groups of students.

In-service teacher education also proves to have substantial effects. Somewhat like the case of physician training, the biggest effects are on teacher knowledge; but effects on classroom behavior and student achievement are also big.

For in-service training, authoritative planning and execution seem to work best; informal coaching by itself seems ineffective. Instructor responsibility for designing and teaching the sessions works better than teacher presentations and group discussions. The best techniques are observation of classroom practices, video-audio feedback, and practice. The best combination of techniques is lecture, modeling, practice, and coaching. The size of the training group, which can range from one (in a tutoring situation) to greater than sixty, makes no detectable difference.

Some apparent effects may be attributable to participant selectivity rather than to superior efficacy: federal-, state-, and university-sponsored programs appear more effective than locally initiated programs. Competitive selection of participants and college credit apparently work better as incentives than extra pay, certificate renewal, and no incentives. Independent study seems to have larger effects than workshops, courses, mini-courses, and institutes.

CONCLUSION

Psychological research provides first-order estimates of the effects of instructional means on educational ends under various conditions. But some practices may be costly—not in dollars but in new or complicated arrangements that may be difficult for some teachers and districts to begin and continue. Thus, the estimates of effects are only one basis for decision making. We need to consider productivity or values of effects in relation to total costs, which include the time and energies of educators and students.

Psychology alone cannot suffice to prescribe practices, since different means bring about different ends. Educators must choose among student-, teacher-, and curriculum-direction of effort; facts and concepts; breadth and depth; short- and long-term ends; academic knowledge and real-world application; equal opportunity and equal results; and Plato's triumvirate of thinking, feeling, and acting. Once these choices are made, the estimates of effects can provide one of the bases for choosing the most productive practices.

REFERENCES

Anderson, Lorin W., and Burns, Robert B. "Values, Evidence, and Mastery Learning," *Review of Educational Research* 57 (1987): 215–223.

Bloom, Benjamin S. *Human Characteristics and School Learning.* New York: McGraw-Hill, 1976.

Carroll, John B. "A Model of School Learning," *Teachers College Record* 64 (1963): 723–733.

Dollard, John, and Miller, Neal. *Personality and Psychotherapy.* New York: McGraw-Hill, 1950.

Druckman, D., and Swets, J. A. *Enhancing Human Performance.* Washington, D.C.: National Academy Press, 1988.

Fraser, Barry J.; Walberg, Herbert J.; Welch, Wayne W.; and Hattie, John A. "Syntheses of Educational Productivity Research," *International Journal of Educational Research* 11, no. 2 (1987): 73–145.

Giaconia, Rose M., and Hedges, Larry V. "Identifying Features of Effective Open Education," *Review of Educational Research* 52 (1982): 579–602.

Guskey, Thomas R., and Gates, Sally L. "Synthesis of Research on the Effects of Mastery Learning in Elementary and Secondary Classrooms," *Educational Leadership* 43 (May 1986): 73–80.

Hoetker, John, and Ahlbrand, William P. "The Persistence of the Recitation," *American Educational Research Journal* 6 (1969): 145–167.

Kulik, James A., and Kulik, Chen-Lin. "Mastery Testing and Student Learning," *Journal of Educational Technology Systems* 15 (1986): 325–345.

Levin, Joel R.; Anglin, Gary J.; and Carney, Russell N. "On Empirically Validating Functions of Pictures in Prose." In *Illustrations, Graphs, and Diagrams,* edited by D. M. Willows and H. A. Houghton. New York: Springer-Verlag, forthcoming.

Mastropieri, Margo A., and Scruggs, Thomas E. *Effective Instruction for Special Education.* Boston: Little, Brown, 1987.

Miller, Neal, and Dollard, John. *Social Learning and Imitation.* New Haven, Conn.: Yale University Press, 1941.

Pallincsar, Anne Marie, and Brown, Anne. "Reciprocal Teaching of Comprehension Fostering and Comprehension Monitoring Activities," *Cognition and Instruction* 1 (1984): 117–176.

Pearson, David. "Reading Comprehension Instruction: Six Necessary Steps," *Reading Teacher* 38 (1985): 724–738.

Slavin, Robert E. "Mastery Learning Reconsidered," *Review of Educational Research* 57 (1987): 175–213.

Vygotsky, Lev. *Mind in Society.* Cambridge, Mass.: Harvard University Press, 1978.

Walberg, Herbert J. "Improving the Productivity of America's Schools," *Educational Leadership* 41, no. 8 (1984): 19–27.

Walberg, Herbert J. "Synthesis of Research on Teaching." In *Handbook of Research on Teaching,* 3d ed., edited by Merlin C. Wittrock. New York: Macmillan, 1986.

Walberg, Herbert J.; Schiller, Diane; and Haertel, Geneva D. "The Quiet Revolution in Educational Research," *Phi Delta Kappan,* 61, no. 3 (1979): 179–183.

Wittrock, Merlin C., ed. *Handbook of Research on Teaching,* 3d ed. New York: Macmillan, 1986.

——— 3 ———

Teacher Effectiveness Research: Theoretical Considerations

Allan C. Ornstein

It is not an exaggeration to say that the literature on teaching is a morass of ill-defined and changing concepts. Investigators have examined teacher personality, traits, behaviors, attitudes, values, abilities, competencies, and many other characteristics. A host of measuring instruments have been employed: personality tests, attitudinal scales, observation instruments, rating scales, checklists, bipolar descriptors, and close-ended and open-ended written statements. The results of teaching have been studied in terms of student achievement, adjustment, attitudes, socioeconomic status, and creativity. Despite all this activity and thousands of studies conducted in the last fifty years, common denominators and agreed-on generalizations are hard to come by; hence, few facts concerning teacher effectiveness have been established (Borich, 1986; Ornstein, 1986a).

Confusion over terms, measurement problems, and the complexity of the teaching act are major reasons for the negligible results in judging teacher effectiveness. The studies themselves are often confirmations of common sense (a "democratic" teacher is an effective teacher) or contradictory ("direct" behaviors are effective; "indirect" behaviors are effective), or the contexts within which the studies take place have little bearing on classroom settings, subject, or grade level of the individual teacher.

Because we are unable to agree on or precisely define what a good teacher is, we can use almost any definition, so long as it makes sense or seems logical. Despite the elusive and complex nature of teaching, research on teaching should continue with the hope we can better understand it. This chapter, then, is concerned with the understanding of teacher effectiveness—and with some of the theoretical issues related to defining effective teaching.

THEORY VERSUS THE PRACTICE OF TEACHING

The test of a good theory is whether it can guide practice. In reverse, good practice is based on theory. By practice, we mean the methods, strategies, and skills that apply to the working world, when a person is on the job and actively involved in his or her profession. These theoretical procedures are teachable and can be applied in different situations. When applied, they should result in the practitioner (the teacher) being considered "successful" or "effective" (Ornstein, 1987). By theory, we mean knowledge gained by research and experience that is generalizable and whereby potential users (teachers) can make informed estimates of the probable effects and effectiveness of practices (Bolin, 1988; Wise et al., 1985). Without theory, we cannot assess whether a particular method or strategy will suit the purpose or effect we are trying to achieve. Also, without theory, we operate haphazardly, intuitively, and instinctively. This is not always bad, but it is often difficult to put confidence in our judgments while teaching because of its swift and complex nature. The nature of teaching, therefore, makes it difficult to repeat and interpret what we are doing when we teach.

Regardless of our theories, those who work with or prepare teachers in one way or another have to deal with practice—that is, with what works. Good theories are workable for practitioners, make sense, can be applied to the real world of classrooms and schools, and are generalizable to the greatest number of real situations. Theories that are not workable and generalizable are not good theories and cannot be translated into practice. Theories about teaching may not provide specific answers or quick solutions to vexing problems. Theories must be adjusted to the situation, given the fact that people (teachers and students) differ—they are not nuts and bolts on an assembly line or tiny transistors in a computer, which can be shaped precisely to specifications. Thus, we commonly hear teachers saying, "That's all good theory, but it doesn't work in practice."

In defense of teachers, most teaching experts have difficulty fusing theory and practice. Perhaps we have trouble connecting theory and practice because the methods of inquiry lend themselves more to theoretical discussions and less to practical matters. Also, while discovering good theory is recognized as a worthwhile endeavor, a repertoire of good practice is often misconstrued by theoreticians as a "cookbook" or as "do's and don'ts" that are second-rate or unimportant. Despite the claims of some theoreticians, we seem unable to make the leap from theory to practice, from the textbook and college course to the classroom and school. Good theory in teaching often gets lost as practitioners try to apply what they have learned in college to the classroom setting in a search for practical solutions to common, everyday problems.

The problem of translating theory into practice is further aggravated by researchers and professors, many of whom are more concerned with the teacher "knowing that" than with the teacher "knowing how." This distinction "refers to the difference between being able to state factual propositions [theory] and being able to perform skills or operations [practice]" (Gage 1978, p. 44). The one kind of knowledge does not necessarily follow from the other; this is the reason why teaching texts and courses can stress either theory or practice. According to Gage, "much of the teacher education program is given over to providing teachers with a great deal of knowledge that certain things are true, in the subject [and grade levels] to be taught" (p. 44). This kind of knowledge is acquired by most prospective teachers at the expense of theory that could help them understand the basic principles and phenomena underlying their work.

The problem is further compounded by practitioners, including teachers, supervisors, and administrators, who feel that practical considerations are more worthwhile than theory; most teachers and supervisors view theory as impractical and "how-to" approaches as helpful. Thus, while many theoreticians ignore the practitioners, at the same time many practitioners ignore the theoreticians. Moreover, many theoretical discussions of teaching are divorced from practical application in the classroom, and many practical discussions of teaching rarely consider theoretical relationships.

Practice involves selecting strategies and methods that apply to specific situations. Theory involves principles and propositions that can be generalized to many situations. The problem is that every situation is unique. This becomes especially evident when practitioners try to apply the theory they learn from the professional literature. Adopting the right method for the appropriate situation is not an easy task and involves a good deal of common sense and experience, which no one can learn from a theoretical discussion. No matter how good our theories may be, they are not always predictable or generalizable from one situation to another.

Teachers need to examine various teaching principles and practices based on theory. According to Stallings and Stipek (1986), teachers should "try different approaches for different subjects" and grade levels, and "ultimately develop their own variations" of what works for their students (p. 750). Teachers need to be encouraged to assess the effectiveness of various theories, and then to modify them for their own classroom setting, students, and subject.

THE SCIENCE VERSUS THE ART OF TEACHING

Another problem with preparing teachers is that we cannot agree on whether teaching is a science or an art. Some readers may say that this is a hopeless dichotomy, similar to that of theory versus practice, because the real world rarely consists of neat packages or either/or situations. Gage (1978) uses this distinction between teaching as a science and as an art to describe the elements of predictability in teaching and what constitutes "good" teaching. A science of teaching is attainable, he contends, because it "implies that good teaching will some day be attainable by closely following vigorous laws that yield high predictability and control." Teaching is more than a science, he observes, because it also involves "artistic judgment about the best ways to teach" (p. 17). When teaching leaves the laboratory or textbook and goes face to face with students, "the opportunity for artistry expands enormously." No science can prescribe successfully all the twists and turns as teaching unfolds, or as teachers respond with "judgment, sudden insight, sensitivity, and agility to promote learning" (p. 15). These are expressions of art that depart from the rules and principles of science.

Is such a limited scientific basis of teaching even worthwhile to consider? Yes, but the practitioner must learn as a teacher to draw not only from his or her professional knowledge (which is grounded in scientific principles), but also from a set of personal experiences and resources that are uniquely defined and exhibited by the teacher's own personality and "gut" reaction to classroom events that unfold (which form the basis for the art of teaching). For Jackson (1968), the hunches, judgments, and insights of the teacher, as he or she responds spontaneously to events in the classroom, are as important as, and perhaps even more important than, the science of teaching.

To some extent, the act of teaching must be considered intuitive and interactive, not prescriptive or predictable. According to Eisner (1983), teaching is based primarily on feelings and artistry, not scientific rules. In an age of science and technology, there is a special need to consider teaching as an "art and craft." Eisner condemns the scientific movement in psychology, especially behaviorism, and the scientific movement in education, especially in school management, as reducing the teaching act to trivial specifications. He regards teaching as a "poetic metaphor," more suited to satisfying the soul than informing the head, more concerned with the whole than with a set of discrete skills or stimuli. Our role as teachers, he claims, should not be that of a "puppeteer," an "engineer," or a manager; rather, it is "to orchestrate the dialogue [as the conductor of a symphony] moving from one side of the room to the other" (p. 8). The idea is to perceive patterns in motion, to improvise within the classroom, and to avoid mechanical or prescribed rules.

Rubin (1985) has a similar view of teaching—that effectiveness and artistry go hand in hand. The interplay of students and teacher is crucial and cannot be predetermined with carefully devised strategies. Confronted with everyday problems that cannot be easily predicted, the teacher must rely on intuition and on "insight acquired through long experience" (p. 61). Rubin refers to such terms as "with-it-ness," "instructional judgments," "quick cognitive leaps," and "informal guesses" to explain the difference between the effective teacher and the ineffective teacher. Recognizing limits to rationality, he claims that for the artistic teacher a "feel for what is right often is more productive than prolonged analysis" (p. 69). In the final analysis, Rubin compares the teacher's pedagogy with the "artist's colors, poet's words, sculptor's clay, and musician's notes" (p. 60)—in all of which a certain amount of artistic judgment is needed to get the right mix, medium, or blend.

Dawe (1984a, 1984b) is most extreme in his analysis of teaching solely as an art, providing romantic accounts and tales of successful teaching and teaching strategies, described in language that could hardly be taken for social science research. He considers the act of teaching akin to drama, and feels that those who wish to teach should audition in a teaching studio before teachers trained as performing artists. Good teaching is likened to good theater, and a good teacher is likened to a good actor.

Blending Science and Art

The more we consider teaching as an art, packed with emotions, feelings, and excitement, the more difficult it is to derive rules or generalizations. If teaching is more of an art than a science, then principles and practices cannot be easily codified or developed in the classroom or easily learned by others. Hence, there is little reason to offer to teachers methods courses in education. If, however, teaching is more of a science, or at least partly a science, then pedagogy is predictable to that extent; it can be observed and measured with some accuracy, and the research can be applied to the practice of teaching (as a physician applies scientific knowledge to the practice of medicine) and also learned in a university or on the job (Bolster, 1983; Ornstein, 1984, 1985b).

But a word of caution is needed. The more we rely on artistic interpretations or on old stories and accounts about teachers, the more we fall victim to fantasy, wit, and romantic rhetoric, and the more we depend on hearsay and conjecture rather than on social science or objective data in evaluating teacher competency. On the other hand, the more we rely on the scientific interpretations of teaching, the more we overlook those commonsense and spontaneous processes of teaching, and the sounds, smells, and visual flavor of the classroom. The more scientific we are in our approach to teaching, the more we ignore what we cannot accommodate to our empirical assumptions or principles. What sometimes occurs, according to Eisner (1985), is that the educationally significant but difficult to measure or observe is replaced by what is insignificant but comparatively easy to measure or observe.

It is necessary to blend artistic impressions and relevant stories about teaching, because good teaching involves emotions and feelings, with the objectivity of observations and measurements and the precision of language. There is nothing wrong with considering good teaching to be art, but we must also consider it to lend itself to a prescriptive science or practice. If it does not, then there is little assurance that prospective teachers can be trained to be teachers—told what to do, how to instruct students, how to manage students, and so forth—and educators will be extremely vulnerable to public criticism and to people outside the profession telling them how and what to teach.

True knowledge of teaching is achieved by practice and experience in the classroom. According to Bolster (1983), the "beliefs, values, and norms—that is, the knowledge—that teachers come to have the most faith in and use most frequently to guide their [teaching] are those consistent with traditions that have 'worked' in the . . . classroom arena." Although it seems to be "more everyday and commonsensical, both in form and structure, than highly specialized and theoretical," the process still includes the giving and receiving of data that can be partially planned and scientifically analyzed (p. 297). There are still cognitive, social, motor, and technical skills that must be taught to teachers and which can be designed and developed in advance with underlying scientific principles—and these principles are based on sound research and objective data.

Indeed, the real value of scientific procedures may not be realized in terms of research or theoretical "generalizations" that can be translated into practice. Research may have limited potential for teachers, but it can help them become aware of the problems and needs of students. Scientific generalizations and theories may not always be applicable to specific teaching situations, but such propositions can help in the formulation of a reliable and valid base for teaching in classrooms. Scientific ideas can serve as a starting point for discussion and analysis of the art of teaching.

TEACHER-STUDENT VARIABLES

The kind of teacher effectiveness studies that make up the mainstream of educational research considers relationships between variables. We can have *predictive* relationships and *causal* relationships. For example, Flanders (1965) in his classic study shows that students who are taught by an "indirect" teacher learn more and exhibit more constructive behaviors than do those who are taught by a "direct" teacher. The results of that study have been cited in thousands of studies on teaching, including some fifteen times in the most recent edition of the *Handbook of Research on Teaching*, edited by Wittrock (1986).

However, such a predictive relationship may not really reflect a causal relationship or a cause-effect relationship. It is possible that students who are nonachievers or unruly cause teachers to exhibit direct behaviors and that students who are achievers and well mannered permit teachers to exhibit indirect behaviors. We can raise this point with about 90 percent of the research on teacher effectiveness, since the results are overwhelmingly correlational.

Researchers have also identified other teacher- and student-related variables:

1. *Presage variables*—certain teacher and student characteristics such as sex, age, social class, or ethnicity.
2. *Context variables*—such as grade level, subject, classroom size, and classroom grouping patterns (homogeneous or heterogeneous; whole group or small group; segregated or integrated).
3. *Process variables*—describe what goes on in the classroom or teaching-learning situation, that is, teacher behaviors, teaching methods, and teacher-student interactions (both verbal and nonverbal).
4. *Product variables*—suggest the amount of learning or achievement or some learner behavior or attitude (Ornstein, 1986a).

Dunkin and Biddle (1974) and Gage (1978) contend that six possible pairings or relationships between these variables are possible: (1) presage-context, (2) presage-process, (3) presage-product, (4) context-process, (5) context-product, and (6) process-product. Ornstein (1985a) points out that researchers can also arrange multiple relationships of these variables, composing the following arrangements: (1) presage-context-process, (2) presage-context-product, (3) presage-process-product, (4) context-process-product; and (5) presage-context-process-product.

Whereas presage, context, and product variables can be precisely defined, process variables are somewhat elusive. Many teacher behaviors and methods that seem to have a positive effect in one situation may be ineffective and inappropriate in another. Different teacher behaviors and methods have different effects on different students, in different grades, subjects, classrooms, and schools. For example, does the "warm" teacher have the same effect on first graders and twelfth graders? In mathematics, history, and physical education? With low-income and middle-income students, with low achievers and high achievers, with boys and girls, and so on? Moreover, it is difficult to isolate the teacher effects from the effects of other agents such as parents, peer group, television, and other teachers (Ornstein, 1986b, 1989). Failure to control for these variables and their interaction effects leads to inappropriate research findings and to non-relevant and misleading data for the teacher. But once we start to analyze the various relationships among the variables, we come to numerous interactions and still other new and untested interactions, which in turn can be analyzed. This process is endless; we enter a hall of mirrors that extends to infinity.

Not only do process variables (different behaviors and/or methods) mean different things to different researchers, but also similar behaviors or methods are sometimes considered effective in one study and ineffective in another study. These are constructs that interact with numerous presage and context variables, and they entail such a diversity of specifics that they defy precise definitions and exact quantification. Moreover, if we break them down into precise, agreed-on, quantifiable constructs and variables, the number would vastly increase to the point of trivia and the importance of each would be reduced to the specific study. How far we extend our analysis depends on our purpose and knowledge; nonetheless, the existing relationships are not linear or clear, but rather multiple and sketchy.

Process Versus Product

Most of the research from the turn of the century to the early 1970s focused on process variables in terms of their relationships to presage or context variables. The idea was to focus on teacher behaviors or methods and to use such measures as ratings, classroom observations, and personality tests to obtain information on what the teacher was doing in the classroom. A basic assumption of many investigators during this period was that assessment of teacher behavior sufficed for describing teaching and learning. The focus was on what the teacher was doing, with little consideration given to the resulting behavior or performance of the students. Although one can make a good case for focusing on teachers, more emphasis should have been given to student outcomes.

Only recently has the research moved from the processes to the products of teaching. Emphasis on the products of teaching makes the behavior of the teacher, or what the teacher is doing, of secondary importance to student outcomes or results, and these are usually measured through standardized tests of achievement. Process variables are still considered part of the research; but, they are often used as part of a process-product paradigm whereby certain teacher behaviors or methods are determined to be "effective" in contributing to student achievement (which is usually based on reading or mathematics tests).

TEACHER STYLE AND TEACHER EFFECTIVENESS

Every teacher has a special way of doing things and a special way of thinking—a manner or style that helps characterize who he or she is. Teaching style is a composite of personality and philosophy, evidenced by behavior and attitude, what the teacher emphasizes, how he or she reacts to different situations. For Rubin (1985), teaching style involves choosing among alternatives, and the choices the teacher makes connote his or her perceived image and roles. Style also involves attitudes, values, and "personality, talents, and ideology" (p. 19). Through their style, teachers integrate the theories they believe in and the practices they adopt in the classroom. Like lifestyles, teaching styles can make the difference—in this case, between a good teacher and a poor teacher, between success and failure in the classroom.

A teacher's style is based on his or her personality and philosophy. Each teacher must develop his or her own style of teaching and feel comfortable in the classroom. If teachers are not themselves, students will perceive them as "phony." In short, teachers must develop a personal repertoire based on their own physical and mental characteristics and on their students. Thus, there is no one ideal type of teacher—there are as many teacher types or styles as there are teachers. Teacher style is a matter of choice and comfort, and what works for one teacher with one set of students may not work for another.

From his discussions with teachers after observing them at work, Jackson (1968) concluded that they were unable to describe precisely their own behaviors in the classroom and that they lack a professional vocabulary with which to describe their teaching. Teaching, however, is full of generalizations and vagueness, just like many other helping professions, and we should not always be expected to define precisely our approaches and actions. Indeed, teaching involves continuous interaction that cannot easily be preplanned or reconstructed. Much of teaching merely unfolds, and much of it is just a matter of individual style that we each have come to adopt over the years, just as we each have adopted a general style for dealing with life.

Teaching style influences how we use teacher effectiveness research. To be of value, the "theories" and "practices" described in the professional literature must be matched to fit the teachers' styles. Experienced teachers learn to use only those recommended behaviors that they feel comfortable with in the classroom. Teachers must learn a body of knowledge (theory) essential for teaching, and how to apply it (practice). They need to learn to be analytical and reflective as they develop and grow as teachers. Teachers learn to choose among alternatives, including the various theories and practices of teaching that can be either adopted "as is" or modified to fit their particular style of teaching.

The current research on teacher effectiveness delineates a host of easily measured businesslike, structured, and tasklike behaviors (i.e., Doyle, 1985; Good and Brophy, 1988; Rosenshine, 1987). But these models fail to consider that teachers differ, that there are many different teacher styles and effective teachers, and that many successful teachers do not exhibit such direct behaviors.

The new and popular teacher effectiveness models lock us into a narrow mold that misses many nuances of teaching. Many of these prescriptions (sometimes called principles) themselves are old ideas bottled under new labels such as "with-it-ness," "smoothness," "clarity," "alertness," "pacing," "momentum," "overlapping," and "student accountability." These terms are rooted in Kounin's (1970) research on classroom management, and in some cases it is not clear that the current crop of researchers on teacher effectiveness gives Kounin his full credit. This explains in part the emphasis on routines, rules, and control—in short, on teaching behaviors and methods that enhance classroom management—and to some extent why Brophy (1986, 1988), Doyle (1985, 1986), and Evertson (1986, 1989) have associated effective teaching with classroom management. Furthermore, much of the new research deals with low achievers and at-risk students—another reason why many of its recommended teacher behaviors and methods coincide with managerial and structured techniques. Indeed, the new research tends to confirm that effective teachers are good classroom managers, which is something most teachers already know and knew even before Kounin established his "principles" of classroom management.

In our efforts to identify good teaching, the teacher effectiveness research is often published as if its findings are new or ground breaking. But the findings are nothing more than behaviors and methods that good teachers have been using for many years. What these product-oriented researchers have done is to summarize what we have known for a long time but have often passed on as "tips for teachers" or "practical suggestions." (And we were once criticized by researchers as being recipe oriented.) These researchers confirm the basic behaviors and methods of experienced teachers; however, they give beginning teachers a better yardstick or starting point to understand effective teaching than did previous researchers, and they give credibility to the teachers' practices by correlating their behaviors (processes) with student achievement (products).

The Purposes of Teacher Effectiveness Research

The fundamental question in the conduct and appreciation of research into teacher effectiveness is whether or not teachers influence student outcomes and, if so, to what extent. The need to establish the relative contribution of the teacher to student learning is particularly important for three reasons:

1. *It provides teacher educators a rationale for their job.* Teacher educators must screen and prepare future teachers, as well as provide in-service education for experienced teachers. If teachers have little or no impact on student outcomes, then there is no reason to guard the gates with credentials or to make such a fuss about teacher education. If teachers have minimal or no impact on students, then there is little or no reason to provide pedagogical knowledge in order to enhance professional competence.

2. *It provides a rationale for the recent reforms regarding teacher evaluation, teacher accountability, teacher performance, and teacher competence.* If teachers have little effect on student outcomes, or if replicable findings of teacher effectiveness cannot be found, then all these new reform policies are at best theoretical exercises and at worst politicize the evaluation of teachers. If such data are lacking, then various methods for effective teaching have been sold unproven, and sound teacher evaluation policies cannot be formulated. Moreover, assessing teachers or making judgments about their competence cannot be supported; making inferences from observations or rating scales to support personnel decisions are invalid; and labels such as "incompetent," "competent," or "master" teacher are premature. The absence of teacher influence on student performance suggests that remediation, probation, or performance-related programs cannot be statistically or legally supported, and it is difficult for supervisors and administrators to give constructive evaluation and feedback to teachers.

3. *It provides support for the ideas that teacher differences exist and that teachers make a difference.* Since the 1980s, the prominent view is that teachers affect student outcomes. This new research assumes that the process (teacher behaviors and/or methods) can be controlled, modified, or taught, and that teacher-student interactions can be analyzed and predicted; it also assumes that what teachers do in the classroom does affect students and that narrowly defined teacher behaviors or methods affect student performance.

In general, the new research on teacher effectiveness opposes a wealth of large-scale research considered conventional wisdom in the 1960s and 1970s, which held that teacher effects were secondary or irrelevant and that each student's IQ, family, home life, peer group, and social class were crucial in determining his or her achievement (Coleman, 1966; Husén, 1967; Jencks, 1972; Thorndike, 1973). This research attributed only a small fraction of the independent variation in student achievement to school variables (about 15 to 20 percent, depending on the research study), and only a small part to teachers (Ornstein, 1982, 1984; Ornstein, Levine, and Wilkerson, 1975). Their analysis points the finger of responsibility for achievement to students, not teachers; thus we should remember their findings and discuss publicly the influence of family structure and parental responsibility on student outcomes.

Caution and Criticism

There is some danger in the new research. The conclusions overwhelmingly portray the effective teacher as task-oriented, organized, and structured—nothing more than Ryans's (1960) Pattern Y or businesslike teacher and Flanders's (1965) direct teacher (who was considered ineffective). These teacher effectiveness models tend to overlook the friendly, warm, and democratic teacher; the creative teacher who is stimulating and imaginative; the dramatic teacher who bubbles with energy and enthusiasm; the philosophical teacher who encourages students to play with ideas and concepts; and the problem-solving teacher who requires that students think out the answers. In their desire to identify and prescribe measurable and quantifiable behaviors, the new researchers overlook the emotional, qualitative, and interpretive descriptions of classrooms, and the joys of teaching. Most of the new research has been conducted at the elementary grade levels, where one would expect more social, psychological, and humanistic factors to be observed, recorded, and recommended as effective.

The new teacher effectiveness models fail to consider that a good deal of effective teaching may not directly correlate with student performance measured by achievement tests. For Greene (1986), good teaching and learning involve such intangibles as values, experiences, insights, and appreciation—the "stuff" that cannot be easily observed or measured. Teaching and learning is an "existential" encounter, a philosophical process involving creative ideas and inquiries that cannot be easily quantified. We might add that much of teaching involves caring, nurturing, and valuing behaviors—attributes not easily assessed by evaluation instruments.

Eisner (1983, 1985) is concerned that what is not measurable goes unnoticed in a product-oriented teaching model. By breaking down the teaching act into competencies and criteria that can be defined operationally and quantified, educators overlook the hard-to-measure aspects of teaching, such as its personal, humanistic, and playful qualities. To say that excellence in teaching mainly requires measurable behaviors and outcomes is to miss a substantial part of teaching—

its artistry, drama, tones, and flavor (Dawe, 1984a; Harmin, 1988; Rubin, 1985).

Unks (1986), also, is concerned that the teacher effectiveness models are too behaviorist and product-oriented. Teacher behaviors that correlate with measurable outcomes often lead to rote learning, "learning bits" and not wholes, memorization, drill, and automatic responses. This current teaching-learning model treats the "mind as a jug" to be filled up with facts that will later be funneled out in a test. The new models also seem to miss moral and ethical outcomes as well as social, personal, and self-actualizing achievements related to learning and life, that is, the affective domain of learning and the psychology of being human.

In their attempts to observe and measure what teachers do and to detail whether students improve their performance on reading or mathematics tests, these models ignore the learners' imagination, fantasy, and artistic thinking, including their dreams, hopes, and aspirations and how teachers influence these hard-to-define but very important aspects of the students' lives. The chief variable in this current research is knowledge of facts, as evidenced by scores on achievement tests; the secondary variable, if there is one, is classroom management and student control. This research also neglects learning experiences that deal with metacognition or learning how to learn, as well as with character, spiritual outlook, and philosophy (Ornstein, 1989).

The current research on teacher effectiveness needs to be revised to include varied teaching styles. Teachers must be permitted to incorporate specific teacher behaviors and methods according to their own unique personality, philosophy, and goals; to pick and choose from a wide range of research and theory; and to discard other teacher behaviors that conflict with their own style, without fear of being considered ineffective. A good many school districts, even state departments of education, have developed evaluation instruments and salary plans based exclusively on these prescriptive and product-oriented behaviors. Even worse, teachers who do not exhibit these behaviors are often penalized or labeled as "marginal" or "incompetent" (Holdzkom, 1987; Ornstein, 1988; Ornstein and Levine, 1989). There is an increased danger that many more school districts and states will continue to jump on this bandwagon and make decisions based on these models without recognizing or giving credibility to other teacher behaviors or methods.

CONCLUSION

Few, if any, activities are as crucial in schooling as teaching; and, as elusive and complex as teaching may be, research toward understanding it must continue. The problem, however, is that most of the research on teaching is not read by the most important group—teachers, who can and should benefit by knowing, understanding, and integrating the concepts and principles of the research on teaching.

It is obvious that certain behaviors contribute to good teaching. The trouble is that there is little agreement on exactly what behaviors or methods are most important. Some teachers will learn most of the rules about good teaching, yet be unsuccessful. Other teachers will break the rules of "good" teaching, yet be profoundly successful. Some teachers will gain theoretical knowledge of "what works," but be unable to put the ideas into practice. And yet other teachers will act effortlessly in the classroom, while others will consider teaching a chore. All this suggests that teaching is more art than science and practice is more important than theory.

While the research on teacher effectiveness provides a vocabulary and system for improving our insight into good teaching, there is a danger that it may lead to some of us becoming too rigid in our view of teaching. Following only the research on teaching can lead to too much emphasis on specific behaviors that cannot be easily measured or prescribed in advance.

Most teacher evaluation processes do not address the question of how to change teacher behavior. The developers of evaluation instruments assume that once they have discovered what ought to be done, teachers will naturally do what is expected. If our purpose is to change or improve the practices of teachers, then it is necessary to come to grips with teachers' beliefs and attitudes and with their concepts of "good" or "effective."

In providing feedback and evaluation to teachers, many factors need to be considered so that the advice or information does not fall on deaf ears. Teachers appreciate feedback processes whereby they can improve their teaching, if the processes are honest and fair and are professionally planned and administered; if teachers are permitted to make mistakes; and if more than one model of effectiveness is considered so that teachers can adopt recommended behaviors and methods that fit their own personality and philosophy of teaching.

REFERENCES

Bolin, Frances G. "Helping Student Teachers Think about Teaching," *Journal of Teacher Education* 39 (1988): 48–55.

Bolster, Arthur S. "Toward a More Effective Model of Research on Teaching," *Harvard Educational Review* 53 (1983): 294–308.

Borich, G. D. "Paradigms of Teacher Effectiveness Research," *Education and Urban Society* 18 (1986): 143–167.

Brophy, Jere E. "Classroom Management Techniques," *Education and Urban Society* 18 (1986): 182–194.

Brophy, Jere E. "Educating Teachers about Managing Classrooms and Students," *Teaching and Teacher Education* 4 (1988): 1–18.

Coleman, James S. *Equality of Educational Opportunity.* Washington, D.C.: U.S. Government Printing Office, 1966.

Dawe, Harry A. "Teaching: A Performing Art," *Phi Delta Kappan* 65 (1984a): 548–552.

Dawe, Harry A. "Teaching: Social Science or Performing Art?" *Harvard Educational Review* 54 (1984b): 111–114.

Doyle, Walter E. "Effective Teaching and the Concept of Master Teacher," *Elementary School Journal* 86 (1985): 27–34.

Doyle, Walter E. "Classroom Organization and Management." In *Handbook of Research on Teaching*, 3d ed. Edited by Merlin C. Wittrock. New York: Macmillan, 1986.

Dunkin, M.J. and Biddle, Bruce J. *The Study of Teaching.* New York: Holt, Rinehart, 1974.

Eisner, Elliot W. "The Art and Craft of Teaching," *Educational Leadership* 40 (1983): 4–13.

Eisner, Elliot W. *The Educational Imagination*, 2d ed. New York: Macmillan, 1985.

Evertson, Carolyn M. "Do Teachers Make a Difference?" *Education and Urban Society* 18 (1986): 195–210.

Evertson, Carolyn M., et al. *Classroom Management for Secondary Teachers*, 2d ed. Englewood Cliffs, N.J.: Prentice-Hall, 1989.

Flanders, Ned. *Teacher Influence, Pupil Attitudes and Achievement.* Washington, D.C.: U.S. Government Printing Office, 1965.

Gage, N. L. *The Scientific Basis of the Art of Teaching.* New York: Teachers College Press, 1978.

Good, Thomas L., and Jere E. Brophy. *Looking in Classrooms*, 4th ed. New York: Harper and Row, 1988.

Greene, Maxine. "Philosophy and Teaching." In *Handbook of Research on Teaching*, 3d ed. Edited by Merlin C. Wittrock. New York: Macmillan, 1986.

Harmin, Merrill. "Value Clarity, High Morality: Let's Go for Both," *Educational Leadership* 45 (1988): 24–27.

Holdzkom, David. "Appraising Teacher Performance in North Carolina," *Educational Leadership* 44 (1987): 40–44.

Husén, Torsten. *International Study of Achievement in Mathematics: A Comparison of Twelve Countries.* New York: Wiley, 1967.

Jackson, Philip W. *Life in Classrooms*. New York: Holt, Rinehart, 1968.

Jencks, Christopher, et al. *Inequality: A Reassessment of the Effect of Family and Schooling in America*. New York: Basic Books, 1972.

Kounin, Jacob. *Discipline and Group Management in Classrooms*. New York: Holt, Rinehart, 1970.

Ornstein, Allan C. "How Good Are Teachers in Effecting Student Outcomes?" *NASSP Bulletin* 66 (1982): 61–70.

Ornstein, Allan C. "A Difference Teachers Make," *Educational Forum* 49 (1984): 109–118.

Ornstein, Allan C. "Considering Teacher Effectiveness," *Clearing House* 58 (1985a): 399–402.

Ornstein, Allan C. "Research on Teaching: Issues and Trends," *Journal of Teacher Education* 36 (1985b): 27–31.

Ornstein, Allan C. "Research on Teacher Behavior: Trends and Policies," *High School Journal* 69 (1986a): 399–402.

Ornstein, Allan C. "Teacher Effectiveness: Current Research and Issues," *Educational and Urban Society* 18 (1986b): 168–175.

Ornstein, Allan C. "Theory and Practice of Curriculum," *Kappa Delta Pi Record* 24 (1987): 15–17.

Ornstein, Allan C. "The Changing Status of the Teaching Profession," *Urban Education* 23 (1988): 261–279.

Ornstein, Allan C. "Theoretical Issues Related to Teaching," *Education and Urban Society* 22 (1989): 95–104.

Ornstein, Allan C., and Levine, Daniel U. "Social Class, Race, and School Achievement," *Journal of Teacher Education* 40 (1989): 17–23.

Ornstein, Allan C.; Levine, Daniel U.; and Wilkerson, Doxey A. *Reforming Metropolitan Schools*. Pacific Palisades, Calif.: Goodyear, 1975.

Rosenshine, Barak. "Explicit Teaching and Teacher Training," *Journal of Teacher Education* 38 (1987): 34–36.

Rubin, Louis J. *Artistry in Teaching*. New York: Random House, 1985.

Ryans, David G. *Characteristics of Teachers*. Washington, D.C.: American Council on Education, 1960.

Stallings, Jane A., and Stipek, Deborah. "Research on Early Childhood and Elementary School Teaching Programs." In *Handbook of Research on Teaching*, 3d ed. Edited by Merlin C. Wittrock. New York: Macmillan, 1986.

Thorndike, Robert L. *Reading Comprehension Education in Fifteen Countries*. New York: Wiley, 1973.

Unks, G. "Product-Oriented Teaching," *Education and Urban Society* 18 (1986): 242–254.

Wise, Arthur; Darling-Hammond, Linda; McLaughlin, Milbrey; and Bernstein, Harriet. "Teacher Evaluation: A Study of Effective Practices," *Elementary School Journal* 86 (1985): 61–121.

Wittrock, Merlin C., ed. *Handbook of Research on Teaching*, 3d ed. New York: Macmillan, 1986.

4

Teaching and Educational Effectiveness: Research Synthesis and Consensus from the Field

Margaret C. Wang and Herbert J. Walberg

Educational research has identified so many variables related to school learning that educators may be perplexed as to which are most influential. Researchers, policymakers, and practitioners require clearer guidance concerning the relative influences of the particular variables that maximize school learning. To this end, this chapter reports the findings from a synthesis of research literature and a survey of professional opinion about teaching and other practices and policies that make for effective education.

The overall purpose of our study was to develop a systematic data base of the most authoritative scholarly opinion and consensus about ways to optimize educational outcomes across a range of educational conditions and settings. We begin by briefly relating the evolution of school learning models in order to provide a conceptual basis and context for our discussion here of the synthesis findings. Then, we report the major findings of the study and their implications for improving instructional effectiveness.

81

RATIONALE AND CONTEXT

J. B. Carroll (1963) introduced educational researchers to theoretical models of student learning in his article, "A Model of School Learning." In his model, he put forth six constructs: aptitude, ability to comprehend instruction, perseverance, clarity of instruction, matching the task to student characteristics, and opportunity to learn. These constructs, which succinctly capture the psychological influences on school learning, became a point of departure for other models that followed. The 1960s and 1970s were marked by the introduction of several additional important models of learning, including those of Bennett (1978), Bloom (1976), Bruner (1966), Glaser (1976), and Harnischfeger and Wiley (1976).

These models all assumed the primary importance of students' characteristics as determinants of the learning process and outcomes. The models included such constructs as aptitude, prior knowledge, and pupil background. Most also addressed the importance of motivation by employing such constructs as perseverance, self-concept of the learner, and attitude toward subject matter. This acknowledgment of individual differences among learners contrasted with narrowly conceived experimental studies of influences on learning, which generally treated individual differences as a source of error (cf. Hilgard, 1964).

In addition to student variables, each of the models of school learning noted above also emphasized teaching constructs. These constructs varied in generality, some being as broad as "clarity of instruction," and others as narrow as "use of cues" or "feedback and correctives."

Although later models refined individual differences and instructional variables, recent models have extended the range of influences considered. Haertel, Walberg, and Weinstein (1983), for example, identified nine theoretical constructs that exhibit consistent causal influences on academic learning: student age (or developmental level); ability (including prior achievement) and motivation; amount and appropriateness of instruction; psychological environments of the classroom, home, and peer group outside the school; and exposure to mass media. They showed that previous models of school learning neglected extramural and social-psychological influences.

The evolution of school learning models was advanced with the introduction of adaptive instruction models that emphasize the centrality of the teacher and the individual student in the learning process (cf. Glaser, 1975; Wang and Lindvall, 1984; Wang and Walberg, 1985). School-based adaptive instruction models are designed to help schools create learning environments that maximize each student's opportunities for success in school. Educators implementing these models paid particular attention to new variables associated with teaching, program design, and implementation. They attended in particular to those features that Glaser (1982) referred to as the "large practical variables." They include efficient use of teacher and student time, practical classroom management systems, feedback and reinforcement for students, teaching interactions based on the learning needs of individual students, and flexible administrative and organizational patterns responsive to program implementation and staffing needs.

Sociologists concerned with the identification of effective schools contributed further to models of school learning. The late Ronald Edmonds (1979) identified characteristics of exceptionally effective schools, especially for the urban poor. Significant contributions to effective schools models were also made by Brookover (1979), Brookover and Lezotte (1979), and Rutter and colleagues (1979). Effective schools are characterized by careful curriculum articulation, staff development, parental involvement, recognition of academic success, maximized learning time, clear goals and high expectations, orderly and disciplined school environment, and leadership of the principal that is characterized by attention to quality of instruction (Purkey and Smith, 1983).

These various models of school learning contribute a variety of practices useful in program development and school improvement. Teachers may wish to focus their research and practice on particular methods, and this chapter provides a synoptic view of the entire panoply of variables for their use.

DEVELOPMENT OF A CONCEPTUAL FRAMEWORK OF VARIABLES IMPORTANT TO LEARNING

The first step in conducting the research synthesis was to delineate a comprehensive set of variables from which we could develop a conceptual framework, one that (a) incorporated variables considered by professionals to be important to learning; (b) set forth a common language that teachers, researchers, and policymakers can use to improve communication about educational effectiveness; and (c) provided guidance for increased collaboration among teachers and other educational professionals in their efforts to improve instruction and learning.

Culled from professional literature and expert opinions, the variables important to learning were identified by considering the following kinds of questions: What aspects of teaching enhance student learning and encourage success for all students? What kinds of social relationships are important to enhance student learning in classrooms? What student characteristics are alterable in improving learning, particularly for students with special needs or otherwise considered to be at risk? What characteristics of learners are important to observe and consider when planning instruction? Answers to questions such as these were analyzed and summarized as the basis for the development of the framework.

The identification of the variables considered important to learning began with a close examination of the models of school learning described above, as well as of selected sources including Brophy (1986), Keogh and colleagues (1982), Wang and Walberg (1985), and Wittrock (1986). Each potential variable was written on a separate index card, then consolidated and organized into a preliminary version of the final coding scheme. This process resulted in a list of more than 200 variables. In the next step of our research, we used the Delphi technique to survey expert opinions about variables considered important to learning. Twelve experts were identified for this phase of information gathering. The expert panel included leading researchers as well as outstanding practitioners and editors of professional journals. The panel was asked to rate on a scale from 1 (low) to 3 (high) the demonstrated importance of each of the variables to student learning.

In accordance with Delphi procedures, results of the "first round" of ratings were then sent back to the experts, and they responded in a "second round," taking into account what other experts had said in the first round. Based on detailed commentaries received from the panel members, a final set of variables was identified for developing a conceptual framework to guide a content analysis of the research literature and to obtain expert and practitioner opinion from the field.

The final framework included 228 variables considered important for learning and "alterable"—that is, conditions and methods that educators can change. In consultation with the expert group, we categorized the variables into six broad categories that formed the conceptual framework shown in Figure 4-1. These categories ranged from remote (state and district variables) to more immediate categories such as program design variables.

THE RESEARCH BASE

The next step in conducting the synthesis involved a detailed reading of the literature to refine the variables in the framework. The preliminary list of sources was reviewed by a technical review panel. The final list—a corpus of book chapters, reports, and other sources considered authoritative—included over 200 items of the past decade or more from the *Review of Research in Education,* the *Annual Review of Psychology,* and the *Annual Review of Sociology,* as well as the *Handbook of Research on Teaching* (Wittrock, 1986), *Designs for Compensatory Education* (Williams, Richmond, and Mason, 1986), more specialized handbooks, and a small number of journal articles chosen to ensure coverage of all of the areas addressed in the comprehensive framework. We read all of these sources but used only the 179 sources relevant to a range of cognitive and affective learning outcomes for K-12 learners in formal educational settings.

The 228 items in the conceptual framework were listed on a fifteen-page coding form, and each of the sources was then coded by our research team, using that form. In all, over 2,500 pages of coding forms were completed. Every point of discussion about each of the 228 variables influencing learning outcomes was coded by page number, together with a notation of the reported strength of its influence on learning. In some cases, multiple discussion points were recorded for a single source. These detailed text citations by page number and ratings have been placed in an archive.

Our research team recorded their average ratings on summary forms, one for each chapter or other source document. Each reference to a variable's relation to learning outcomes was coded on a three-point scale, with "1" representing a weak, uncertain, or inconsistent relation to learning; "2" representing a moderate relation; and "3"

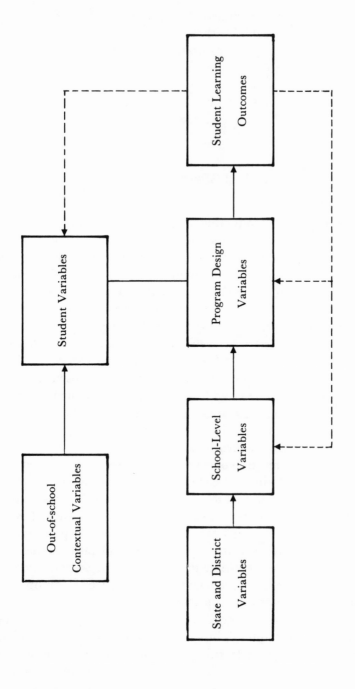

Figure 4-1

A Conceptual Framework of Variables Important to Learning

representing a strong relation. The average ratings for each of the 179 sources were themselves averaged to determine the emergent consensus on which variables exert the most powerful influence on learning outcomes. The initial coding tabulated well over 10,000 separate statements concerning the strength of association between one of the 228 variables and learning outcomes. These were reduced to about 3,700 summary ratings for individual source documents, which were then averaged across documents. Finally, average ratings of similar variables were themselves averaged within the subcategories discussed below.

Briefly, the content analysis confirms the importance of the quality of schooling for learning outcomes. Of the six broad categories, the highest ratings overall were assigned to "Program Design Variables," followed by "Out-of-School Contextual Variables." The category reflecting the quality of instruction as delivered ("Classroom Instruction and Climate Variables") ranked third in importance, closely followed by "Student Variables." The last two categories ("School-Level Variables" and "State and District Variables") received markedly lower ratings overall. This overall ranking of sources of influence contrasts sharply with the "conventional wisdom" since the time of the Equality of Educational Opportunity survey (Coleman et al., 1966), which seemed to suggest that the quality of schooling has little impact on outcomes compared with the impact of socioeconomic variables.

The variables included in each of these six broad categories were further classified into subcategories of variables, shown in Table 4-1. Our content analysis of the literature relevant to each of these subcategories enabled us to rate each subcategory according to its importance for students' learning. The subcategories of variables that obtained the highest mean ratings (2.00 or greater on our three-point scale) were Metacognition (2.08), Classroom Management (2.07), Quantity of Instruction (2.02), Student-Teacher Interactions: Social (2.02), Classroom Climate (2.01), and Peer-Group Influences (2.00). These ratings reflect the importance of proximal psychological variables.

These broad conclusions are supported by a number of more specific findings from the research synthesis that are highlighted in the remainder of this section. The following comments are based on the judgments of our research team of the importance the literature attaches to certain variables.

Table 4-1
Categories of Variables Important to Learning

I. State and District Variables

   A. District-level demographics and marker variables
   B. State-level policy variables

II. Out-of-School Contextual Variables

   A. Community variables
   B. Peer-group variables
   C. Home environment and parental-support variables
   D. Student use of out-of-school time variables

III. School-Level Variables

   A. Demographic and marker variables
   B. Teacher/administrator decision-making variables
   C. School culture variables (ethos conducive to teaching and learning)
   D. Schoolwide policy and organizational variables
   E. Accessibility variables
   F. Parental-involvement policy variables

IV. Student Variables

   A. Demographic and marker variables
   B. History of educational placements
   C. Social and behavioral variables
   D. Motivational and affective variables
   E. Cognitive variables
   F. Metacognitive variables
   G. Psychomotor variables

V. Program Design Variables

   A. Demographic and marker variables
   B. Curriculum and instructional variables
   C. Curriculum design variables

VI. Implementation, Classroom Instruction, and Climate Variables

   A. Classroom implementation support variables
   B. Classroom instructional variables
   C. Quantity of instructional variables
   D. Classroom assessment variables
   E. Classroom management variables
   F. Student-teacher interactions: social variables
   G. Student-teacher interactions: academic variables
   H. Classroom climate variables

Student characteristics. Individual differences among students have long been recognized as critical determinants of learning outcomes. "Metacognition," or self-regulation of one's learning, turned out to be most important. Two additional student characteristics accorded importance in the research literature were "perseverance on learning tasks" and "motivation for continual learning." Both of these reinforce the conclusion that consistent engagement with the subject matter to be learned is critical for school success.

Quality and quantity of instruction. Classroom management and climate and student-teacher interactions represent an important constellation of variables related to effective instruction. Examination of the highly rated items in these areas reveals a portrait of cooperative, cohesive, goal-directed classrooms in which a variety of educational approaches and activities are employed. Items heavily cited in the research literature include sound organization and systematic sequencing of instruction, and effective use of direct, teacher-centered instruction. Among other instructional approaches frequently linked to positive learning outcomes were peer and cross-age tutoring and cooperative group learning strategies.

Several variables associated with quantity of instruction also emerged as important, including amount of student time on task, length of school day and of school year, amount of time allocated to direct instruction in basic skills, and amount of time spent out of school on homework and on leisure reading. Of these, the most highly rated variable is time on task.

Out-of-school context. Research literature is expanding on the role of parents in promoting student learning. The synthesis confirmed the importance of variables related to this, as well as of peer-group influences. These findings were reflected in ratings for parental involvement in school activities, interest in schoolwork, and monitoring of school attendance and homework completion. Parental support might also be mediated through influence on students' selection of friends. The research literature described peer-group variables, especially academic and occupational aspirations, as strongly related to school success.

Strength of influences on school learning. Physical processes can often be explained as functions of a small number of variables strongly interacting in simple ways. In contrast, many influences appear to moderately affect learning outcomes. Authors of original research studies and of reviews and syntheses are appropriately cautious in stating the importance of particular variables. Taken together, nonetheless, the variables in our content analysis of the research literature constitute a powerful set of determinants of learning.

CONSENSUS FROM THE FIELD

From the conceptual framework of variables important to learning and our content analysis of the literature, we designed a survey to investigate educators' opinions on the importance of the variables. Eight groups of professionals were asked to respond to the survey. Through the cooperation of the Council for Exceptional Children, we sent surveys to a random sample of 1,001 of the organization's members, all of whom are special education teachers: 449 (45 percent) responded. Each of the special education teachers was asked to recruit as an additional respondent the "regular" teacher whose classroom was nearest to his or her own classroom; 182 regular teachers responded. A sample of 526 school psychologists was selected randomly from the membership list of the National Association of School Psychologists; 207 responded. Each psychologist was asked to recruit a school principal in a building he or she served. Fifty school principals responded. All state directors of special education and state directors of Chapter I programs were asked to complete the survey, which they did at relatively moderate rates: 64 percent (N = 36) and 58 percent (N = 40) respectively. A group of special education researchers was identified by assembling names of recipients of federal research grants in the field of special education relating to services for mildly handicapped students in regular education settings; 55 responded of the 197 approached. A final category of educational researchers/authors was created by assembling names of the first-listed authors of 134 major chapters in the various research reports and reviews used in our content analysis; 61 (46 percent) responded.

The survey instrument containing the 228 variables (arranged by category) in the framework was responded to by a total of 1,123 persons. They were asked to rate on a three-point scale the importance of each variable for learning. Table 4-2 lists all 228 variables and designates by a double asterisk (**) the items that respondents regarded as "highly important" (mean rating of 2.6 and above) and

Table 4-2
Summary of Survey Findings of Educators' Opinions on Variables Important to Student Learning

I. *State and District Variables* (These are variables associated with state- and district-level school governance and administration. They include state curriculum and textbook policies, testing and graduation requirements, teacher licensure, specific provisions in teacher contracts, and some district-level administrative and fiscal variables.)

A. District-Level Demographics and Marker Variables

    1. School district size
    2. Degree of school district bureaucratization
    3. Degree of school district centralization
    4. Presence of contractual limits on after-school meetings
    5. Limits on class size
    6. Presence of contractual restrictions on activities performed by aides
* 7. Degree of central-office assistance and support for programs
* 8. Degree of board of education support for instructional programs
* 9. Per-pupil expenditure
  10. Efficiency of transportation system

B. State-Level Policy Variables

* 1. Teacher licensure requirements
  2. Degree of state control over textbooks
  3. Degree of state control over curriculum
* 4. Academic course and unit requirements
  5. Minimum competency test requirements
* 6. Adherence to least restrictive environment/mainstreaming

II. *Out-of-School Contextual Variables* (These are variables associated with the home and community contexts within which schools function. They include community demographics, peer culture, parental support and involvement, and amount of time students spend out of school on such activities as television viewing, leisure reading, and homework.)

A. Community Variables

** 1. Socioeconomic level of community
 * 2. Ethnic mix of community
 * 3. Quality of social services for students

** = highly important (mean rating of 2.6 and above on 3-point scale)
 * = moderately important (mean rating of 2.0–2.5 on 3-point scale)

Table 4-2 *continued*

B. Peer-Group Variables

** 1. Level of peers' academic aspirations
** 2. Level of peers' occupational aspirations
 * 3. Presence of well-defined clique structure
** 4. Degree of peers' substance abuse
** 5. Degree of peers' criminal activity

C. Home Environment and Parental Support Variables

** 1. Educational environment (e.g., number of books and magazines at home)
** 2. Parental involvement in assuring completion of homework
** 3. Parental involvement in assuring regular school attendance
** 4. Parental monitoring of student's television viewing
 * 5. Parental participation in school conferences and related activities
** 6. Parental application of appropriate, consistent discipline
** 7. Parental expression of attention to children
** 8. Parental interest in student's school work
** 9. Parental expectation for academic success

D. Student Use of Out-of-School Time Variables

 1. Student participation in clubs and extracurricular school activities
 * 2. Amount of time spent on homework
 * 3. Amount of time spent on leisure reading
 * 4. Amount of time spent viewing educational television
 * 5. Amount of time spent viewing noneducational television

III. *School-Level Variables* (These are variables associated with school-level demographics, culture, climate, policies, and practices. They include demographics of the student body, whether the school is public or private, levels of funding for specific categorical programs, school-level decision making, and specific school-level policies and practices, including policies on parental involvement in the school.)

A. Demographic and Marker Variables

 1. Public versus private school
 2. Size of school
 * 3. Level of Chapter I (compensatory education) funding
 4. Level of Title VII (bilingual) funding
 * 5. Level of PL 94–142 (handicapped) funding
 * 6. Mix of socioeconomic levels in the school
 7. Mix of cultural/ethnic groups in the school
 8. Mix of students' language backgrounds in the school

B. Teacher/Administrator Decision-Making Variables

** 1. Teacher-administrator consensus on school values, norms, and roles
** 2. Principal actively concerned with instructional program

Table 4-2 *continued*

** 3. Teacher involvement in curricular decision making
** 4. Teacher involvement in instructional decision making
 * 5. Teacher involvement in resource allocation decisions
** 6. Teacher involvement in finding ways to increase academic performance

C. School Culture Variables (Ethos Conducive to Teaching and Learning)

 * 1. Use of cooperative, not exclusively competitive, goal structures
** 2. Schoolwide emphasis on and recognition of academic achievement
 * 3. Low staff absenteeism
 * 4. Low staff turnover
** 5. Low staff alienation
** 6. Active collaboration between regular classroom teachers and special education teachers
** 7. Safe, orderly school climate
** 8. Degree of school personnel-professional collaboration

D. Schoolwide Policy and Organizational Variables

 * 1. Presence of "effective schools program"
 * 2. Explicit school grading and academic progress policies
 * 3. Explicit schoolwide discipline policy
 * 4. Explicit schoolwide attendance policy
 * 5. Coordination of pullout programs for handicapped students with regular instructional programs
   6. Use of multi-age grouping
 * 7. Use of instructional teaming
 * 8. Use of cross-age tutoring
 * 9. Use of peer tutoring
 * 10. Use of academic tracking for specific school subject areas
   11. Minimization of external classroom disruptions (e.g., broadcast announcements)
 * 12. Adherence to least restrictive environment/mainstreaming
 * 13. Minimum use of suspension and expulsion as discipline tools

E. Accessibility Variables

 * 1. Accessibility of educational program (overcoming architectural, communication, and environmental barriers)

F. Parental-Involvement Policy Variables

 * 1. Parental involvement in improvement and operation of instructional programs
 * 2. School-sponsored parenting skills workshops (e.g., behavior modification, parent effectiveness training)

IV. *Student Variables* (These are variables associated with individual students themselves, including demographics, academic history, and a variety of social, behavioral, motivational, cognitive, and affective characteristics.)

Table 4-2 *continued*

A. Demographic and Marker Variables

    1. Chronological age
   * 2. Socioeconomic status
    3. Gender
   * 4. Ethnicity
   * 5. First or native language
   * 6. Physical and health status
   * 7. Special education classifications (e.g., EMR, LD)

B. History of Educational Placements

   * 1. Prior grade retentions
   * 2. Prior special placements
   * 3. Current placement in regular class versus self-contained special
       education class

C. Social and Behavioral Variables

  ** 1. Positive, nondisruptive behavior
  ** 2. Appropriate activity level
  ** 3. Cooperativeness with teacher
  ** 4. Cooperativeness with peers
   * 5. Ability to make friends with peers

D. Motivational and Affective Variables

  ** 1. Attitude toward school
  ** 2. Attitude toward teachers
  ** 3. Attitude toward subject matter instructed
  ** 4. Motivation for continual learning
  ** 5. Independence as a learner
  ** 6. Perseverance on learning tasks
  ** 7. Self-confidence
  ** 8. Academic self-competence concept in subject area instructed
  ** 9. Attributions for success and failure in subject area instructed

E. Cognitive Variables

   * 1. Piagetian stage of cognitive development
  ** 2. Level of reasoning (fluid ability)
   * 3. Level of spatial ability
  ** 4. Memory
  ** 5. Level of general academic (crystallized) knowledge
   * 6. Level of specific academic knowledge in subject area instructed
  ** 7. Level of reading comprehension ability
   * 8. Level of writing ability
   * 9. Level of computational ability
   * 10. Level of oral fluency
  ** 11. Level of listening skills

Table 4-2 *continued*

* 12. Learning styles (e.g., field independent, visual/auditory learners, high cognitive complexity)

F. Metacognitive Variables

** 1. Self-regulatory, self-control strategies (e.g., control of attention)
** 2. Comprehension monitoring (planning; monitoring effectiveness of attempted actions; monitoring outcomes of actions; testing, revising, and evaluating learning strategies)
** 3. Positive strategies for coping with failure
** 4. Positive strategies to facilitate generalization of concepts

G. Psychomotor Variables

* 1. Psychomotor skills specific to area instructed

V. *Program Design Variables* (These are variables associated with instruction as designed, and with the physical arrangements for its delivery. They include the instructional strategies specified by the curriculum, and characteristics of instructional materials.)

A. Demographic and Marker Variables

** 1. Size of instructional group (whole class, small group, one-on-one instruction)
* 2. Proportion of students with special needs served in regular classes
* 3. Number of classroom aides required
* 4. Resources needed

B. Curriculum and Instructional Variables

** 1. Clearly presented academic, social, and attitudinal program goals/outcomes
* 2. Use of explicit goal/objective setting for instruction of individual student (e.g., individualized educational plans [IEPs])
** 3. Use of mastery learning techniques, including use of instructional cues, engagement, and corrective feedback
* 4. Use of cooperative learning strategies
* 5. Use of personalized instructional program
* 6. Use of prescriptive instruction combined with aspects of informal or open education
* 7. Use of diagnostic-prescriptive methods
* 8. Use of computer-assisted instruction
* 9. Use of crisis-management techniques to control classroom disruptiveness
* 10. Use of program strategies for favorable affective climate
** 11. Alignment among goals, contents, instruction, assignments, and evaluation
* 12. Curriculum units integrated around key discipline-based concepts
* 13. Use of multidisciplinary approaches to instructional planning

Table 4-2 *continued*

(including diagnosis in educational planning)

* 14. Presence of information in the curriculum on individual differences and commonalities (including handicapping conditions)

* 15. Presence of culturally diverse materials in the curriculum

C. Curriculum Design Variables

  * 1. Materials employ alternative modes of representation

** 2. Materials presented in a cognitively efficient manner

** 3. Materials employ explicit and specific objectives

  * 4. Materials employ advance organizers

  * 5. Materials employ learning hierarchies

  * 6. Materials are tied to assessment and diagnostic tests

  * 7. Availability of materials and activities prepared specifically for use with whole classroom, small groups, or one-on-one instruction

** 8. Degree of structure in curriculum accommodates needs of different learners

  * 9. Student interests guide selection of a significant portion of content

** 10. Availability of materials and activities for students with different abilities

** 11. Availability of materials and activities for students with different learning styles

  * 12. Developmental issues considered

  * 13. Student experiences considered

VI. *Implementation, Classroom Instruction, and Classroom Climate Variables* (These are variables associated with the implementation of the curriculum and the instructional program. They include classroom routines and practices, characteristics of instruction as delivered, classroom management, monitoring of student progress, and quality and quantity of instruction provided, as well as student-teacher interactions and classroom climate.)

A. Classroom Implementation Support Variables

  * 1. Creation and maintenance of necessary instructional materials

  * 2. Adequacy in the configuration of classroom space

  * 3. Availability of classroom aides

     4. Use of written records to monitor student progress

     5. Establishing efficient classroom routines and communicating rules and practices

** 6. Developing students' responsibility for independent study and planning of one's own learning activities

B. Classroom Instructional Variables

  * 1. Prescribing individualized instruction based on perceived match of type of learning tasks to student characteristics (e.g., ability, learning style)

  * 2. Use of procedures requiring rehearsal and elaboration of new concepts

** 3. Use of clear and organized direct instruction

Table 4-2 *continued*

** 4. Systematic sequencing of instructional events and activities
* 5. Explicit reliance on individualized educational plans (IEPs) in planning day-to-day instruction for individual students
* 6. Use of instruction to surface and confront student misconceptions
* 7. Use of advance organizers, overviews, and reviews of objectives to structure information
* 8. Clear signaling of transitions as the lesson progresses
* 9. Significant redundancy in presentation of content
** 10. Teacher conveys enthusiasm about the content
** 11. Directing students' attention to the content
** 12. Using reinforcement contingencies
** 13. Setting and maintaining clear expectations of content mastery
** 14. Providing frequent feedback to students about their performance
* 15. Explicitly promoting effective metacognitive learning strategies
* 16. Promoting learning through student collaboration (e.g., peer tutoring, group work)
** 17. Corrective feedback in the event of student error
** 18. Flexible grouping that enables students to work to improve and change status/groups
** 19. Teaching for meaningful understanding
** 20. Degree to which student inquiry is fostered
* 21. Scaffolding and gradual transfer of responsibility from teacher to student
* 22. Degree to which assessment is linked with instruction
** 23. Skills taught within the context of meaningful application
** 24. Good examples and analogies to concretize the abstract
** 25. Consideration of the teacher's use of language in the instructional process
** 26. Explicitly promoting students' self-monitoring of comprehension

C. Quantity of Instruction Variables

1. Length of school year
* 2. Length of school day
** 3. Time on task (amount of time students are actively engaged in learning)
** 4. Time spent in direct instruction on basic skills in reading
** 5. Time spent in direct instruction on basic skills in mathematics
** 6. Time allocated to basic skills instruction by regular classroom teacher
** 7. Time allocated to basic skills instruction by special education teacher
* 8. Difference between academic learning time and allocated learning time
* 9. Time spent out of school on homework
* 10. Time spent out of school viewing educational television
* 11. Time spent out of school in informal learning experiences (e.g., museum trips, scouts)
* 12. Nature of regular classroom content missed by students during participation in pullout programs

Table 4-2 *continued*

D. Classroom Assessment Variables

* 1. Use of assessments to create detailed learner profiles rather than simple classifications or unelaborated total scores
* 2. Use of assessment as a frequent, integral component of instruction
* 3. Accurate, frequent measurement of basic skills in reading
* 4. Accurate, frequent measurement of basic skills in mathematics

E. Classroom Management Variables

** 1. Minimal disruptiveness in classroom (e.g., no excessive noise, no students out of place during instructional activities, no destructive activities)
** 2. Group alerting (teacher uses questioning/recitation strategies that maintain active participation by all students)
** 3. Learner accountability (teacher maintains student awareness of learning goals and expectations)
** 4. Transitions (teacher avoids disruptions of learning activities, brings activities to a clear and natural close, and smoothly initiates new activity)
** 5. Teacher "with-it-ness" (teacher is continually aware of events and activities and minimizes disruptiveness by timely and nonconfrontational actions)

F. Student and Teacher Interactions: Social Variables

* 1. Student initiates positive verbal interactions with other students and with teacher
** 2. Student responds positively to questions from other students and from teacher
** 3. Teacher reacts appropriately to correct incorrect answers
** 4. Teacher reinforces positive social interactions with students rejected by peers
** 5. Teacher provides explicit coaching on appropriate social behaviors
** 6. Teacher provides explicit coaching to reduce aggression

G. Student and Teacher Interactions: Academic Variables

** 1. Teacher asks academic questions frequently
* 2. Teacher asks questions predominantly low in difficulty
* 3. Teacher asks questions that are predominantly low in cognitive level
* 4. Teacher maintains high post-question wait time
* 5. Frequent calls for extended, substantive oral and written response (not one-word answers)

H. Classroom Climate Variables

* 1. Cohesiveness (members of class are friends sharing common interests and values and emphasizing cooperative goals)

Table 4-2 *continued*

** 2. Low friction (students and teacher interact in a considerate and cooperative way, with minimal abrasiveness)

 * 3. Low cliqueness (students work with many different classmates, and not just with a few close friends)

** 4. Satisfaction (students are satisfied with class activities)

** 5. Speed (the pacing of instruction is appropriate for the majority of students)

** 6. Task difficulty (students are continually and appropriately challenged)

** 7. Low apathy (class members are concerned and interested in what goes on in the class)

** 8. Low favoritism (all students are treated equally well in the class, and given equal opportunities to participate)

 * 9. Formality (students are asked to follow explicitly stated rules concerning classroom conduct and activities)

** 10. Goal direction (objectives of learning activities are specific and explicit)

 * 11. Democracy (all students are explicitly involved in making some types of classroom decisions)

** 12. Organization (class is well organized and well planned)

 * 13. Diversity (the class divides its efforts among several different purposes)

** 14. Environment (needed or desired books and equipment are readily available to students in the classroom)

 * 15. Competition (students compete to see who can do the best work)

by a single asterisk (*) those items regarded as "moderately important" (mean rating of 2.0–2.5).

Correlations among the eight educator groups' mean ratings of items showed that the groups strongly agree on which variables are most important. All correlations tended to be high, with a median for the 28 correlations of 0.88. This consensus, moreover, largely coincides with the content analysis reported in the preceding section of this chapter.

The responses from the survey were analyzed to explain further the extent to which expert opinions on variables important to learning correspond to the framework as a way of thinking about effective practices. Table 4-3 provides a summary of the results of factor analysis.

We extracted seven factors, which account for 73 percent of the variance in the variables. Some of the factors relate to the cells shown in Figure 4-1. The first factor, "Instruction," concerns how the curriculum is implemented through instruction. The variables loaded on this factor are closely related to variables included under the

Table 4-3
Patterns of Contributing Variables of Factors Influential to Learning
(number of respondents = 945)

Factors	Subcategories of Salient Variables	Variance Explained
Factor 1 Instruction	1. Classroom instruction 2. Curriculum design 3. Curriculum and instruction	16.46
Factor 2 Classroom environment	1. Student and teacher interactions 2. Classroom climate 3. Classroom management 4. Social and behavioral	14.30
Factor 3 School characteristics	1. Teacher/administrator decision making 2. Schoolwide policy and organization 3. Demographic and marker variables	12.12
Factor 4 Instructional time and assessment	1. Quantity of instruction 2. Ongoing classroom assessment	8.41

Factor 5
Parent involvement and
   peer influence
	1. Home environment and parental
	   support
	2. Peer-group variables
		8.36

Factor 6 Cognition and motivation	1. Motivation and affect 2. Cognition 3. Metacognition	7.10
Factor 7 Demographic variation	1. School-level demographics 2. Student demographics 3. Community demographics	6.67
	Total Variance Explained	73.42

general category of "Program Design Variables" in the conceptual framework shown in Figure 4-1. The second factor, "Classroom Environment, concerns psychological and managerial relations among students and teachers within the class. The third factor, "School Characteristics," refers to the school as a unit (i.e., its culture, policy, and organization), included under "School-Level Variables" in Figure 4-1. The fourth factor, "Instructional Time and Assessment," measures the amount of time devoted to instruction and the extent to which each student's progress is measured and accommodated. The fifth factor, "Parent Involvement and Peer Influence," is related to variables included under the category of "School-Level Variables" in the framework. The sixth factor, "Cognition and Motivation," assesses student aptitude and enthusiasm for academic tasks; it includes student variables relevant for planning instruction and monitoring student learning. These variables are included in the framework under the "Student Variables" category. The seventh factor, "Demographics," indexes student, school, and community socioeconomic and ethnic variations. The variables loaded on this factor are referenced in the "Out-of-School Contextual Variables" category of the conceptual framework.

The factor analysis is plausible in that similar subcategories grouped together reflect ways that many educators and researchers think about education. The variables loaded on factor 1, for example, clearly concern the design of curriculum and instruction, while factor 2 concerns classroom management and in-class social relations. The factors also characterize the special interests of somewhat distinct groups of educators. Factor 3, for example, concerns school-level variables, perhaps of greatest interest to principals and administrators; factors 1 and 4 may be of greatest interest to teachers, curriculum and program developers, and psychometricians; factors 2 and 6 may be of greatest interest to teachers, teacher educators, educational psychologists, and providers of in-service staff development; and factors 5 and 7 involve relationships beyond the school, especially with parents.

CONCLUSION

Our study suggests several factors and many specific variables that researchers and practitioners indicate are important in arranging effective learning environments. Such information has several uses. The variables identified are among the dimensions of knowledge and instructional practice that deserve attention in the initial preparation and continuing education of teachers. There is remarkable agreement among regular and special education teachers, principals, school psychologists, and researchers about what factors and variables are most important. These can be foci in the preparation and continuing education of special and regular teachers in colleges and universities.

The important variables may also be viewed as a basis for

studying individual students. This idea has not been widely explored, but appears to be sensible. For example, it might be observed that time on task tends to be low in a particular class or school. Perhaps a great deal of time is being given to management functions or to transitions between activities, at the expense of time devoted to instruction. In such a situation, plans and remedies can be implemented to improve the use of time in the classroom. But, equally, it may be important to observe individual differences among students in their use of time and to identify those for whom time on task needs to be increased. Most of the variables can be used in this dual way, that is, to study both teaching and individual differences.

This study calls attention to alterable variables and to the "level of the lesson"—the practical realities of teaching—rather than to such practices as IQ testing or hypothesizing about "underlying deficits." We believe that these latter approaches are mistaken and that, at least in the present state of knowledge about teaching, instruction should be based on directly observable and manageable factors in the learning environment. Much can be gained in improving the current practice through rigorous efforts organized around principles identified as important to learning.

The validated framework can have a variety of applications: ensuring consistency in teacher education; encouraging consensus among teachers about methods that work; and designing and implementing programs that meet scholarly standards as well as teacher, student, and community needs. Program designers and teachers, for example, may use the framework as a basis for making decisions about choosing and implementing particular programs or practices, by weighing research findings against their own needs and priorities (Wang et al., 1990). These processes involve systematic analysis of specific features of educational approaches and assessing them in relation to the needs of local schools.

The framework may also prove useful to curriculum designers and developers of innovative programs. The list of variables can serve as a checklist to determine which variables are critical to consider in program development and evaluation. The checklist can help ensure that the program design incorporates features that research suggests are important to enhance learning efficiency and productivity. Thus, from the outset, consideration can be given to the variety of ways in which approaches or practices can be implemented, given site-specific constraints and needs.

REFERENCES

Bennett, S. N. "Recent Research on Teaching: A Dream, a Belief, and a Model," *British Journal of Educational Psychology* 48 (1978): 127–147.

Bloom, Benjamin S. *Human Characteristics and School Learning.* New York: McGraw-Hill, 1976.

Brookover, Wilbur, ed. *School Social Systems and Student Achievement: Schools Can Make a Difference.* New York: Praeger, 1979.

Brookover, Wilbur B., and Lezotte, L. W. *Changes in School Characteristics Coincident with Changes in Student Achievement.* East Lansing: Institute for Research on Teaching, Michigan State University, 1979. ERIC ED 181 005.

Brophy, Jere. "Research Linking Teacher Behavior to Student Achievement." In *Design for Compensatory Education: Conference Proceedings and Papers*, edited by B. I. Williams, P. A. Richmond, and B. J. Mason, pp. 121–179. Washington, D.C.: Research and Evaluation Associates, 1986.

Bruner, Jerome S. *Toward a Theory of Instruction.* New York: W. W. Norton, 1966.

Carroll, John B. "A Model of School Learning," *Teachers College Record* 64 (1963): 723–733.

Coleman, James S., et al. *Equality of Educational Opportunity.* Washington, D.C.: U. S. Department of Health, Education, and Welfare, 1966.

Edmonds, Ronald. "Effective Schools for the Urban Poor," *Educational Leadership* 37, no. 1 (1979): 15–27.

Glaser, Robert. "The School of the Future: Adaptive Environments for Learning." In *The Future of Education: Perspectives on Tomorrow's Schooling*, edited by Louis Rubin, pp. 121–133. Boston: Allyn Bacon, 1975.

Glaser, Robert. "Components of a Psychological Theory of Instruction: Toward a Science of Design," *Review of Educational Research* 46 (1976): 1–24.

Glaser, Robert. "Instructional Psychologist: Past, Present, and Future," *American Psychologist* 37 (1982): 292–305.

Haertel, Geneva D.; Walberg, Herbert J.; and Weinstein, Thomas. "Psychological Models of Educational Performance: A Theoretical Synthesis of Constructs," *Review of Educational Research* 53 (1983): 75–92.

Harnischfeger, Annagret, and Wiley, David E. "The Teaching-Learning Process in Elementary Schools: A Synoptic View," *Curriculum Inquiry* 6 (1976): 5–43.

Hilgard, Ernest R. "A Perspective of the Relationship between Learning Theory and Educational Practices." In *Theories of Learning and Instruction*, edited by Ernest R. Hilgard, Sixty-third Yearbook of the National Society for the Study of Education, Part 1, pp. 402–415. Chicago: University of Chicago Press, 1964.

Keogh, B. K.; Major-Kingsley, S.; Omori-Gordon, H.; and Reid, H. P. *A System of Marker Variables for the Field of Learning Disabilities.* Syracuse, N.Y.: Syracuse University Press, 1982.

Purkey, Stewart C., and Smith, Marshall S. "Effective Schools: A Review," *Elementary School Journal* 83 (1983): 427–452.

Rutter, Michael; Maughan, Barbara, Mortimore, Peter; Ouston, Janet; and Smith, Alan. *Fifteen Thousand Hours: Secondary Schools and Their Effects on Children.* Cambridge, Mass.: Harvard University Press, 1979.

Wang, Margaret C., and Lindvall, C. Mauritz "Individual Differences and School

Learning Environment." In *Review of Research in Education,* Vol. 11, edited by E. W. Gordon, pp. 161–225. Washington, D.C.: American Educational Research Association, 1984.

Wang, Margaret C., and Walberg, Herbert J. *Adapting Instruction to Individual Differences.* Berkeley, Calif.: McCutchan, 1985.

Wang, Margaret C.; Walberg, Herbert J.; Reynolds, M. C.; and Rosenfield, S. "A Decision-Making Framework for Description of Innovative Education Programs." In Margaret C. Wang, *Designing and Evaluating School Learning Environments for Effective Mainstreaming of Special Education Students: Synthesis, Validation, and Dissemination of Research Methods.* Final Report for project funded by the Office of Educational Research and Improvement, U. S. Department of Education. Philadelphia, Penn.: Center for Research in Human Development and Education, Temple University, 1990.

Williams, D. I.; Richmond, P. A.; and Mason, B. J., eds. *Design for Compensatory Education: Conference Proceedings and Papers.* Washington, D.C.: Research and Evaluation Associates, 1986.

Wittrock, Merlin C., ed. *Handbook of Research on Teaching,* 3d ed. New York: Macmillan, 1986.

Part II

Classroom Observations of Teaching

5

Observation for the Improvement of Teaching

Jane Stallings and H. Jerome Freiberg

INTRODUCTION

In 1969, Stanford Research Institute (SRI) held a contract with the National Institute of Education to evaluate National Head Start and Follow Through Planned Variation programs. Project Follow Through was established by the U. S. Congress in 1967 (the legislative authority was the Economic Opportunity Act of 1964, as amended) when it became apparent that a program was needed in the early grades of public school that was articulated with Project Head Start goals and approaches and, therefore, would provide a comparable educational program for economically disadvantaged children over a longer period of time. A clearly stated purpose of the Follow Through program was the enhancement of the life chances of the economically deprived child.

According to Deutsch (1967), "children from backgrounds of social marginality enter the first grade already behind their middle-class counterparts in a number of skills highly related to scholastic achievement. They are simply less prepared to meet the demands of the school and the classroom situation. . . . In other words, intellectual and achievement differences between lower-class and middle-class children are smallest at the first-grade level, and tend to increase through the elementary school years" (pp. 64–65). However, an evaluation by Wolff and Stein (1966) of the first summer program of Head Start in 1965 had indicated that the initial achievement gains of the children had not been maintained in the public school. These early findings were believed to indicate that a more sustained program of longer duration might produce lasting gains. The result was the establishment of Follow Through Planned Variation as a longitudinal quasi-experimental program that would evaluate the ability of an intervention program to enhance the educational achievement of economically disadvantaged children.

Project Follow Through was originally set up in a "planned variation" research design; that is, the goal was to examine the differential effectiveness of programs based on divergent educational and developmental theories. The program began when researchers and other educational stakeholders were invited by the government to submit plans for establishing their various programs in public schools in order to test whether their individual approaches could improve the educational achievement of economically disadvantaged children. From the group that came forward, twenty-two were selected to implement their programs as Follow Through sponsors. We refer to "sponsors" here as those responsible for constructing and implementing the educational programs (or models). Eleven of the twenty-two sponsors of educational programs had developed and tried their models in university settings, eight were affiliated with private research institutes, and three were community-developed programs.

The sponsors of educational programs described their models to an audience that included representatives from school districts around the country at a conference in Kansas City, Kansas, in 1968. Ultimately, these models were implemented in 154 Follow Through projects within 136 urban and rural communities throughout the nation. The Follow Through sponsors then faced the challenge of program implementation, including guiding the behavior of teachers toward specified goals set by the sponsors. Egbert (1973) provides a historical view of the Follow Through project.

In other evaluations of Follow Through Planned Variation, the major emphasis was to determine if the models affected children's performance. Yet it was clear that if such effects were found, and if the effects were different from one model to another, we would not know what caused the differences. Therefore, we needed to know what was actually happening in the classrooms. In order to determine whether the sponsors were effective in getting teachers to practice their methods in the classroom, it was necessary to observe the classrooms systematically. We wanted to know whether a child's day in the classroom corresponded with the sponsor's educational prescriptions. To assess this, we needed a comprehensive observation instrument.

In the fall of 1969, the SRI staff, with assistance from twelve sponsors' representatives, developed an observation system with which a wide range of classroom behaviors could be recorded and with which objective information could probably be recorded that would provide a fair assessment of all sponsors' models. The procedures that were developed could record activities, materials used, groupings, and interactions. This chapter presents the fourth and most comprehensive report of Follow Through classroom observation data. The data for this study were collected in spring 1973 from thirty-six sites representing seven sponsors. The seven models of the chosen sponsors represent a wide spectrum of innovative educational theories and were selected because each model was being implemented in at least five locations. The models selected for this study include two models based on positive reinforcement theory (from the University of Kansas and from the University of Oregon), a model based primarily on the cognitive developmental theory of Jean Piaget (High/Scope Foundation), an open-classroom model based on the English Infant School Theory (Education Development Center), and three other models drawn from Piaget, John Dewey, and the English Infant Schools (Far West Laboratory, the University of Arizona, and Bank Street College).

The study focuses on whether sponsors can deliver their educational models to diverse communities, and explores the effects of training classroom personnel to use specific procedures in the classroom. An educational theory can be proved effective only if the teachers and aides carry out program specifications. Such specifications set by sponsors include the physical arrangement of the classroom, utilization of the prescribed curricula, and interactions with children. This study addresses the following issues:

1. Are the observed classroom programs consistent with their sponsors' stated intentions? That is, does the model show a relatively high frequency of occurrence of those elements of the program that the sponsor rated as important?

2. Are the sponsored classrooms consistent within a site and between sites? That is, do the four third-grade classrooms at site A score similarly on specific program components and do they resemble the third-grade classrooms at sites B, C, D, and E?
3. How do selected classroom processes relate to scores on the following: Metropolitan Achievement Test (MAT) (reading and arithmetic), Raven's Coloured Progressive Matrices, Cooper-smith's Self-Esteem Inventory, and Intellectual Achievement Responsibility Scale (IAR)?

SAMPLE

Four first-grade and four third-grade classrooms were observed in each of thirty-six cities and towns. These represented five projects for each of six of the Follow Through educational models and six projects for the University of Arizona's model. One first-grade and one third-grade non-Follow Through classroom were selected for comparison at each project site. These non-Follow Through classrooms were combined to form two pooled comparison groups, thirty-five first grades and thirty-six third grades. The projects included in the sample represented all geographic regions, urban and rural areas, and several racial and ethnic groups.

Observation sites were selected according to the following criteria: (1) they were among the sites where pupil testing was to occur in spring 1973 as part of the Follow Through evaluation; (2) each sponsor would, as much as possible, have a balanced geographic distribution of sites, which included urban-rural and north-south projects; and (3) each sponsor would have included at least two sites where he thought the model was well implemented.

In addition to identifying classrooms for observation, we randomly selected four children from each classroom for individual observations. At each site, the primary consideration in identifying the classrooms and children to be observed was the availability of baseline data for the children when they entered school in kindergarten or first grade.

In those projects where baseline data were not available, the Follow Through classrooms were nominated by the sponsor, and the non-Follow Through classrooms were selected by the SRI Field

Operations staff. The SRI staff selected children for individual observation on a random basis from classroom roster lists.

MEASUREMENT INSTRUMENTS

Behavior Observation

The Classroom Observation Instrument (COI) is designed to record classroom arrangements and elements of events considered educationally significant by the Follow Through sponsors.

Formation of Variables. Many of the individual codes are too molecular to serve effectively as measures of classroom educational characteristics. Hence, it was necessary to form theoretically significant variables by combining certain codes. The COI consists of 602 categories describing behaviors of teachers and children in the classroom situation. The items identify materials used in the classroom, the grouping arrangements of teacher and children, the activities that occur, the behavior of an individual, and the interactions that occur between two or more people.

Interaction observations were made in five-minute sequences. A form of shorthand was used to record the continuous action and interaction of selected persons in the classrooms. On two of three days of observation, there was an adult focus, that is, the classroom adults were the subjects of observation. On the remaining day, the four randomly selected children were the focus. Hence, the data provide one set of measures of classroom process (adult focus) and one set of child behaviors (child focus) with the same set of categories, or codes.

Observers were instructed to complete approximately four observations each hour during the five-hour observation day; hence, it was hoped that a total of twenty observations would be completed each day, or sixty for each classroom. For the 1,011 observation days of all observers, the adjusted mean number of observations completed each day was 18.88, with a standard deviation of 2.17. Fewer observations occurred for certain classrooms because of intervening events during the class day that prohibited observations. Data from any day that had fewer than twelve observations were deleted.

The data were collected on three consecutive days in spring 1973. In most cases, the teachers had been working with the sponsors' educational models for two or three years. No beginning teachers were selected for observation.

Since there are over 100,000 possible combinations of codes that could form variables, it was important to formulate only those variables considered relevant to the study of sponsor implementation. The following sections will describe the transformation of codes from each portion of the classroom observation instrument into variables.

Because this study evaluated classroom environments and classroom instructional processes, the classroom rather than the child was the unit of analysis. Classroom mean scores were also computed for the sample of individually observed children. Each classroom was assigned a value on a given variable based on the sum of the frequency of occurrence of the variable for the observation days.

Classroom Summary Information (CSI) Variables. Once a day, before the observation with the COI started, the observer recorded information that identified the classroom by sponsor, site, teacher, grade, and observer. The observer also noted the numbers of adults and children present. To obtain the ratio of children to teachers and aides, the total number of children present on each observation day was divided by the total number of teachers and aides present. An average ratio over the three days was then computed. Total class duration was computed by averaging the number of class hours recorded for the three days of observations.

Physical Environment Information (PEI) Variables. This section of the COI, completed once each observation day, provided two kinds of information: (1) seating and workgroup patterns, and (2) equipment and materials present and used in the classroom. The scores for a classroom were based on the sum of all three days.

Classroom Checklist (CCL) Variables. The CCL variables define the frequency of occurrence of specific activities (e.g., group time, mathematics, dramatic play) that denote the frequency of occurrence of the different groupings of adults and children (e.g., aide with small group of children, one child without an adult), grouping within particular activities (e.g., teacher with two children in mathematics activity), and the use of special materials or equipment (e.g., texts or workbooks, audiovisual equipment) within the activities of mathematics, reading, social studies, and science. Some metavariables were formed, such as "How frequently does a child receive individual attention from an adult?" This metavariable was formed by adding many discrete subvariables, such as "How frequently does a child receive individual attention from an aide during mathematics?" plus "How frequently does a child receive individual attention from a volunteer during reading?" plus all other variables that describe an incident where one child is working with an adult.

Five-minute Observation (FMO) Variables. This main portion of the COI is used to record, in the form of coded sentences, interactions that occur in the classroom. The Flanders Interaction Analysis Observation system served as the model for this section of the COI. The Who, to Whom, What, and How codes have functions and operational definitions similar to the Flanders system (1970). For this purpose, the observer used a series of four-celled frames (see Figure 5-1 for frames used in preschool or kindergarten classrooms). To record each interaction, the observer made a check mark in the appropriate circle in each of the four cells of a frame. These marks identified the speaker, the person being spoken to, and the message

	Who	To Whom	What	How
*				
Ⓡ	Ⓣ Ⓐ Ⓥ	Ⓣ Ⓐ Ⓥ	① ② ③ ④ ⑤	Ⓗ Ⓤ Ⓝ Ⓣ
Ⓢ	Ⓒ Ⓓ ②	Ⓒ Ⓓ ②	⑥ ⑦ ⑧ ⑨ ⑩	Ⓞ Ⓖ Ⓟ
Ⓒ	Ⓢ Ⓛ Ⓐⓝ Ⓜ	Ⓢ Ⓛ Ⓐⓝ Ⓜ	⑪ ⑫ ⓃⓋ Ⓧ	Ⓞ Ⓦ ⒹⓅ Ⓐ Ⓑ

Figure 5-1
Frames Used for Observations in Preschool and Kindergarten Classrooms

Who and *To Whom* categories: T–teacher, A–aide, V–volunteer, C–child, D–different child, 2–two children, S–small group, L–large group, An–animal, M–machine. *What* categories: 1–command or request; 1Q–direct question (Q from *How* col.); 2–open-ended question; 3–response; 4–instruction, explanation; 5–general comments/general action; 6–task-related comment; 7–acknowledge; 8–praise; 9–corrective feedback; 10–no response; 11–waiting; 12–observing, listening; NV–nonverbal; X–movement. *How* categories: H–happy; U–unhappy; N–negative; T–touch, Q–question; G–guide/reason; P–punish; O–object; W–worth; DP–dramatic play/pretend; A–academic; B–behavior.
  * R–Repeat the Frame, S–Using Second Language, C–Cancel the Frame

being delivered. The How column describes the emotional affect and whether the conversation had an academic content or referred to behavior. Each frame represents a sentence. If one person asks a question, it is coded in the first frame. A second frame is used for the response of the other person, and so on.

For example, the following three interactions would require three frames:

1. TEACHER: Maria, what did you like best about the story *Peter Pan?*
   [In our shorthand, this sentence is coded TC2QA. The teacher (T, Who column) has asked Maria (C, To Whom column) a thought-provoking question (2Q, What column). The question is about the academic subject in the How column (A, How column).]

2. MARIA: Tinkerbell. She was very brave.
   [Shorthand: CT3A. The child (C, Who column) responds (3, What column) with academic content (A, How column) to the teacher's (T, To Whom column) question.]

3. TEACHER: Oh yes, she was brave, wasn't she?
   [Shorthand: TC7A. The teacher (T, Who column) acknowledges (7, What column) the child's (C, To Whom column) academic (A, How column) response.]

Seventy-two of these frames represent a five-minute interaction period. The variables formed from these complex codings were those that seemed most appropriate to the sponsors' models and to the analysis planned for this study.

The FMO variables were selected and named to describe interactions relevant to sponsors' implementation. The variables are defined by appropriate code combinations or sentences. Generally, the FMO variables describe child-adult verbal interactions (i.e., questions, responses, instruction, comments, and feedback) and nonverbal interactions (i.e., nonverbal requests, responses, self-instruction, feedback, waiting, and observing/listening). In some cases, these FMO variables are further defined by the How category modifiers (such as academic, social behavior, happy, negative). A few variables are defined by the sequential ordering of certain interaction frames (e.g., adult question followed by child response followed by adult feedback).

Observer Reliability

All observers were trained in a seven-day intensive training course delivered at four national training sites. Potential observers watched a specimen videotape, and only those who met the final criterion of coding interactions with a reliability of 70 percent or above were employed to collect data for this study. Of the original seventy-two who were trained, sixty-three met this criterion. Nine more observers were trained in a special session to fill these vacancies.

The observers began work in classrooms; after approximately two weeks, twenty simulated classroom situations were videotaped and shown to the observers to code. Each simulation was approximately twenty interaction frames long. These simulations attempted to present several concise, clear examples of each code used in the COI. Each simulation began with a still frame in which the narrator identified the focus of the observation (a teacher or a child). Each skit was shown with a two-second pause between interactions. The observers were instructed to code one interaction frame during each pause.

Matrices were constructed for each observer. A form was prepared that listed all sixteen What codes across the top of the matrix and down the side. Those across the top were the "true" codes as judged by the investigators; the numbers of instances of each occurring in the twenty situations were listed in the row under the labels. The codes listed down the side were the actual codes ascribed by the observer being tested. The reliability booklets for each observer were examined frame by frame, and tallies were made of each observer's coded interaction sequences. If the observer's coding agreed with the criterion, a tally was placed in the intersection of the row and column. The principal diagonal, then, contains the cells indicating the observer's correct coding; other cells contain incorrect coding. The row totals are the total number of times an observer recorded each code, whether correctly or not. The number of criterion examples shown across the top could be compared with the diagonal to compute the observer's reliability for each code. An examination of a particular cell in the row reveals whether the code was recorded correctly or incorrectly, and, if recorded incorrectly, the row cells show exactly which codes were confused with one another. (This is reported in great detail by Stallings and Gieson, 1977.)

Thus, observer bias can be assessed by examining the overuse, underuse, or confusion of codes. In this study, each observer was responsible for observing one grade level at a single location and therefore the data collected by each observer is identifiable in analysis. The value of this method for measuring accuracy is that it contributes directly toward interpreting the data.

Other Child Measures

The children's ability when they began school was assessed by the Wide Range Achievement Test (WRAT). It was administered to children when they entered school, either at the kindergarten or first-grade level.

Reading and mathematics skills were assessed by the MAT in both first and third grades. Problem-solving skills (perceptual) were assessed in third grade only, using the Raven's Coloured Progressive Matrices. This test, designed as a culture-fair, fluid intelligence test, was adopted for use in the evaluation as a measure of nonverbal reasoning and problem-solving ability in visual perceptual tasks. The Intellectual Achievement Responsibility Scale (IAR), used in third grade only, assessed the extent to which the child takes responsibility for his own successes or failures (i.e., internal locus of control) or attributes his achievements to the operation of external forces (e.g., luck or fate). Child behaviors were assessed through systematic observations recorded on the COI. Absences from school were determined from school records.

CONSISTENCY OF CLASSROOM PROCESSES

We examine in this section the day-to-day variability of what occurs in the classroom. For the purposes of this chapter, we would like to have consistent descriptions of what was occurring in a classroom during spring 1973. The activities and interactions that occur in a classroom no doubt change radically over the course of a school year as adults and pupils become acquainted, as the subject matter changes, and as holiday seasons pass. Even when inferences are confined to the spring of the school year, after the Follow Through teacher has had approximately six months to implement a sponsor's model, classroom processes no doubt vary from day to day. It was, therefore, important to find out how stable our descriptions of these processes could be when based on only a few days of observation.

Three consecutive days of observation were scheduled for each classroom, both Follow Through and non-Follow Through. The values of the Classroom Check List (CCL) variables are based on all three days of observation; the values of the adult/activity focus Five-Minute Observation (FMO) interaction variables were based on two days of observation, while the child-focus observations were based on a single day per class.

A subset of CCL and FMO variables was chosen for the assessment of the stability of the classroom processes. The variables were selected on the basis of how well they described sponsors' programs. Results from previous evaluations (Stallings, 1973; Stallings, Baker, and Steinmetz, 1972) were used in the selection.

For each variable, the correlations were computed between the observed values on the two days of adult/activity focus observations. The Spearman-Brown formula was applied to the correlations to derive the consistency of two or three days of observation for the FMO and CCL variables, respectively. (Since there was only a single day of child-focus observations per class, the child-focus FMO variables were not included in this analysis.)

The consistency coefficient reflects the variability of the obtained classroom means, part of which is a product of "true" variance in classroom variables, while the remainder stems from measurement errors. Because of the method of determining observer reliability (measurement error), there is no satisfactory way to untangle the two by a correction for attenuation.

A primary factor contributing to less-than-perfect consistency is the assumed variability of the classroom processes from day to day. Another factor is the variability of the children's absences from day to day and differences in the number of absences across classrooms. A high-consistency coefficient, say above 0.70, indicates that the classrooms maintain approximately the same rank order on observed scores from day to day. This would indicate that error due either to day-to-day variability within classrooms or to absences is slight, although it would not rule out the possibility of systematic error operating across absences.

For all classrooms combined, both sponsored and non-Follow Through, the coefficients are reasonably high. Those for the CCL variables are above 0.70, with the exception of variable 66 (numbers, mathematics, arithmetic) for the third grade, where the coefficient was 0.68. For the adult/activity focus FMO variables, the coefficients were all above 0.85, with the exception of variable 374a (adult instruction, academic) for first grade, where the coefficient was 0.74.

For the individual sponsors, approximately 84 percent of the 140 coefficients had a value of 0.70 or more. The reliability coefficient for variable 66 (numbers, mathematics, arithmetic) was below 0.70 in six out of the fourteen cases. In particular, the coefficients were extremely low for both grade levels of the University of Arizona and for the third grades of Bank Street and of the University of Oregon. The negative coefficient for Bank Street's third grade is the result of one classroom in which an extremely high proportion of the class time was spent in mathematics on the first day and a small proportion on the second day. The extremely low-consistency coefficients for the University of Oregon on variable 66 in the third grade and variable 67 in the first grade are notable because this sponsor's program is considered more structured than others.

In summary, the coefficients computed over all classrooms indicate that the consistency of instructional processes was surprisingly high. The differences among classrooms account for a substantial portion of the variability among the variables we have selected. The same conclusion holds with a few exceptions for the coefficients computed for each sponsor and grade level. The only variable for which the day-to-day consistency was low for several sponsors was variable 66 (average amount of time that a child was observed to be engaged in numbers, mathematics, arithmetic).

MEASUREMENTS OF APPROXIMATION TO THEORETICAL MODEL

The first step in the assessment of classroom implementation was to describe each educational model in detail. These descriptions were prepared by our staff and reviewed by the sponsors, then revised according to the sponsors' specifications. The second step was to create variables from the codes used in the observation instrument that would describe representative elements of each sponsor's model. Each sponsor identified those variables that were (1) important to his model and (2) expected to occur more frequently than in conventional classrooms. A list of variables was made for each of the seven models. The number of variables ranged from sixteen for the University of Oregon to twenty-eight for Far West Laboratory (see Table 5-1). The critical list of variables describes a sponsor's model only in part; the observation instrument employed in the study is not designed to capture the important subtle processes of some of the programs. For example, a goal of Far West Laboratory is to have teachers establish environments where a child can search for solutions to problems in his own way and can risk, guess, and make discoveries without serious negative psychological consequences. It was not possible for us to measure directly the extent to which such an environment had been established.

Since the Follow Through programs are intended to be innovative and to represent alternatives to the conventional classroom, a pool of non-Follow Through classrooms was used as the standard from which Follow Through classrooms were expected to differ in specified ways. The standards were established separately for first and third grades.

With observational data, the distribution of scores rarely follows a normal curve; thus a nonparametric scaling technique was used in the implementation analysis. Implementation scores for each sponsor were determined by rank-ordering the non-Follow Through classrooms' mean scores on each sponsor variable and then dividing the distribution into five equal parts, or quintiles. Each sponsor classroom has a score on each variable and falls within a quintile range. A sponsor's implementation score on any variable is always a score between 1 and 5. This represents the position of a Follow Through classroom score relative to the distribution of non-Follow Through scores.

Using each variable designated as critical by the sponsor of a model, a total implementation score was computed for each classroom in each project location and for each sponsor. In order to assess the degree of implementation achieved by Follow Through classrooms, a total implementation score was also computed for each non-Follow Through classroom on each sponsor's set of implementation variables. The mean and standard deviation of the non-Follow Through pooled classrooms are reported for each sponsor separately for first and third grades. One-tailed "t" tests were computed to test for the significance of the differences between each Follow Through sponsor's classrooms and the non-Follow Through classrooms. Analyses of

Table 5-1
List of Critical Variables Selected by Sponsors

Variable	Far West Laboratory	University of Arizona	Bank Street	University of Oregon	University of Kansas	High/Scope	Education Development Center (EDC)
24, child selection of seating and work groups	X	X	X			X	X
25, games, toys, play equipment present	X	X	X			X	X
39, general equipment, materials present	X						X
65, guessing games, table games, puzzles		X	X		X	X	
66, numbers, mathematics, arithmetic	X	X	X	X	X	X	X[a]
67, reading, alphabet, language development	X	X	X	X	X	X	X[a]
70, sewing, cooking, pounding		X				X	
71, blocks, trucks						X	
74, practical-skills acquisition	X[b]		X				
83, wide variety of activities, over one day	X	X	X			X	X
86, teacher with one child	X	X	X			X	
87, teacher with two children			X				
88, teacher with small group		X	X	X	X	X	
92, aide with one child	X		X	X	X		
94, aide with small group		X	X				
114, one child independent	X	X	X				X
115, two children independent							X
116, small group of children independent	X		X				X
239, mathematics or science equipment/academic activities	X	X	X			X	
240, texts, workbooks/academic activities				X	X		
343, child to adult, all verbal except response			X				X

Variable						
344, individual child verbal interactions with adult	X	X	X	X	X	X
350, child questions to adults	X	X	X	X	X	X
363, child group response to adult academic commands, requests, or direct questions			X		X	
372, child presenting information to a group	X		X		X	X
375, adult instructs an individual child				X		
376, adult instructs a group		X	X		X	X
390, adult task-related comments to children	X		X	X	X	X
394, all adult acknowledgment to children		X	X	X	X	
398, all adult praise to children		X		X		
412, adult feedback to child response to adult academic commands, requests, direct questions		X	X	X	X	
420, adults attentive to a small group	X	X		X	X	
421, adults attentive to individual children	X	X		X	X	X
423, positive behavior, adults to children	X	X				
435, total academic verbal interactions						
438, adult communication or attention focus, one child	X	X	X	X	X	X
440, adult communication or attention focus, small group			X		X	
444, adult movement	X					
450, all child open-ended questions						X
451, adult academic commands, requests, and direct questions to children	X	X		X		
452, adult open-ended questions to children	X	X	X		X	X
453, adult response to child's question with a question		X			X	X
454, child's extended response to questions	X	X	X		X	X

continued

Table 5-1, continued

Variable	Far West Laboratory	University of Arizona	Bank Street	University of Oregon	University of Kansas	High/Scope	Education Development Center (EDC)
456, all child task-related comments	X					X	
457, all adult positive corrective feedback	X			X	X		
460, all child positive affect	X	X					X
469, all adult reinforcement with tokens				X	X		
509, child self-instruction, academic				X[a]			
510, child self-instruction, objects			X			X	X
513, child task persistence			X		X	X	
514, two children working together, using concrete objects						X	
515, small group working together, using concrete objects						X	
516, social interaction among children	X		X				X
574, child movement	X		X				X
599, child self-instruction, nonacademic	X	X				X	
Total N critical variables	28[b] 27[a]	21	27	16[b] 17[a]	17	29	20[b] 22[a]

[a] Third-grade only
[b] First-grade only

variance were also computed to examine the within-site and among-site differences in total implementation scores for each sponsor. Implementation is judged on two criteria: (1) Do the sponsored classrooms differ significantly from non-Follow Through classrooms? and (2) Are the classrooms similar in implementation both within projects and among projects? (See Stallings, 1975, p. 26, for this statistical procedure.)

RESULTS

The data obtained from this large sample indicated that the models in Head Start and Follow Through Planned Variation programs were very effective in training teachers in diverse locations to instruct in compliance with the models (i.e., Bank Street teachers in Tuskeegee looked similar to Bank Street teachers in New York City).

Further analyses of the observation data indicated that instructional processes identified with exploratory models explained 45 percent of the variance in scores on the Ravens Progressive Matrices. Instructional variables identified with direct instruction models explained 37 percent of the variance in reading achievement and 64 percent in mathematics achievement (Stallings, 1975). This was one of the first national evaluations of educational models to use a comprehensive observation system linking classroom processes to student outcomes.

OTHER STUDIES USING THE COI

Early Childhood Education

Following the initial study, the COI was used in a California study of an early childhood education program (Stallings, Cory, Fairweather, and Needels, 1979). The evaluation focused on the instructional processes of teachers in schools classified as having students with increasing achievement scores, compared with the instructional processes of teachers in schools where students' achievement scores were decreasing. This evaluation indicated more variance in instructional processes within schools than among schools. Overall observation variables identified with direct instruction methods were significantly related to higher student achievement scores regardless of how the school had been classified.

Puerto Rican—English as a Second Language

The versatility of the coding system allows each coded interaction to be identified as English or Non-English. This capability was used in an evaluation of the quantity and quality of English being spoken in Puerto Rican classrooms. Puerto Rican observers were trained in a ten-day session to collect data reliably on the COI. Data were collected in urban and rural elementary and secondary schools, and observations occurred over two full days in randomly selected classrooms. The use of English was calculated as a percentage of the total recorded interactions. The quality of English used was assessed by reviewing tape recordings. (See Rivera-Medina, 1981.)

MODIFICATION FOR SECONDARY SCHOOL

For a study of teaching basic reading skills in secondary schools (Stallings, Fairweather, and Needels, 1978), the COI was modified to record the activities and instructional processes occurring in secondary classrooms. This study identified forty-one observation variables that were significantly related to a gain in reading achievement scores. Modifications in the coding and in the training program have been made to accommodate other subject areas such as science, social studies, mathematics, and physical education. For example, in a study of factors influencing women to take advanced mathematics classes (Stallings and Robertson, 1979), the COI was modified to identify when teachers were speaking to male or female students. The coding system provided variables that could be used to compare the nature of the interactions between male students and teachers with those between female students and teachers. Counter to our prediction, we found no significant differences in the classroom interactions among teachers and their male and female students. Because modifications to the program have occurred over the past ten years, we changed the name of the observation system to Stallings Observation System (SOS).

Table 5-2
Self-Analytic Model of Staff Development

Baseline/Pretest
  Observe teachers
  Prepare individual profiles of behavior
  Teachers assess what change is needed
  Teachers set goals
  Start where teachers are in skill development
Inform
  Provide information about research findings on effective practice
  Link theory, research, and practice
  Check for understanding by eliciting practical examples
  Ask, Why might that be? How does that work in your classroom?
Guided Practice: Integration
  Provide conceptual units one at a time
  Teachers adapt to own context and style
  Teachers assess and provide feedback via peer observations
  Teachers make a commitment to try a new idea in class the next day
Post-Test Observations
  Observe teachers: prepare second profile
  Teachers analyze profiles
  Teachers set new goals
  Assess training program for effectiveness

STAFF DEVELOPMENT BASED ON OBSERVATION

Phase I of the study of secondary basic reading skills was a year-long quasi-experiment in which very specific instructional variables were identified. Using these variables we constructed a staff-development program (named the Effective Use of Time [EUOT]). This training program, which was Phase II of the study and was based on an interactive theory of adult education, guided teachers to use the effective strategies. (See Table 5-2 for the model.)

In the year-long experiment, the teachers in the experimental classes successfully implemented the EUOT program, and their students gained six months more on reading achievement tests than did students in control classrooms. Findings from Phase I and II correlations and analysis of variance were remarkably similar. Summarizing the two data sets, we established the criteria shown in one teacher's profile (see Figure 5-2). These criteria then formed the basis for our recommendations for change in the teacher's behavior. The

Figure 5-2
The Percentage of Time Devoted by a Teacher to Certain Classroom Activities, in Relation to Established Criteria, with Recommendations for Change.

Activities	R*	Criterion***	Criterion Percentage	Teacher Baseline Percentage
Preparation				
Making assignments	Less	—X	7	8
Organizing	Less	—X	5	9
Teacher working alone	Less	——X	3	15
Interactive Instruction				
Review/Discussing	More	X—	10	6
Informing	More	X——	20	14
Drill and practice	OK	X	2	2
Oral reading	More	X——	9	2
*Noninteractive**				
Doing written work	OK	X—	25	20
Silent reading	Less	——X	9	20
Off Task				
Students socializing	Less	—X	4	8
Students uninvolved	Less	——X	5	15
Teacher disciplining	Less	—X	1	6

* R= Recommendations
** Students work alone
*** Shows how much teachers exceeded (horizontal line to the right of vertical criterion line) or fell short of (line to left) the criterion for time devoted to the activity in question.

criteria are adjusted according to the achievement level of the students (Stallings, 1986).

DISSEMINATION

Federal and state education agencies, concerned for the many students in secondary schools who could not competently read, write, or compute, found the findings from the secondary reading studies of considerable interest. Subsequently, under the auspices of the Stallings Teaching and Learning Institute, the EUOT program was disseminated through the National Diffusion Network, and funding to assist in dissemination has continued from 1980 through 1990. The

EUOT program has been widely disseminated. Trainers for the EUOT program were certified at the Stallings Teaching and Learning Institutes at Vanderbilt University and the University of Houston. These participants included college of education faculty, school staff developers, and state department of education personnel. A body of research has evolved from these participants and from numerous student dissertations. The development of lap-top computer technology has allowed for more in-depth analysis and immediate feedback to teachers by providing instant profiles.

EUOT has been implemented in Branson, Missouri, over a three-year period. There, selected teachers were certified as trainers and observers to disseminate the program to all teachers in the district. Significant behavior change has been recorded for teachers and students throughout the project. In fall 1986, the Missouri Department of Elementary and Secondary Education identified Branson as a "Successful Project." Governor Ashcroft stated, "In the Branson school district, teachers and administrators have reported significant success with their Effective Use of Time (EUOT) program. This in-service experience helps teachers see how well they use class time and gives them strategies for using class time more effectively. The teachers involved in the program reported that EUOT helped them improve their skills significantly" (Orth, 1987, p. 4).

EUOT RESEARCH

Anderson (1984) examined the use of the SOS variables combined with Effective Use of Time (EUOT) training to improve instruction in the Washington, D.C., public schools. Her study focused on the changes in the teaching behavior of twenty-nine junior high school teachers who were trained by five different EUOT trainers. The SOS was used to determine the degree of change from the beginning to the end of the semester. The study examined the difference between the change of groups taught by four district trainers and one taught by an external trainer consultant. The teachers in the external consultant's group were found to change their behavior more than did teachers in the other groups. Anderson found that the most change occurred when the trainer (1) provided frequent teacher interactions, (2) discussed the observation variables frequently, (3) made frequent supportive statements to try new ideas, and (4) stayed focused on the topic of the seminar (i.e., managing and motivation, student behavior, asking higher-level questions).

Longitudinal Study

Devlin-Scherer, Schaffer, and Stringfield (in press) conducted a follow-up observation study of an Effective Use of Time Program, for which they selected a sample of ten teachers who reflected high and low implementors from the original EUOT observations. They had three points of observation data (before the training, after the training, and two years later). High implementors had scores above the mean at the end of the training and the low implementors had post scores below the group mean. The ten teachers were observed and interviewed two years after receiving training in order to determine the long-term impact of the training on their teaching. The follow-up observations were compared with the initial observations on thirty-two variables. The average for the group of ten remained about the same over the elapsed time (i.e., change on eighteen of the observed variables was maintained at the same level as at the end of the training). On eight of the variables, the group's average was reverting to their initial behavior. Analyses of individual teacher's profiles revealed that teachers who had initially implemented the variables successfully were more likely to sustain their change than were teachers who implemented at a lower level. The high-implementing teachers indicated in interviews that the workshops provided them with present and future assistance. The low-implementing teachers indicated that sessions were confirmations of what they knew. They enjoyed the workshops more as opportunities to interact with peers. High implementors were able to identify specific skills they used in their classrooms. Low implementors were more global in their responses and less likely to identify specific skills.

Teacher Commitment

A study by Devlin-Scherer and colleagues (1985) entitled "The Effects of Developing Teacher Commitment to Behavioral Change" responds to the concern of measuring the effectiveness of training programs.

Seventeen elementary and secondary teachers were trained by pairs of university, principal, or teacher trainers in the Stallings Effective Use of Time Program. Workshop sessions were audio-recorded and analyzed to determine the impact of verbal commitment behavior on changes in classroom teaching behavior. Using the SOS, a comparison of pre- and post-classroom observations indicated that teachers who stated public commitments to behavioral changes each week more often followed through and made these behavioral changes in their classroom teaching than did teachers who did not make such public commitment. [P. 31]

SOS FOR EVALUATION

Stringfield, Teddlie, and Suarez (1985) used the SOS to examine the classroom instructional processes of two Louisiana schools. One was identified as high achieving and the other was identified as low achieving. The majority of the students in both schools are white, and black, Hispanic, and Asian students form the minority population. Each school is located in middle-class, single-family-dwelling neighborhoods. The site team observers (who were blind to the achievement status of the schools) noted that students at the low-achieving school spent about one hour less a day doing academic tasks. During six days of observations, few classes began at 8:30 A.M. as scheduled. Many students were in the halls when the bell rang. The researchers indicated that there was "a constant stream of children to and from bathrooms, the office, the library, and in some cases, just hanging out in the halls" (p. 34). According to the SOS data, students in the high-achieving school received nearly twice as much interactive instruction as did students in the low-achieving school.

STUDENT TEACHING

A study by Harris (1988) included a sample of fifty student teachers. Over a fifteen-month period, twenty student teachers participated in full treatment of SOS feedback plus EUOT workshops and seven in feedback from SOS treatment only; there were twenty-three controls. Change was measured with eleven variables aggregating specific SOS variables. Analysis of variance indicated full-treatment subjects improved (moved toward criterion levels) for eight of eleven variables, with change significant at the 0.05 level for teachers' monitoring students, students in interactive instruction, and students off task. SOS feedback-only subjects improved for nine variables, with change significant for teachers' interactively instructing, teachers' managing, and students in interactive instruction. Implications for teacher education suggest that the feedback portion of the EUOT program is effective during the preservice teaching experience, that the portion of the EUOT workshops dealing with interactive instruction effects a change beyond that of SOS feedback only, and that trainer as observer increases student teachers' classroom management.

Freiberg and Waxman (1988) used three approaches for providing feedback to student teachers that have not been widely used but have great potential for improving the classroom instruction of preservice teachers. The methods include (a) feedback from pupils, (b) systematic feedback from classroom observation system (SOS), and (c) self-analysis of classroom lessons through an audiotape analysis (Low Inference Self-Assessment System; see Freiberg, 1987). The authors found that these feedback approaches, individually or collectively, provide student teachers, cooperating teachers, and university supervisors with excellent data for strengthening the preservice teaching experience. (See Freiberg, Waxman, Houston, 1987.)

Student Teaching in Inner-City Schools

The purpose of the Learning to Teach in Inner-City Schools project (LTICS) is to develop teachers who choose to teach in inner-city schools and are effective in teaching inner-city children. Historically, most new teachers did their student teaching in the suburbs. Those hired for inner-city schools had little preparation to serve children who come from a wide variety of cultural backgrounds and from low socioeconomic families. The dropout rate of new teachers in inner-city schools is reported to be twice the average for the nation (Stallings, Martin, and Bossung, in press).

The goal of LTICS is to change this history of failure by novice teachers in inner-city schools to one of success. To this end, a partnership was established between a school district serving inner-city students and a college of education that trains student teachers. The partnership created a professional development school that provides a structure in which a group of supervising teachers, college supervisors, and ten to twelve student teachers per semester learn to implement effective instructional strategies for inner-city school populations. This occurs through shared required weekly seminars that follow the EUOT format. The seminars focus on the problems and solutions of teaching inner-city children (e.g., holding high expectations, working with parents and their children, assessing children's prior knowledge and experiences, planning appropriate lessons, managing classroom time, motivating and managing positive student behavior, and developing reflectivity and thinking skills). Seminars are taught by school and college faculty and community/parent representatives.

Student teachers and supervising teachers are observed with the SOS at the beginning of each semester and set goals for instructional change. The percentage of time children spend on academic tasks is computed and analyzed for change; these statistical analyses have indicated significant change each semester in student teacher and teacher behavior. The impact of LTICS is also evaluated by calculating the percentage of student teachers graduating from LTICS who choose to teach inner-city or other at-risk populations (85 percent at this time). Follow-up interviews with LTICS graduates indicate job satisfaction, and their principals give them high ratings.

SUMMARY

Observation in classrooms serves many purposes. Most often observation is used to evaluate teachers and students. The flexibility of the SOS has provided a means to identify effective instructional practices in a wide range of classroom settings. The specificity of the SOS variables and their face validity have made it relatively easy to translate them into teaching behaviors, and these data from the study have provided the content for extensive in-service and preservice professional development. The profiles of teaching behaviors observed in a pretest and posttest design provide a continuing basis for evaluation and improvement of the EUOT program.

REFERENCES

Anderson, Sandra Lee. "Teacher Training Techniques from Four Observational Perspectives," *Journal of Classroom Interaction* 20, no. 1 (1984): 16–28.

Deutsch, Martin. *The Disadvantaged Child.* New York: Basic Books, 1967.

Devlin-Scherer, Roberta; Devlin-Scherer, Wade; Schaffer, Eugene; and Stringfield, Samuel. "The Effects of Developing Teacher Commitment to Behavioral Change," *Journal of Classroom Interaction* 21, no. 1 (1985): 31–37.

Devlin-Scherer, Roberta; Schaffer, Eugene C.; and Stringfield, Samuel C. "A Two-Year Follow-up of a Staff Development Program Designed to Change Teacher Behavior," *Journal of Classroom Interaction,* in press.

Egbert, Robert L. "Planned Variation in Follow Through." Paper presented at the Brookings Institute Conference on Social Experimentation, Washington, D.C., April 1973.

Flanders, Ned A. *Analyzing Teacher Behaviors.* Reading, Mass.: Addison-Wesley, 1970.

Freiberg, H. Jerome. "Teacher Self-evaluation and Principal Supervision," *National Association of Secondary School Principals Bulletin* 71 (1987): 85–92.

Freiberg, H. Jerome, and Waxman, Hersholt C. "Alternative Feedback Approaches for Improving Student Teachers' Classroom Instruction," *Journal of Teacher Education* 39, no. 4 (1988): 8–14.

Freiberg, H. Jerome; Waxman, Hersholt C.; and Houston, W. Robert. "Enriching Feedback to Student Teachers through Small Group Discussion," *Teacher Education Quarterly* 14, no. 3 (1987): 71–82.

Harris, Alene Hawes. "Sources of Treatment Effects in a Teacher Effectiveness Training Program." Doctoral dissertation, Vanderbilt University, August 1988.

Orth, Lee J. "A Good Time Was Had by All." In *School and Community.* Branson: Missouri State Teachers Association, 1987.

Rivera-Medina, Eduardo. *Assessment of the In-service Training Needs of Teachers of English and of Spanish to Returned Migrants in Puerto Rico.* Final Report. Washington, D.C.: National Institute of Education, 1981.

Stallings, Jane A. *Follow Through Program Classroom Observation Evaluation, 1971–1972.* SRI Project URU-7370. Menlo Park, Calif.: Stanford Research Institute, August 1973.

Stallings, Jane A. "Implementation and Child Effects of Teaching Practices in Follow Through Classrooms," *Monographs of the Society for Research in Child Development* 40 (1975), Serial No. 163.

Stallings, Jane A. "Effective Use of Time in Secondary Reading Programs." In *Effective Teaching of Reading: Research and Practice.* Newark, Del.: International Reading Association, 1986.

Stallings, Jane A.; Baker, Phil; and Steinmetz, Gerald. "What Happens in the Follow Through Program: Implications for Child Growth and Development." Paper presented at the meeting of the American Psychological Association, Honolulu, September 1972.

Stallings, Jane A.; Cory, R.; Fairweather, James S.; and Needels, Margaret. *Early Childhood Education Classroom Evaluation.* Final Report for the Department of Education, State of California. Menlo Park, Calif.: SRI International, 1979.

Stallings, Jane A.; Fairweather, James S.; and Needels, Margaret. *A Study of Teaching Basic Reading Skills in Secondary Schools*. Final Report for the National Institute of Education. Menlo Park, Calif.: SRI International, 1978.

Stallings, Jane A., and Gieson, Philip. "The Study of Reliability in Observational Data." In *Phi Delta Kappa Occasional Paper*, no. 19. Bloomington, Ind.: Phi Delta Kappa, 1977.

Stallings, Jane A.;Martin, Anna; and Bossung, Joan. "Houston Teaching Academy: A Partnership in Developing Teachers," *Teaching and Teacher Education*, in press.

Stallings, Jane A., and Robertson, A. *Factors Influencing Women's Decisions to Enroll in Advanced Mathematics Courses*. Final Report for the National Institute of Education. Menlo Park, Calif.: SRI International, 1979.

Stringfield, Samuel C.; Teddlie, Charles; and Suarez, Sandra. "Classroom Interaction in Effective and Ineffective Schools: Preliminary Results from Phase III of the Louisiana School Effectiveness Study," *Journal of Classroom Interaction* 20, no. 1 (1985): 31–37.

Wolff, M., and Stein, A. "Study I: Six Months Later—A Comparison of Children Who Had Head Start Summer 1965 with Their Classmates in Kindergarten." (A Case Study of Kindergartens in Four Public Elementary Schools, New York City). Yeshiva University, August 1966.

6

The Social Construction of Classroom Lessons

Carolyn M. Evertson and Regina Weade

Recent research has revealed an intricate picture of the classroom as a complex communication environment. As students and teacher interact, multiple messages are being signaled and interpreted simultaneously. These messages convey expectations about what participants should do, in what ways, for what purposes, and with what intended outcomes. As participation evolves, norms become established that serve to guide action. At the same time, recurrent cycles of activity emerge that begin to characterize the ordinary ebb and flow of classroom life. Expectations, however, are never fully set. Rather, as the teacher and students move from topic to topic and from activity to activity, expectations are continually being adjusted, negotiated, modified, elaborated, and refined. Classroom events and instructional arrangements are continually shifting in both overt and subtle ways (Cazden, 1986; Doyle, 1986).

Changes in what is expected for appropriate participation, both socially and academically, occur even when the physical setting and physical organization of the classroom remain the same. For instance, when a lesson moves from "doing" a set of practice mathematics problems to "checking" the problems, students are expected to monitor the need for adjustments that are essentially social. That is, the "rules" about who may talk to whom, when, about what, in what ways, and for what purposes are adjusted. In an academic sense, the expectation moves from reading problems and writing responses to reading responses, providing rationales for answers, and verifying accuracy. Both socially and academically, students are expected to construct and interpret meaning as guides for action during the ongoing flow of talk and activity. Inferences are drawn about what is to be learned and how competence is to be displayed (cf. Bloome, 1987). Students and teacher alike are faced with the challenges of continually monitoring what is occurring and what is implied as their rights and obligations for participating change. As they do so, they are also actively engaging in the cooperative and joint construction of classroom events and activities in which opportunities for meaningful learning are embedded.

Over the last two decades, research on classroom processes has revealed important insights about the structural features, including identification of social and academic participation structures, of well-organized classrooms (Doyle, 1986). Knowing that these structures exist, however, is probably an insufficient basis for understanding how they evolve in any given classroom. Unfortunately, progress toward capturing and understanding the dynamic interplay among participants, and among the assorted features, structures, and factors that influence what occurs in classrooms, has been slow.

Many difficulties can hinder our advancing understanding of classroom processes. These difficulties stem in part from an apparent allegiance to traditional research designs that have evolved within separate and highly specialized domains of knowledge. A case in point is the false dichotomy that has emerged in the ways we view relationships between classroom management and instructional processes (Weade and Evertson, 1988). That is, effective management is typically regarded as a matter of first-order importance, or a necessary precondition, after which effective instruction follows (cf. Evertson, Emmer, Sanford, and Clements, 1983; Emmer, Sanford, Clements, and Martin, 1983). Fortunately, awareness of the dualism inherent in such a view is growing. Observers note, for instance, that when they watch the ongoing stream of talk and interactions in the real time and space of a classroom, distinctions between management and instruction become blurred (Zumwalt, 1986). As these processes evolve, they are intertwined, intermingled, and in continual dynamic relation (Brophy, 1988; Erickson, 1986; Weade, 1987).

As new directions are forged in research on classroom processes, the resolution of discrepancies between what domain-specific knowledge has taught and what is observed first-hand in classrooms will present a significant challenge. Clearly, more holistic approaches are needed to enable close examination of the situated dynamics within which classroom processes naturally occur (cf. Evertson and Smylie, 1987; Shavelson, Webb, and Burstein, 1986). Holistic approaches, however, do not require the wholesale rejection of the traditional frameworks that have been constructed in research on teaching. Instead, they entail building on our prior understandings of classroom processes through the design of studies that selectively blend perspectives and methods across both domain-specific knowledge bases and alternative research traditions. Gage's (1989) call for drawing convergence among separate strands of knowledge and diverse modes of inquiry could not be more timely. New directions for research on classroom processes will require a weaving together of perspectives, findings, and methods that have accrued through a range of alternative traditions. The search will be not only for what an expanded picture of classroom processes might reveal, but also for ways in which each tradition, in its own right and in a reciprocal fashion, might contribute depth and refinement to another.

The purpose of this chapter is twofold: (1) to demonstrate one way in which alternative perspectives and methods of observing classroom processes were brought together in a study of classroom management and instruction, and (2) to illustrate what such an approach reveals about the ways student and teacher jointly construct meanings in the dynamic and interactive/reactive context of the classroom. We will argue that the orchestration of opportunities for learning is accomplished by members of a classroom through communicative processes. By looking at and understanding classrooms as complex yet differentiated communication environments, it is possible to ascertain what members of a classroom need to know, produce, predict, and evaluate in order to participate appropriately and to gain access to learning. Further, when a social interaction perspective is merged with a more traditional, process-product view of classroom management and instruction, processes that differentiate effective and less effective classrooms can be identified. Our intent is to make visible what is ordinarily invisible, that is, the social processes through which the academic content of instruction evolves.

CLASSROOM MANAGEMENT AND INSTRUCTION:
A CONVERGING PERSPECTIVE

Illustrations presented in this chapter are taken from a larger study of the effects of training teachers in the principles of effective classroom management[1] (Evertson, Weade, Green, and Crawford, 1985). The design of that study consisted of a series of planned comparisons that were organized into separate, yet linked, investigations. Each was designed so that its findings could provide part of the entry framework for what was to follow. By the same token, findings in each also served to further inform what had come before. In order, these investigations (a) identified and substantiated the effects of classroom management training workshops on teachers' classroom management practices; (b) examined relationships between classroom management practices and student achievement; (c) produced detailed descriptions of classroom management processes as they evolved in a purposely selected subsample of effective and less effective classrooms; and (d) generated comparative data on the similarities and differences across classrooms in the strategies used by teachers to set expectations and monitor lesson content. Taken together, this linked set of investigations demonstrates a progression that moves from broad and general observations of classroom and instructional characteristics across multiple settings to specific and particular exemplars of the face-to-face interactions that were occurring in selected classrooms. Like a camera lens that can focus at a wide angle to capture the larger picture and then zoom in for close-up shots of some of the elements of that larger picture, each investigation concentrates on progressively closer examinations of classroom management phenomena. By acknowledging both limitations and opportunities in the types of generalizations and inferences that could be drawn within any given investigation, the design of the linked set underscores the

---

[1] The study from which this chapter is drawn was supported in part by the National Institute of Education (OERI) grant NIE–G–83–0063 and by the Arkansas Department of General Education, Little Rock, Arkansas (Principal Investigator: Carolyn M. Evertson). The opinions expressed in this chapter are those of the authors and do not necessarily reflect the position or policy of either agency. No official endorsement should be inferred.

problematic nature of observation itself as a method of inquiry (cf. Evertson and Green, 1986).

Investigations 1 and 2: Observations and Findings Across Multiple Classrooms

At the outset, a broad angle of vision incorporated observations conducted in 102 classrooms from six school districts in a midwestern state (70 teachers in grades 1–6, with 36 in an experimental group and 34 in a control group; 32 teachers in junior and senior high schools, 16 experimental and 16 control). A central purpose at this point was to identify a set of appropriate elements for use in a statewide training model. As data were collected and initial findings were reviewed by the researchers and state and local administrators, concerns emerged about a range of differential effects of training among teachers in the treatment group. That is, although generally effective, training was not equally effective for all teachers. Interest emerged in finding ways to understand the processes and effects better in order to make the statewide training model maximally useful for all teachers. Outcomes of this initial study included design of a second study to examine the effects of the training more closely in a smaller sample of classrooms.

The second study in this linked series involved a subsample of teachers drawn from two schools in a single school district. Of the sixteen seventh-, eighth-, and ninth-grade teachers of English and mathematics, eight participated in two in-service workshop training sessions. The initial workshop was held prior to the opening of school, and the other took place six to eight weeks later in the school year. Classroom observations of all teachers were conducted at least six times over the course of the school year. During these observations, a variety of data collection methods were used, including (a) narrative notes with periodic time designations and class activity descriptions, (b) classroom rating scales, (c) categorizations of student engagement, (d) pre- and postachievement test scores on standardized and district-wide criterion-referenced tests in English and mathematics, and (e) audiotapes and verbatim transcripts for each classroom observation. In addition to these data, investigators had access to curriculum and textbook materials used in any given classroom and during any of the observations as well as opportunities to interview individual teachers and local district personnel.

Findings in both the first and second investigations, which generally confirmed those in earlier studies conducted elsewhere (Evertson, Emmer, Sanford, and Clements, 1983), indicated that trained elementary teachers rated significantly higher than untrained teachers in the following ways: they were clearer in describing objectives and lesson content to students, they had more efficient and appropriate classroom procedures and routines, they were more consistent in managing student behavior, and they had less student off-task behavior and more task-oriented classroom focus (Evertson, in press). In addition, trained secondary teachers paced lessons more appropriately than untrained teachers, had more efficient routines for lesson management, monitored and controlled student behavior more appropriately, and had higher student engagement in classroom activities (Evertson, 1985).

For the sixteen middle grades, comparisons on achievement measures indicated that students in the trained teachers' classrooms gained more in both mathematics and English than did their counterparts in the control group. By juxtaposing management ratings and achievement-gain scores as separate dimensions, the researchers were able to make rank-order comparisons among the sixteen teachers. (For detailed reports of data analyses, see Evertson et al., 1985, and Weade and Evertson, 1988.) Organization of the data in this way was intended to provide a framework for the principled selection of effective and less effective classrooms for the detailed case comparisons that were to follow. Sampling objectives for the subsequent analyses included representation of both effective and less effective classroom managers, based on observers' ratings, and effective and less effective instruction, based on achievement gain scores, as well as inclusion of both trained and control group teachers representing each of the two junior high schools in the district.

A 2 x 2 typology, presented in Figure 6-1, was constructed to facilitate comparisons across the management and achievement dimensions. Natural breaks in the rank-order data were used to designate divisions between effective teachers and less effective teachers on both dimensions. Teachers could then be classified within one of four cells: (1) high management effectiveness and high student achievement, (2) low management effectiveness but high achievement, (3) high management effectiveness but low achievement, and (4) low management effectiveness and low achievement. Ultimately, a subsample of four English teachers was selected; letter designations as

ACHIEVEMENT

	Effective	Less Effective
Effective	Teacher A Experimental group[a] School M—Ninth-grade English Teacher B Experimental group School N—Seventh-grade English	Teacher C Control group School M—Seventh-grade English
Less Effective		Teacher D Control group School N—Eighth-grade English

MANAGEMENT

[a]Experimental treatment was participation in a program of classroom management training.

Figure 6-1
Description of Teachers Selected for Sub-sample by Level of Management Effectiveness and Achievement Effectiveness.

Teacher A, Teacher B, and so forth were assigned following selection to reflect relative and parallel positions (A = highest; D = lowest) on both management and achievement dimensions.

An Emergent Finding: The Relationship Between Classroom Management and Instruction

The empty cell in the management/achievement typology is representative of the larger sample. No cases were available in which a teacher (either trained or untrained) whose students had demonstrated notable achievement gains could be classified as a less effective manager. This pattern may be an anomaly. Nonetheless, it can also be viewed as a reflection of theoretically expected differences between teachers trained in classroom management and those not trained. Multiple cases were available for selection into the other three cells, but the intersection between low management effectiveness and high achievement drew an absolute blank. The typology, therefore, mirrors support for the existence of a causally dependent relation between management effectiveness and student achievement. Moreover, the pattern also suggests a finding that was unanticipated by the researchers: *management effectiveness is a necessary, but insufficient, condition for bringing about student achievement gains.* The difference between what is necessary and what is sufficient emerged as a central concern in the set of case comparisons that follow.

Investigations 3 and 4: Focused Observations in Selected Classrooms

The investigations described thus far followed the process-product tradition of research on teaching. Accordingly, observations were conducted in relation to a normative, or aggregate, model of management practices recommended for use in all classrooms (cf. Evertson, 1987). As the power of the observational lens is adjusted, however, the perspective guiding the observations also shifts. This shift marks a merging point of two different yet complementary bodies of literature. The first undergirds the normative model used in the organization and delivery of the management-training workshops. The second is grounded in theoretical constructs that have emerged from the fields of sociolinguistics, ethnography of communication, conversational analysis, and discourse processes[2] (cf. Green, 1983).

---

[2] The analyses of classroom conversations conducted for the study from which illustrations for this chapter are drawn cannot be described as sociolinguistic or ethnographic due to limitations in the way data were collected. Rather, these analyses reflect the application of a sociolinguistic/ethnographic perspective to data that were available. Because conversations were audiorecorded, much of the nonverbal actions of participants in the classrooms, which contributed to construction of meanings, were not available for analysis.

The principal interest is in the ways everyday interactions serve to support or constrain access to social and academic participation and, in turn, opportunities for meaningful learning.

Recent work from the sociolinguistic/ethnographic perspective has shown that teachers with the same goals, similar groups of students, and similar content do not deliver classroom lessons in the same ways (Green, Weade, and Graham, 1988). This work demonstrates that the ways in which a teacher orchestrates lessons, signals instructional participation, presents academic information, and uses language influence the nature of student engagement and student learning. At the same time, evidence from this tradition is available that models of effective and less effective teaching can be reliably identified (Erickson, 1982). Although teaching is context-specific, there are patterns of similarity for both effective and less effective teachers within lessons, even though these patterns contrast across groups. In the present study, as the perspectives shift from normative to situated, a portion of the focus also changes from classifying *teachers* to describing the *strategies* used by the teacher as generally more or less effective. That is, even though patterns contrast across cases, both effective and less effective teachers might demonstrate a range of more and less effective strategies in relation to particular instructional goals (Green, Weade, and Graham, 1988). At the root of the identification of these patterns is a set of assumptions that much of the daily life in classrooms is conducted through action, and that communication is the dominant means of constructing actions. Gumperz (1986) captures the perspective in a way that makes the linkages to a more traditional process-product approach especially visible:

> The teacher's efforts to organize class settings, set up learning environments, and label and define instructional tasks must be understood. Speakers and hearers depend on each other's good faith in creating such understandings which set the preconditions for effective information transfer. By the above actions, teachers create the conditions that make learning possible.
>
> The interactional sociolinguistic approach focuses on the interplay of linguistic, contextual, and social presuppositions which interact to create the conditions for classroom learning. Analysis focuses on key instructional activities that ethnographic observations have shown may be crucial to the educational process. These activities are realized through definable speech events which stand out against the background of everyday conversation; they have characteristics which can be understood and can be described by ethnographers and recognized by participants. Moreover, knowledge of the events and what is accomplished by them is common to groups of people; they are not

occasional occurrences, but have a place in the daily conduct of affairs of groups. From this perspective, language in the classroom can be seen as part of the language of the school setting; characteristics of particular classroom situations of children of different ages are seen to occur regularly as speech routines held together through the daily practices of teacher and students; that is, there are features of these routines which are similar across all classroom contexts and some that vary as schooling progresses. [P. 65]

Type case analytic procedures (Erickson and Shultz, 1981; Green, Weade, and Graham, 1988) were used for the analysis reported in this phase of the study. Initially, single class period lessons that had taken place in early November in the year of the training study were selected for each teacher. Following procedures developed by Green (1977) and working from verbatim transcriptions of audiotape recordings, detailed descriptive accounts of lesson structure were generated for each of the selected lessons. The resulting type case models existed as four separate, situation-specific inventories of recurrent patterns and themes in the unfolding lessons. They also served as a base from which particular instructional variables (e.g., interactions, instructional units, and topical content) could be identified. Patterns of interaction and instructional sequencing were further explored by frequency of occurrence in order to identify what was normal or ordinary, and to assess consistency and variability both within and across identified patterns. Based on sample selection, the type case models were referred to as descriptions of effective management and instruction (two cases), effective management and less effective instruction (one case) and less effective management and instruction (one case) (see Figure 6-1).

Representativeness of the November sample had to be estimated prior to drawing credible comparisons across the type case models. This was accomplished by comparing and contrasting identified patterns in each lesson with the larger sample of six lessons for each teacher. In this way, questions about stability and variability in teaching style and management and instructional processes could be explored and the influence of factors such as the time of year and the nature of lesson content could be examined. Thus the representativeness of the November lessons was not an *a priori* determination. Rather, it was a judged outcome of the analysis that had been initiated on the basis of a principled selection of cases. (See Heap [1985] for a discussion of distinctions between the context of discovering how classroom events are organized and accomplished and the context of presenting findings that result from such analyses.)

Investigation 3 assessed the stability and variability of interaction and instructional patterns over the school year for each teacher. Findings suggested that for both effective and less effective teachers, the manner of establishing social procedures such as turn-taking and eliciting student participation remain stable across lessons. For the effective teachers, variations in style paralleled topic-by-topic and item-by-item variations in academic content, students' familiarity with the content (new versus review), and the level of difficulty of the content. For less effective teachers, variations in style occurred when procedural expectations for students were not clear, in particular when functional procedures were necessary for students to "get through the lesson." (See Evertson and Weade [1989] and Evertson et al. [1985] for comparisons of patterns over time for each teacher.)

For Investigation 4, several charts were generated to summarize the findings and to focus pattern analysis on interactions between teacher and students, among students, and among teacher, students, and materials. Several aspects of lesson management were considered in each case; the findings illustrated next provided evidence on (a) relationships between the academic and social demands placed on students and (b) the thematic development accomplished through conversational exchanges.

Observation of Social and Academic Task Structures in Four Classrooms

Examination of structural features of the four November lessons revealed that they evolved as a series of lesson phases, each varying in the expectations signaled to students for appropriate participation. Expectations were categorized in terms of the demands placed on students for social responses (e.g., speak when called on) and those for academic responses (e.g., name the verb in the sentence). Observation confirmed that these demands co-occurred. Thus, "lesson" is not a unitary phenomenon. Rather, classroom lessons are structured as highly differentiated parts through which the teacher, more or less consistently and continually, shifts the expectations for participation and demonstration of both procedural and academic competence. Similar findings on the multifaceted nature of lessons have been reported in the classic work of Gump (1967) and, more recently, Stodolsky (1984), both of whom proceeded from a social-interaction perspective in which the basic unit of analysis was defined as an activity segment.

Comparison across the four November lessons suggested a pattern of relationships between the ways teachers sequenced their lessons and their placements within the management/achievement typology (see Figure 6-1). Frequencies were tallied for the number of changes required at each transition between lesson phases, first for changes in social participation and then for appropriate academic participation. A quantitative index, useful for drawing systematic comparisons across the four lessons, could then be calculated by summing row and column totals. (See Weade and Evertson [1988] for quantitative comparisons.) The numbers, however, tell only part of the tale. Qualitative examination of the expectations and the ways they shift over time also reveals the patterns. The illustrations outlined below provide a "bird's-eye view" of lesson structure and instructional sequencing in each of the four November lessons.

Teacher A. In this lesson, teacher and students were reviewing a teacher-made grammar test that students had taken on a preceding day. The teacher had graded the tests and returned them to students as they entered the classroom. The structure of the lesson paralleled the five sections of the test. The following structural outline lists social expectations on the left and the co-occurring academic expectations on the right.

Social	*Academic*
Respond when called on (at random).	Name the past and past participle of each given verb.
Volunteer by raising hand; then respond if called on.	Name the tense for each verb.
Respond when called on (at random).	Read sentence aloud, supply verb in the correct tense (given present tense verb).
Respond when called on (at random); then volunteer another response	Given sentence with incorrect verb, read the sentence, correcting the

(there is more than one correct answer) by raising hand; then respond when called on.	verb as you read.
Listen as teacher (T) gives answers; ask questions at the end, if you have any.	Check your paper, identifying verbs as active or passive, as T gives answers.

The academic expectations listed above evidence a comparatively tight, sequential progression in the evolving academic structure. Students first identify principal parts of verbs, and then name the verb tense when given a principal part. The third phase of the lesson requires students to apply the knowledge required in the first two phases; students must place the verbs in context. Here, students shift away from focusing on single, isolated words and begin working with sentences. The progression continues through the remaining two lesson phases, and as the level of complexity gradually increases, each of the final phases also focuses on slightly different aspects of verb usage. Socially, as will be seen in the comparisons that follow, the requirements for participation do not change appreciably. In some phases, students are called on by name at random, and in others, students are to raise hands to bid for a turn. At the beginning of each phase of the lesson, Teacher A not only verbally signals what procedure will be used, but also provides a publicly stated rationale for her choice. Rationales are typically related to the group's performance, as she announces her memory of it, from grading the tests (e.g., the level of difficulty students experienced with the content). The entire lesson requires working with a single sheet of paper, moving through items one-by-one, section-by-section. The social demand changes most noticeably in the last phase when it becomes "listen as the teacher gives the answer" (the teacher's publicly stated rationale is that time is running short and that it is important to get all the answers checked).

Teacher B. In Teacher B's November lesson, students are also studying verbs. From our bird's-eye view, we again see a social structure on the left and the evolving academic demand on the right.

Social	*Academic*
Number paper 1–23; then take test, working from test paper and separate reference list; pass paper to front when told to; receive another paper for what will happen next.	Identify auxiliary verbs in each of 23 sentences.
Volunteer for turn by raising a hand; respond when called on.	Give verb phrase, then main verb, then auxiliary verb.
Open book to p. 55; volunteer for turn by raising a hand; respond when called on.	Give answer about verbs, depending on question asked by the teacher.
Number paper 1–10; do exercise on p. 56.	Identify verb phrase and auxiliary verb in 10 given sentences.

Examination of the academic structure reveals a consistent focus on auxiliary verbs. In contrast, changes in expected social performance require shifting from the test paper to "the paper just returned to you" to the workbook (distributed by students in the front row) and then to a new sheet of paper in the final phase of the lesson. In comparison with Teacher A, there is a relative increase in the demands placed on students for interpreting changes in their rights and obligations for appropriate social participation.

Teacher C. The lesson in Teacher C's classroom reveals dramatic shifts in both social and academic tasks across seven lesson phases.

Social	*Academic*
Listen as T reads, and write the numbers 1–25 on your paper.	Spell each of 25 words correctly.
Listen as T rereads; when told, pass in your paper.	Check accuracy.
Get your workbook, turn to	Say "anything you can

page 18; respond when called on.	remember about verbs."
Look on page 18; listen.	Hear about the "he/they" test.
Give choral response (yes or no) after T says "He (and then a word); They (and then a word)" from the list in the workbook.	Identify each word as a verb, or not a verb.
Respond when called on; work from list on board.	Identify the verb.
Number your paper 1–20; write one word on paper from each sentence in book; raise your hand if you have a question.	Identify the verb.

Academically, Teacher C's lesson shifted from spelling to verbs at the transition between its second and third phases. In addition, the teacher's opening series of messages in the third phase indicated that the introductory part of the lesson on verbs had been presented two days earlier, with no attention to verbs on the intervening day. Changes in social expectations appeared to be substantial. Students moved from the spelling paper used in the first two phases of the lesson to text and workbook materials in the discussion phase that followed. The discussion phase required bidding for a turn; students were called on at random in the fourth phase of the lesson. The fifth phase required a unison/choral response pattern with no bidding. The sixth phase required shifting back to Teacher C's designation of individual responders as well as movement from the books to a focus on the chalkboard. Finally, students shifted to a written exercise in the last lesson phase that required a return to workbooks. Given both the number and complexity of transitions in Teacher C's lesson, the demands placed on students to monitor changes in what is expected appear to be relatively major.

Teacher D. The bird's-eye view of Teacher D's classroom reveals the following.

Social	*Academic*
Listen for your group assignment; get materials according to your placement in one of three different groups.	----------------------------------
Group 1: Respond when called on; work from your homework paper.	Pronounce and correctly spell the words you wrote on your homework paper.
Listen to instructions for a spelling test.	----------------------------------
Take the spelling test.	Identify the correctly spelled word in each series of words.
Exchange your paper with another student; then listen as T gives the answers.	Check accuracy on identification of the correctly spelled word in each series.

Review of the academic expectations in the column on the right finds a logical progression in Teacher D's lesson. However, the number of changes required is minimal; the two complete lesson phases are procedural—they contain no academic expectations. The social-participation structure, in contrast, is complex. As indicated in the opening phase of the lesson, the day's activities were organized for three separate groups. Hence, although the researchers followed only the group that stayed with Teacher D for the remainder of the class period, three separate structures were evolving simultaneously within the classroom. While the teacher directed Group 1 in the spelling lesson, a student could be heard in the background reading a separate list of spelling words for another small group. A third group, which actually consisted of only a single student ("group" was the term used by Teacher D), was engaged in a journal-writing activity. The relative balance between changes in social and academic expectations appears to be heavily weighted on the social side, both within this lesson and in comparison with the structural features of the lessons in the other three classrooms.

Summary. In comparing the management and achievement effectiveness dimensions of the lessons, two patterns become evident. One relates to the number of transitions in instructional events initiated by the teachers. In the less effective classrooms, Teachers C and D initiate a higher number of transitions. Students, in turn, must interpret changes in what they are to do and how they are to proceed more frequently than must students in the more effective classrooms. In the effective classrooms, the focus at any given point on "what we are doing now" is relatively more sustained, more enduring, and less transitory than in the less effective classrooms.

A second pattern becomes evident by looking at the relative balance between social shifts and academic shifts. Students in Teacher C's and Teacher D's classrooms must attend to matters of who may talk to whom, when, about what, and in what ways in order to know how to participate appropriately, and these expectations change more frequently than the academic tasks. Teacher A and Teacher B, in contrast, orchestrate a relative balance at the major transition points in their lessons. The chance to interpret changes in what is expected academically is not overshadowed by the need to focus on shifting social demands.

When examining the four November lessons, it is important to note the differences between what we can see from the bird's-eye view and what is available to students and their teachers. The differences suggest both opportunities and limitations in what the aerial vantage point reveals. First, a view of each lesson as a whole from its beginning to its end is a necessary antecedent to continuing analyses of more isolated conversational exchanges. A sense of the whole provides important background and contextual information to frame what is occurring at any given turn in the lesson. Nonetheless, the distance needed to capture a whole lesson has focused our attention on transitions between lesson phases as the most visible points of contrast. What is happening within the lesson phases remains relatively unexplored—a closer look is warranted. In addition, our aerial view is retrospective. What we can see by looking back over what has already occurred contrasts sharply with what is available to participants as they engage in the processes of constructing what can and will occur. Future lesson events may be more or less predictable, but there are inevitable limits to a participant's certainty about what will occur next, what will be meant, and what will happen as a result. Thus, although surface appearances might suggest that the lessons are simple, the picture that emerges from a participant's point of view is both complex and problematic. As expectations continually shift in both overt and subtle ways, both within and across different parts of a lesson, participants are constantly monitoring what is happening in order to know how to demonstrate competence and appropriate performance.

A final factor in examining these lessons is related to decisions about how they could best be represented in written form. Since our interest has been to highlight distinctions between the social and academic features of the evolving participation structures, each has been graphically depicted in parallel, yet separate, lists. The purpose is heuristic; the distinctions lend clarity to our understandings of these structures. Nonetheless, when considered as separate phenomena, it is all too easy to assume that the social participation structure is just another way of talking about classroom management and, likewise, that the academic participation structure is a label for patterns of subject matter content delivery. Both assumptions are faulty ones. Social and academic participation structures evolve in a mutually interdependent fashion. Adjustments in expectations for social participation influence what can and will occur academically, and vice versa. Further, changes in what is expected are neither random nor accidental. Rather, they reflect decisions, changes, and responses to changes in such factors as the nature of the activity, cognitive demands, and variable levels of difficulty of the subject matter, as well as the degree of conversational cooperation among members of the classroom and institutional factors such as time and materials. In short, although the bird's-eye view provides an important background perspective about what is occurring in these classrooms, it fails to fully capture the complexity of communicative demands faced by participants. In the following discussion, the power of the observational lens will be adjusted to zoom in more closely on what is occurring in *one* part of a single lesson phase in *one* classroom. While the scope of what can be seen is more narrow, the closer view permits a more detailed investigation of the naturally evolving dialogue in the classroom and the ways that social and academic expectations are embedded in this dialogue. What emerges is a picture of the conversational work that teacher and students jointly construct and accomplish as they come together to reach instructional goals.

CONVERSATIONAL WORK IN A LEARNING-ORIENTED CLASSROOM

When viewed from a social-interaction perspective, classroom lessons are products; they are outcomes of dynamically evolving actions and interactions of teacher and students. A social expectation is not merely stated and adhered to, just as it might be listed in a student handbook or among a set of "rules" posted on a classroom wall. In a similar vein, the academic content of a lesson is not a given; it cannot be inferred by reading a curriculum guide or a scripted lesson plan. Instead, expectations are signalled and various interpretations of these signals are supported or rejected through the participants' talk and actions. Information is revealed to participants in a time-ordered, topic-by-topic, and bit-by-bit fashion. As these bits emerge, they link together to form a coherent "text" of the evolving lesson. Meanings, however, are not simply extracted by students; they are actively constructed. In order to gain access, participants must monitor what is being said (or written or read), how it is being considered, what is getting accepted or rejected in relation to the topic at hand, and how others are responding to the information provided.

To illustrate, a short segment of the conversational exchanges in Teacher A's grammar-review lesson follows. As discussed earlier, Teacher A ranked highest among sixteen comparison teachers on traditional measures of observed management practices and students' gains on achievement tests. Additional, external factors also support the judgment that this is a well-organized, learning-oriented classroom (cf. Marshall and Weinstein, 1988). Teacher A has a strong reputation in the school and in the district as an excellent teacher; she had also been recently selected as runner-up in the state's teacher-of-the-year competition.

The excerpt that follows is from the opening segment of the fourth lesson phase in the November grammar-review lesson. Students and teacher are checking through each item on the test one-by-one. This section of the test listed sentences with incorrect verb forms, and students were to rewrite the sentences using an acceptable verb form. Since the required response pattern for this task was open-ended, more than one way of correcting each sentence was possible. As students read aloud the sentences they had written on their test papers, variations in their responses became apparent. We can "listen-in" as the range of alternative responses becomes available for all to hear.

907   All right,
908   Let's see how you corrected these sentences.
909   Most of you did a good job of these.
910   There's a couple of things we still need to work on a little bit though.

911   Now I think we've all decided
912   That "ain't" is not acceptable.

913   But some of us are so used to saying "ain't"
914   That we really have to think about an alternative. Don't we?

915   We have to think about what else is going to go in its place
916   And write it down on paper.

917   What did you put for number one, in place of it?
918   Read your whole sentence.
919   Maria,

920   And if anybody has another sentence you want to read us
921   Raise your hand.

922   *Maria*: We don't have any money.

923   That's a good choice.
924   You don't have any money.

925   I like the way that sounds.
926   That
927   *Tony*: We have no money.
              (lines 926–927 delivered simultaneously.)
928   Sounds good to you.
929   Raise your hand Tony.

930   All right
931   Brian

932   *Brian*: We haven't got any money.

933   "We haven't got any money" would be good.
934   Katy
935   *Katy*: We do not, uh, got any money.

936   We do not got any money.
937   *Several*: (laughter)
938   *Katy*: I mean
939   we do not
940   got any money.

941   All right
942   You know what would sound good Brian?
943   If you change it to "We do not have any money".

944   See we got to be careful
945   We
946   We have to be careful
947   How we use got
948   Don't we?

949   I include myself in that too
950   *Several*: (laughter)

951   Okay
952   Does anybody have another one? (pause)

953   *All*: (silence)

954   All right
955   What did you do with number two?

At the opening of this lesson phase, Teacher A's general intent was overtly stated: "Let's see how you corrected these sentences" (line 908). The ways the lesson would proceed and how turns would be allocated, however, had to be inferred from what immediately followed. That is, in order to ascertain an expected pattern for responding, students had to observe what the teacher was doing and how she was interacting with other students. As Teacher A calls on

Maria to respond to the first item (lines 917–919), she is also signalling that students will be called on by name to speak one at a time. In addition, students were to read their whole sentence, not just the verb or verb phrase (line 918). An expectation that more than one student might volunteer a response for any given item is signalled in lines 920–92. This signal is overt in both its statement of procedure and its indication about how to get a turn. The demands for social participation in this lesson phase require observation of multiple signals and the ability to infer a pattern from these signals.

Consideration of the interactions that follow responses to the first item indicates that at least one student, Tony, had not interpreted all of the expectations the teacher signalled. He did volunteer an alternative response (line 927), and his response was given in a whole sentence. His response could have been judged as academically appropriate. The teacher's subsequent response, however, reinforces what Tony had failed to observe: the direction to raise a hand before responding (line 929). Tony's error was a social error. Teacher A responds to Tony by not acknowledging his turn and by calling on Brian for a turn.

Later in this segment, Teacher A receives a response from Katy that is socially appropriate but not academically acceptable (lines 934–950). The teacher's response to an academic error differs from her response to Tony's earlier social error. She accepts Katy's turn to talk but not her use of "got." The difference in Teacher A's responses to these errors, one social and one academic, provides information to students about the expectations for participating: A response must be given in a socially acceptable way to be considered; errors are permissible and will be considered, but a social error results in a limited turn to talk. The contrast in Teacher A's responses to errors illustrates that the social and academic dimensions of classroom participation structures are interrelated.

The teacher's sensitivity to students is displayed in the portion of the excerpt that follows Katy's academic error. Examination of lines 944–950 suggests that Teacher A made a deliberate error herself by using "got" in the same way Katy had incorrectly used it, thus sharing in the difficulty in the usage of the word. The teacher illuminates that Katy's difficulty is not hers alone; the error is one that all must consider and avoid. The two instances of laughter (lines 937 and 950) sound alike in the audio recording of this lesson. However, line-by-line examination of what occurs in between these two points reveals that the teacher's responses to each instance were not similarly constructed. Following generation of the second bit of laughter, Teacher A redirects attention by asking if anyone has another sentence (line 952). Seeing no volunteers, she moves the class to the second item on this section of the test. As she does so, a replication of the response pattern initiated at the outset of this lesson phase appears imminent. That is, Teacher A's delivery of line 955, "What did you do with number two?" is closely tied to the expectation signalled in line 908: "Let's see how you corrected these sentences." Moreover, exploration of subsequent interactions (not illustrated in this excerpt) confirms that expectations were not only signalled but also communicated. Teacher A "got" what she asked for, both socially and academically.

CONCLUSIONS

The discussions and illustrations in this chapter are derived from a study in which different perspectives and alternative, yet complementary, research traditions converged. Together, each of these alternatives contributed depth and refinement to the other. Together, they also demonstrate what can be seen and what can be learned about processes of classroom management and instruction. In particular, the approach illustrated here explores the classroom as a communicative environment in which expectations for participating are continually shifting and opportunities for learning are constructed through participants' interactions.

As a rule, generalizations cannot be drawn from case examples when sample sizes are limited. Any generalizations readers might make from the illustrations in this chapter will be the result of an interaction between what the illustrations reveal and what readers recognize from their own experiences in classrooms. The intent of this chapter is to stimulate continuing dialogue about the observation and exploration of teaching and learning events and the classroom as a communicative environment.

REFERENCES

Bloome, David. "Reading as a Social Process in a Middle School Classroom." In *Literacy and Schooling*, edited by David Bloome. Norwood, N.J.: Ablex, 1987.

Brophy, Jere. "Educating Teachers about Managing Classrooms and Students," *Teaching and Teacher Education* 4, no. 1 (1988): 1–18.

Cazden, Courtney. "Classroom Discourse." In *Handbook of Research on Teaching*, 3d ed., edited by Merlin C. Wittrock. New York: Macmillan, 1986.

Doyle, Walter. "Classroom Organization and Management." In *Handbook of Research on Teaching*, 3d ed., edited by Merlin C. Wittrock. New York: Macmillan, 1986.

Emmer, Edmund T.; Sanford, Julie; Clements, Barbara; and Martin, Jeanne. "Improving Junior High Classroom Management." Paper presented at the Annual Meeting of the American Educational Research Association, Montreal, 1983.

Erickson, Frederick. "Classroom Discourse as Improvisation: Relationships between Academic Task Structure and Social Participation Structure in Lessons." In *Communicating in Classrooms*, edited by Louise Cherry Wilkinson. New York: Academic Press, 1982.

Erickson, Frederick. "Tasks in Times: Objects of Study in a Natural History of Teaching." In *Improving Teaching*, edited by Karen K. Zumwalt. Alexandria, Va.: Association for Supervision and Curriculum Development, 1986.

Erickson, Frederick, and Shultz, J. "When Is a Context? Some Issues and Methods in the Analysis of Social Competence." In *Ethnography and Language in Educational Settings*, edited by Judith Green and Cynthia Wallat. Norwood, N.J.: Ablex, 1981.

Evertson, Carolyn M. "Training Teachers in Classroom Management: An Experiment in Secondary School Classrooms," *Journal of Educational Research* 79 (1985): 51–55.

Evertson, Carolyn M. "Managing Classrooms: A Framework for Teachers." In *Talks to Teachers*, edited by David C. Berliner and Barak V. Rosenshine. New York: Random House, 1987.

Evertson, Carolyn M. "Improving Elementary Classroom Management: A School-based Training Program for Beginning the Year," *Journal of Educational Research*, in press.

Evertson, Carolyn M.; Emmer, Edmund T.; Sanford, Julie P.; and Clements, Barbara S. "Improving Classroom Management: An Experiment in Elementary School Classrooms," *Elementary School Journal* 84, no. 2 (1983): 173–188.

Evertson, Carolyn M., and Green, Judith L. "Observation as Inquiry and Method." In *Handbook of Research on Teaching*, 3d ed., edited by Merlin C. Wittrock. New York: Macmillan, 1986.

Evertson, Carolyn M., and Smylie, Mark. "Research on Teaching: Views from Two Perspectives." In *Historical Foundations of Educational Psychology*, edited by John A. Glover and Royce R. Ronning. New York: Plenum, 1987.

Evertson, Carolyn M., and Weade, Regina. "Classroom Management and Teaching Style: Instructional Stability and Variability in Two Junior High English Classrooms," *Elementary School Journal* 89, no. 3 (1989): 380–393.

Evertson, Carolyn M.; Weade, Regina; Green, Judith L.; and Crawford, John.

Effective Classroom Management and Instruction: An Exploration of Models, Final report, NIE G–83–0063. Washington, D.C.: National Institute of Education, 1985. ERIC ED 271 423.

Gage, N. L. "The Paradigm Wars and Their Aftermath: A 'Historical' Sketch of Research on Teaching Since 1989," *Educational Researcher* 18, no. 7 (1989): 4–10.

Green, Judith L. "Pedagogical Style Differences as Related to Comprehension Performance: Grades One through Three." Doctoral dissertation, University of California, 1977.

Green, Judith L. "Research on Teaching as a Linguistic Process: A State of the Art." In *Review of Research in Education*, vol. 10, edited by Edmund W. Gordon. Washington, D.C.: American Educational Research Association, 1983.

Green, Judith L.; Weade, Regina; and Graham, Kathy. "Lesson Construction and Student Participation: A Sociolinguistic Analysis." In *Multiple Perspective Analyses of Classroom Discourse*, edited by Judith L. Green and Judith O. Harker. Norwood, N.J.: Ablex, 1988.

Gump, Paul V. *The Classroom Behavior Setting: Its Nature and Relation to Student Behavior*, Final Report. Washington, D.C.: U.S. Office of Education, Bureau of Research, 1967. ERIC ED 015 515, 1967.

Gumperz, Jenny J. "Interactional Sociolinguistics in the Study of Schooling." In *The Social Construction of Literacy*, edited by Jenny Cook-Gumperz. Cambridge, Mass.: Cambridge University Press, 1986.

Heap, James. "Getting There from Here, in Ethnomethodological Research: Steps and Maxims." Paper presented at the Annual Meeting of the International Reading Association, New Orleans, La., 1985.

Marshall, H. H., and Weinstein, R. S. "Beyond Quantitative Analysis: Recontextualization of Classroom Factors Contributing to the Communication of Teacher Expectations." In *Multiple Perspective Analyses of Classroom Discourse*, edited by Judith Green and J. O. Harker. Norwood, N.J.: Ablex, 1988.

Shavelson, Richard J.; Webb, Norine M.; and Burstein, Leigh. "Measurement of Teaching." In *Handbook of Research on Teaching*, 3d ed., edited by Merlin C. Wittrock. New York: Macmillan, 1986.

Stodolsky, Susan S. "Frameworks for Studying Instructional Processes in Peer Work Groups." In *The Social Context of Instruction: Group Organization and Group Processes*, edited by Penelope L. Peterson, Louise C. Wilkinson, and Maureen Hallinan. New York: Academic Press, 1984.

Weade, Regina. "Curriculum 'n' Instruction: The Construction of Meaning," *Theory into Practice* 26, no. 1 (1987): 15–25.

Weade, Regina, and Evertson, Carolyn M. "The Construction of Lessons in Effective and Less Effective Classrooms," *Teaching and Teacher Education* 4, no. 3 (1988): 189–213.

Zumwalt, Karen K. "Working Together to Improve Teaching." In *Improving Teaching*, edited by Karen K. Zumwalt. Alexandria, Va.: Association for Supervision and Curriculum Development, 1986.

7

Schools as Affectors of Teacher Effects

Sam Stringfield and Charles Teddlie

Effective teaching does not occur with equal frequency among schools or school districts. This is so obvious that many parents make both career-move and home-purchasing decisions based largely on the quality of schooling (which includes, for example, the teaching within schools) they believe their children will receive in a new neighborhood or city. To avoid exposing prospective teachers to the worst examples of instruction and instructional settings, schools of education concentrate their student teachers in specific, more effective districts and schools. Also in this vein, in efforts to bring in large, high-paying industries, communities and states often make extraordinary offers of concentrated educational opportunity to the families of would-be incoming executives. In short, the knowledge that some schools are more effective than others is so common that were there not a body of research demonstrating the differential performance of schools in providing effective teaching, even the most casual observers would be inclined to wonder, "Why not?"

In this chapter we examine recent developments in school effects research. We use the terms "teacher effects" and "school effects" to refer specifically to studies linking classroom and school processes to measures of basic skills achievement. The terms "teacher effectiveness" and "school effectiveness" will be used when considering aggregated data relative to a wide variety of desired outcomes, often including academic achievement. The chapter is organized in three sections. A medical analogy leads into a brief history of pre-1985 studies of school effects. (For reviews of the school effects research base, see Geske and Teddlie [forthcoming], Good and Brophy [1986], and Purkey and Smith [1983]). Most of the chapter is devoted to a discussion of three studies that have nested classroom data within school effects designs. After presenting our current hypotheses regarding the building of more and less effective schools, we close with a discussion of needed research.

SCHOOL EFFECTS RESEARCH: AN ANALOGY AND A HISTORY OF PRE-1985 STUDIES

In "Medical Lessons from History," Thomas (1979) concluded that the most important breakthrough in medical research was not, as is widely recorded, the discovery of "miracle drugs." He argues persuasively that the more important finding had been made decades earlier. The greater realization was that much of what had been previously marketed as medical science was bunk. Subsequent "debunking" cleared the way for "one hundred years of scientific inquiry," which produced the miracle drugs, penicillin, the major psychotropics, and the astounding wealth of medical knowledge from which we benefit today.

We believe that future historians of education will note a similar paradox in the development of educational "effects" research. They will conclude that the most important studies in the history of school effects were *Equality of Educational Opportunity* (Coleman et al., 1966) and *Pygmalion in the Classroom* (Rosenthal and Jacobson, 1968). The first examined a great many variables and was widely interpreted as indicating that "schools don't make a difference." The later study appeared to add insult to injury by indicating that while schools on their own may not have effects, the infusion of a fairly simple artifact may have measurable effects on desired student characteristics. Together, they cleared much debris from the field, and the challenge of research on the effects of schooling began anew.

From these humble ashes have risen many good studies of teaching and schooling. In part, because the study of behavior patterns of individual teachers is less complex than the study of entire schools of teachers and other professionals, the teacher effects field progressed more rapidly. It has made a full cycle through the descriptive-correlation-experimental loop called for by Rosenshine and Furst (1973), and has branched in a variety of productive directions, the diversity of which is represented in this book.

School effects studies require much more data per unit of interest, offer compounded unit-of-analysis problems, require considerable long-term teamwork, and, as they have evolved, often require measures of teacher-classroom effects. Thus it is not surprising that school effects studies have evolved more slowly. Past research includes a moderate number of descriptive studies, a few reasonably rigorous process-outcome studies, and a considerable number of reform-oriented "school improvement" projects. Many of the school improvement studies have involved heroic efforts, but to date none has met reasonable standards for the independent gathering of detailed process and outcome data in experimental and control conditions, such as those established by Gage and Needels (1989) for evaluating teacher effects in quasi-experiments. Lacking rigorous quasi-experiments for measuring school effectiveness, the state of the art in school effects research rests on descriptive and process-outcome studies.

Post-Coleman and pre-1985, three reasonably large-scale process-outcome school effects studies were conducted in England and the United States. The two U.S. studies—Brookover and colleagues (1979), in Michigan, and Teddlie and colleagues (1984), in Louisiana—each gathered student, teacher, and principal attitudinal data and student achievement data in over seventy elementary schools. Rutter and associates (1979) reported on a longitudinal analysis of fourteen secondary schools in London.

These three studies offered replicating evidence that, controlling for the social and economic backgrounds of students, some schools consistently obtain greater achievement gains and other desired outcomes than do others, and that the educational value added can be significant. Second, the three studies, in very different locations, found similar school processes associated with greater student achievement. Explicit in the Rutter analyses, and implicit in Brookover's, was the conclusion that the association between the combined measure of overall school process and each of the outcome measures was stronger than the relationship between any individual process variable and outcome measure. This suggested to Rutter (1983) that the cumulative effect of these social factors may be the creation of an overriding

school ethos, or set of values, attitudes, and behaviors that characterizes each school.

All three studies found that characteristics of more effective
schools were more likely to be prevalent in schools serving students
from more affluent families. That is, there were high levels of multi-
collinearity between desirable school characteristics and the conditions in the communities being served. Brookover was sufficiently
concerned with the multicollinearity problem that he conducted
separate analyses for inner-city black schools and suburban-to-rural
predominantly white schools, and found somewhat differing patterns
of results. Teddlie and Stringfield (1985) and, on a smaller set of
California schools, Hallinger and Murphy (1986) examined socioeconomic status (SES) differences that related to school-level academic
success, and came to similar conclusions. For example, all of the
studies found that principals in higher-effect schools protected
academic time; yet all concluded that principals in higher-effect,
low-SES schools achieved their results through a more forceful,
directive leadership than did high-effect principals in middle-SES
schools.

Nonetheless, to the extent it was possible to isolate the effects of
SES from school effects, Phase II of the Louisiana School Effectiveness
Study (Teddlie et al., 1984) found the following predicted school
effects: (1) students' and principals' sense of positive academic climate, including the principals' sense of school efficacy, (2) families'
practical commitment to education (e.g., parents come to school
events, stay in contact with the school), and (3) the absence of a
negative school climate (principals and teachers did not absent themselves from school as often as possible; students reported reasonably
positive self-images). Other school climate factors, such as teachers'
reports of positive school climate, proved to be more closely associated
with the SES of the community than with non-SES-related achievement.

In summary, pre-1985 studies provided data in support of the
plausible hypothesis that schools make a difference. They produced a
reasonably stable set of school effects correlates, including the presence of an overriding school ethos. Finally, they provided evidence of
the multicollinearity of desirable characteristics of schools and the
SES of students served by those schools.

The question of *how* school climate affected student achievement
was relatively unexplored in the early studies. For example, it seemed
clear that a central role existed for the instructional leader of a school,

yet it was equally clear that very few students learned mathematics at their principal's knee. None of the pre-1985 studies provided detailed, classroom-level behavioral data. Quoting Good and Brophy (1986): ". . . to date not a single naturalistic study of effective schools provides basic data (means and standard deviations for each classroom) to demonstrate that the behavior of individual teachers in one school differs from the behavior of teachers in other schools" (p. 586).

RECENT U.S. SCHOOL EFFECTS STUDIES

During the last five years, three school effects studies have been undertaken in the United States. (For classroom-based school effects studies in England and Europe, see Mortimore and colleagues [1988] and Peters [1990].) Each of the three studies has nested teacher-level, process-product data within a larger study on school effectiveness. A limitation of the three is that all have been conducted in one state, and all involve an overlapping set of principal investigators. The three are Phases III and IV of the Louisiana School Effectiveness Study (Stringfield, Teddlie, and Suarez, 1985; Stringfield et al., 1990; Teddlie and Virgilio, 1988; Teddlie, Kirby, and Stringfield, 1989). We next describe each of these studies.

The Louisiana School Effectiveness Study, Phase III

For the third phase of the Louisiana School Effectiveness Study (LSES-III), schools were chosen through a seven-step process involving the examination of data from the state's Basic Skills Test for two years for each school, controlling for the socioeconomic status of the schools, and the identification within districts (among contiguous districts in some rural contexts) of matched stable positive and negative "outliers." Eight matched outlier pairs (sixteen schools) were selected. High, or positive, outlier schools were schools that scored above their predicted academic achievement, while low, or negative, outlier schools were schools that scored below their predicted academic achievement.

Observation teams were trained in the use of eight separate low- and high-inference, school and classroom observation systems. Each school was visited by a team of two persons who were not informed of the school's outlier status. Observation teams visited for three days during both the fall and the spring of the 1984–1985 school year. The goal of twenty-four in-class observations per visit was achieved for most schools. Observers gathered half of their in-class data from third-grade classes, and the remainder were obtained from classrooms of other grade levels. At the end of each set of observations, a detailed case history was constructed, and an integrative review was recorded on audiotape.

Analyses of this large data base have focused on students, teachers, and schools. Both low- and high-inference systems indicated considerable differences in time use among students. For example, an observer at a negative outlier school serving a predominantly middle-class community noted, "Had student time been water, and the classrooms swimming pools, the halls of the school would have been flooded, and the pools virtually empty." On average, students in the positive outlier schools were engaged in interactive instruction, a positive predictor of achievement, during 42 percent of the academically scheduled time, compared with 34 percent in the negative outlier schools.

Analyses of the extensive case histories indicated that students at high outlier schools were experiencing school days that were much more likely to make academic sense. Students there appeared to better understand the *whys* of their academic tasks. They were less likely to be spending time mechanically completing sets of intellectually unconnected ditto sheets, responding to fact-level questions, or simply complying with seemingly arbitrary demands. Students were more likely to be involved in tasks that connected academic demands to various other aspects of their larger lives. For example, all the primary-grade students at one school kept a daily diary.

Not surprisingly, measures of teachers' use of academic time also varied among the schools. Data from the Classroom Observation System (COS), a high-inference classroom observation system based in part on Rosenshine's (1983) discussion of direct instruction, yielded clear differentiations between teaching in high and in low outlier schools. As shown in Table 7-1, teachers in higher-achieving schools were consistently more successful in keeping students on task, spent more time presenting new material, provided more independent practice, demonstrated higher expectations for student success, provided more positive reinforcement, experienced fewer classroom interruptions, had fewer discipline problems, generated more consistently friendly classroom ambiences, and provided classrooms that appeared

Table 7-1
Means and Standard Deviations for Ratings of Classrooms on Ten Teaching Effect Dimensions, by Schools' Outlier Status[a]

Variable	Positive Outlier Schools[b]		Negative Outlier Schools[c]		Difference[d]
	Mean	Standard Deviation	Mean	Standard Deviation	$M_{pos.} - M_{neg.}$
Time on task	2.62	0.58	1.97	0.84	0.65****
Present new material	2.44	0.72	2.08	0.77	0.36*
Independent practice	2.47	0.74	1.90	0.74	0.57***
High expectations	2.73	0.50	2.18	0.77	0.55****
Positive reinforcement	2.59	0.56	2.27	0.71	0.32**
Interruptions minimal	2.61	0.58	1.89	0.75	0.72****
Discipline	2.69	0.59	2.15	0.75	0.54****
Friendly ambience	2.73	0.48	2.22	0.71	0.51****
Student work displayed	2.37	0.83	2.20	0.87	0.17
Classroom appearance	2.64	0.49	2.35	0.57	0.29**

[a] Rating of 1 = no evidence of desired pattern/behavior; 2 = weak or contradictory evidence of desired pattern/behavior; 3 = clear evidence of desired pattern/behavior

[b] Based on 65 classroom observations

[c] Based on 51 classroom observations

[d] *—$p < 0.05$; **—$p < 0.01$; ***—$p < 0.001$; ****—$p < 0.0001$

to be more academically focused and generally more pleasant than did their peers in matched, stable, low outlier schools (Teddlie, Kirby, and Stringfield, 1989).

Field notes indicated that teachers in positive outlier schools were more likely to be engaged in planned academic push. They covered more material faster than their peers at matched schools. Asked why no students in an affluent, suburban school were in the fastest track of their district's curriculum, a teacher at a negative outlier school explained, "Piaget was right. You can't push kids to learn before they are ready." But fully one-third of the students at the matched positive outlier school were progressing successfully in the fastest track.

Teachers at negative outlier schools often had difficulty explaining either the "whys" of their curriculum or how much progress they intended to have made through their curriculum during the following two to six weeks. Many gave every indication of simply "going through the paces."

Seven broad differences in school characteristics between outlier groups were found in LSES-III (Stringfield et al., 1990). We believe that each of these often had an impact on teacher behavior. Positive outlier schools displayed a serious but friendly atmosphere. While a primary purpose of the schools was the transmission of knowledge, the task was being achieved in ways that the principals, teachers, and students seemed to enjoy. Observers often reported "feeling good" about their visits to positive outlier schools.

At positive outlier schools, academic time was regarded as a scarce commodity—something to be protected. Intercoms, for example, were used much less frequently at positive outlier schools. Special classes (music, physical education, Chapter I [compensatory education], special education, foreign languages) were thoughtfully coordinated within the regular academic framework. Students never left reading to go to Chapter 1 math, or math to go to band. Effective routines were in place to facilitate the smooth handling of such uncontrollable events as rainstorms during scheduled physical education classes.

Principals at positive outlier schools provided realistic appraisals of their schools' strengths and weaknesses. At the end of three-day visits to negative outlier schools, LSES observers often felt that they knew more about the schools' instructional functioning than did the schools' principals.

In positive outlier schools, principals recruited new teachers intensely, provided targeted staff-development for their teachers, and found ways to move ineffective teachers quietly out of their schools. Brophy (1988) has noted that the literature on process-product teacher effects can most accurately differentiate the bottom 25 percent of teachers from the remaining 75 percent. However, some schools recruit and retain very few of that bottom 25 percent, and others are composed primarily of teachers in the lower 25 percent. Principals who blandly recited, "All our teachers are good teachers, and always have been," were rarely at positive outlier schools. Principals who volunteered detailed descriptions of how they "worked" the district's personnel department in order to bring known high-energy teachers to their schools, who described specific, behavioral strengths and weaknesses of individual staff members, and who quietly recounted successful efforts to retire incompetent teachers early, to refuse them tenure, or to transfer them were always at positive outlier or improving schools.

Schools in which academic challenges, recognition, and rewards were clearly posted were always positive outliers or improving. Some schools posted honor rolls outside their principals' offices; others gave pencils to students who made "A's." One rural school raised money and took its "principal's list" students to dinner at a restaurant. The event was some students' first experience with "eating out."

Finally, some schools obtained much greater benefits from their library and, where available, their librarian. A passive or hostile librarian and a too-quiet, too-empty, too-isolated library were almost always indicators of a negative outlier school.

We interpret LSES-III as indicating that there is variance in student-, teacher-, and school-level activities within all SES levels. That variance can explain significant differences in student achievement. LSES-III schools obtained greater academic performance by helping students spend a relatively high percentage of the school day on tasks that made educational sense to them. Teachers typically achieved those goals through planning, push, clear discipline, and direct instruction. Teachers' actions expressed high academic expectations, and the students responded to this. Positive outlier schools obtained higher levels of the desired student and teacher behaviors by providing a friendly but serious academic atmosphere, one in which academic time was sheltered and programs were smoothly coordinated. Principals stayed on top of the schools' events; actively hired, trained, and sometimes dismissed teachers; clearly posted recognitions for academic achievement; and energetically involved the library in the school's life.

Teddlie and Virgilio (1988)

The study by Teddlie and Virgilio (1988) sought to replicate the LSES-III findings related to teachers' behavior, while involving more types of schools. Their study examined teacher behaviors in typical as well as negative- and positive-outlier schools. The authors sampled junior high schools as well as elementary schools. Schools were chosen using the same process as in LSES-III. Nine teachers were selected at random from each of six junior high schools, and six teachers from each of nine elementary schools in the study.

Two classroom observation instruments were used in the study. The first, the Classroom Snapshot (Stallings, 1980), was used in LSES-III as a measure of time on task (TOT). The second was the

Virgilio Teacher Behavior Inventory (VTBI). Development of the VTBI (Teddlie, Virgilio, and Oescher, in press) reflected a desire to refine measurement on the high-inference Classroom Observation System used in LSES-III. VTBI includes three major scales, measuring classroom management, classroom instruction, and classroom climate. A multivariate analysis of variance and post-hoc tests revealed that all four measures differentiated high outlier plus typical schools from low outlier schools, and that the three VTBI subscales were also able to differentiate the high outlier schools from typical schools. Within school levels (elementary and junior high), the Classroom Snapshot and all three VTBI scales differentiated between high outlier and typical schools versus low outlier schools. However, attempts to discriminate between high outlier and typical schools at the junior high level were not successful.

All schools were sampled from one large suburban school district, and the study involved fewer than 150 hours of classroom observation: thus, data should be interpreted as suggestive. Yet the quantification of a high-inference observation system, and the expansion of high- and low-inference classroom process measures into a study of junior high school effects advanced the field. The data from both the LSES-III and Teddlie and Virgilio studies indicated that mean differences in teachers' and students' use of time were partially a function of the truncated or smaller range of behaviors in the high outlier schools. The best teachers at both the positive and negative outlier schools were roughly similar in their time usage and their ability to obtain high student TOT rates. However, the lowest TOT rates in negative outlier schools were almost invariably much lower than in high outlier schools. In other words, the worst teachers in the negative outlier schools had much lower student TOT rates than the worst teachers in positive outlier schools. In the Teddlie and Virgilio study, for example, the range of student TOT scores for teachers in high outlier elementary schools was only 19 percent, while it was a huge 71 percent in low outlier elementary schools. We believe that severely ineffective teachers' negative impact on the learning of twenty to twenty-five students extends beyond their one year of teaching the students.

In addition, Teddlie and Virgilio concluded that the principal of a school, through clear goal orientation, the exercising of instructional leadership within classrooms, and the thoughtful scheduling of teach-

Table 7-2
Mean Percentage of Time Spent in Interactive Instruction in the Third Grades of a Matched Pair of Schools [1]

School	October 1984 Mean	(N)[2]	April 1985 Mean	(N)	October 1989 Mean	(N)
		Observation Period				
Positive Outlier	48.5	(2)	42.7	(2)	42.5	(4)
					50.1*	(3)*
Negative Outlier	26.3	(3)	20.8	(3)	27.8	(4)
Mean Difference	22.2		21.9		14.7	
					22.3*	

[1] All cells based on a minimum of twelve class-period observations/grade.
[2] Number of teachers in third grade during the observation cycle.
* Deletes one teacher who was new to the positive outlier school effective September 1989.

   All other comparisons involve only teachers with over 2 years' experience within their school.

ers' and students' time, serves as the human link between teacher effects and school effects.

LSES-IV

   LSES-IV is progressing as this volume goes to press. In Phase IV, we are revisiting the sixteen LSES-III schools. In addition to the three days of observation in fall and spring and achievement testing at three points in time (fall 1989, spring 1990, fall 1990), the study is employing the more refined VTBI for high-inference observing and revised interview protocols, plus teacher-induction and Chapter 1 studies nested within this longitudinal school effects format.

   At the completion of data gathering in fall 1989, and before analysis of several major data bases has begun, a few conclusions are apparent. First, most schools appear to have remained stable positive or negative outliers for at least seven years (the two years before LSES-III plus the five years since.)

   Table 7-2 presents interactive teaching (Stallings, 1980) data from a pair of schools serving a suburban community. This pair was originally discussed in Stringfield, Teddlie, and Suarez (1985). In the five years since LSES-III, both schools had experienced considerable growth in their catchment area populations. This resulted in both schools losing their sixth grades to a middle school. The positive outlier school changed principals. Both schools responded to over a 20 percent increase in Asian, Hispanic, black, and other minority students, and both benefited from a new state law that reduced elementary grade class sizes to a maximum of twenty-three students. Only one of the third-grade teachers at each school during the 1984–1985 school year was teaching third grade at the same school during the October 1989 observations (e.g., six of the teachers were new either to the schools or to third grade between 1985 and the fall 1989.) Finally, it should be noted that the intervening half-decade had been a time of extraordinary debate about national and state educational reform. Yet if one ignores the one teacher who joined her school only a month before the data were gathered (and thus may not have yet been acculturated to the school), the grade-within-school differences in interactive teaching varied by less than one-half of 1 percent across the three data points and five years.

Other schools changed in predicted directions. Stringfield and Teddlie (1986) had noted at the end of LSES-III that four negative outlier schools were attempting self-directed program improvement. The two most active of them demonstrated marked improvements in classroom processes during the fall 1989 observations.

For us as observers, it is proving rewarding to observe the classes and to see a few teachers gain in professional maturity. At the same time, it is disheartening to watch a few teachers who could not manage a group of primary grade students five years ago, cannot manage or meaningfully instruct them today, and are getting neither training nor guidance nor dismissal notices. Cuban's (1983) metaphor of the churning effects of a hurricane on the top few feet of an ocean (policy level), and the sustained calm below (classroom level) seems appropriate here, where poor teachers seem unaffected by the push for educational excellence at the policy level.

The data from the LSES and Teddlie and Virgilio studies, however interesting, are rather causal-comparative. While they represent considerable progress in bringing together teacher- and school-effects research bases, they lack the firmness of well-controlled quasi-experiments. Not forgetting that limitation, we believe that the three studies provide enough information to justify hypotheses of how more effective and less effective schools are created, reasons for the multi-collinearity between school climate and SES variables, and the generation of a more refined research agenda.

The long-term goal of LSES is to provide a model that describes more effective school processes, explains how schools improve, and can be used to facilitate that improvement. While we are impressed with the work of school improvement researchers, we are concerned that virtually the entire study of change has taken place within the context of planned and often mandated programmatic shifts. We believe that the great majority of schools—to the extent they change at all—become more effective or less effective independent of external programs.

THE CREATION OF MORE EFFECTIVE AND LESS EFFECTIVE SCHOOLS

Both effective schools and ineffective schools result from naturally occurring processes that take years. deCaluwe, Marx, and Petri (1987), working in the Netherlands, have proposed that ten years is not an unreasonable unit of time for discussing the institutionalization of meaningful school innovation. We Americans are not accustomed to planning over such time frames, or to studies of such duration. LSES is only nine years old, and our relationships with some schools span nearly that entire time. In a previous paper (Stringfield and Teddlie, 1988), we reached a little beyond our quantified research to describe how schools become either more effective or less effective. We summarize that reach next.

The process of becoming a highly effective school:

1. In schools that eventually become effective, an instructional leader or leadership group, ideally including the principal, emerges or, more often, arrives.
2. The principal/group conducts an instructional audit of the school.
3. Principals and staff are actively involved in hiring teachers.
4. Principals at positive outlier and improving schools visit classrooms often. During their frequent classroom visits, the higher-

effect principals expect to see students and teachers at work.

5. The principals find resources for targeted staff- and school-development. Teachers who do not respond to targeted staff-development are put on probation, improve, or are moved out of the school.

6. Over time, positive outlier schools develop a minimum daily homework policy, and thoughtfully integrate all "special" activities into their school's days and weeks.

7. The school provides visible student, class, and school rewards for academic success.

The process of becoming a highly ineffective school:

1. The principal envisions his job as bureaucratic, centered on paper-and-pencil administration.

2. The principal accepts whatever prospective teachers are sent to him.

3. Beyond rarely visiting classrooms, avoiding curricular involvement, and passivity in hiring and staff development, principals at negative outlier schools almost never fire or force the transfer of a staff member. Given the annual "floating" of ineffective teachers from school to school (Bridges [1986] referred to this process as "the dance of the lemons"), and the fact that high-effect principals do not accept their share of floated teachers, a disproportionate share of ineffective teachers eventually work at ineffective principals' schools, which typically serve low-SES students. Ineffective teachers usually like teaching for ineffective principals because they are left in their rooms to do as they please.

4. The long-term school effect of several ineffective teachers is considerably greater than the sum of the individual teacher effects. A linear increase in the number of ineffective teachers produces a geometric decrease in positive school effects. This is because competent-to-excellent teachers must spend greater and greater percentages of their time designing and implementing instruction appropriate for ever greater numbers of students who arrive at their grade significantly below grade level. In an ineffective school, the task of teaching a full year's curriculum for a grade level to all students borders between requiring heroic efforts and being impossible. Learned help-

lessness among teachers is not a school characteristic likely to produce great student gains on any desired attribute.

5. Over years, the school develops a reputation as an unpleasant place in which to attempt to educate young people. Such a reputation can develop quickly if the building serves an economically disadvantaged neighborhood. Competent teachers within the system then resist transferring to the school.

6. If the school is becoming ineffective in a low-SES neighborhood, the staff develop elaborate rationalizations for their behavior, and for the school's performance. By contrast, in an upper-middle-class ineffective school, teachers and principals observe that their students are scoring above the national average, and congratulate themselves on a job well done.

7. The principal reinforces the above norms by writing only "good" teacher evaluations.

The process of remaining ineffective is often resistant to school improvement efforts. After several years of increasing ineffectiveness, a school develops elaborate cultural supports for ineffective schooling patterns.

Why do we have ineffective schools? We believe that ineffective schools serve valuable functions for school districts. They provide warehouses in which teachers and administrators whom central administrators do not wish to confront and/or fire can be stored. Second, many people in the United States believe that a significant percentage of our own population cannot learn much. For an administrator who believes this, the presence of a school obtaining minimal achievement from disadvantaged students actually reduces dissonance. More benignly, some administrators know that schools are being ineffectively operated, but are unaware of, or lack confidence in, potential intervention programs. Seeing no viable options, they resign themselves to an imperfect situation. So long as many districts perceive many benefits and few costs to having ineffective schools, they will continue to ill-serve students.

Across the LSES-III, LSES-IV, and Teddlie and Virgilio studies, schools serving more affluent communities were much more likely to be able to hold together the scarce resources required for positive school effects. We visited several low-SES schools that lacked *any* qualified applicants for vacant teaching positions. This created a doubly disastrous effect. Students spent days, months, and sometimes years being instructed by less qualified, often less competent, "long-term substitutes." Second, having no attractive replacement teachers available, principals were loath to criticize or evaluate firmly the certified staff they had. By contrast, schools serving affluent clienteles often had long waiting lists of prospective teachers. This allowed some principals to demand high levels of performance from the teachers.

From libraries to air conditioners to workbooks, computers, and staff development, money did not always buy positive effects, but it bought opportunity. All other things being equal, good teachers and affluent families gravitate toward opportunity. As previous sections have made clear, this gravitation need not be overwhelming. A school's inability to fill even a few positions with qualified, enthusiastic staff can have disastrous results to its overall effectiveness.

RESEARCH NEEDS

First, there is a great need for more school effects studies of any reasonably rigorous description. The school effectiveness movement has had a significant impact on U.S. educational policy in the absence of the breadth of data associated with, for example, the teacher effects field. A half-dozen studies on teacher-within-school effects would significantly strengthen any confidence researchers and practitioners can have in the generalizability of findings from this field. Such process-outcome and quasi-experimental studies focusing on the classroom would be strengthened by the gathering of multiple outcome measures.

There have not been good studies that have nested programs within schools. Special education and compensatory education (e.g., Chapter 1) are two near-universal programs that seek to further students' academic achievements. Many prior analyses of Title 1 and Chapter 1 data have treated programs as though they existed in the midst of otherwise homogeneous schools. Program effects logically interact with and ideally build on regular classroom and school effects.

The area of teacher induction has received much needed attention of late. We believe that this area would benefit from differential induction-by-school analyses. In LSES-IV we are gathering data on behaviors of new teachers, and on perceptions of their inductions into outlier schools.

Finally, we believe that the models of school effects implicit in school effects research are inadequate. From Coleman through LSES, we have treated socioeconomic status as a static, input variable. In fact, affluence-generating industries choose to locate in communities with good schools. Once middle-class families have committed to following their careers to a given city, they typically choose a particular home, based, among other things, on the reputation of the schools. Thus, SES is a powerful, directional predictor of point-in-time school-level achievement. However, when viewed from the perspective of decades, the widely held (and wall-charted) reputations of California, Massachusetts, and New Hampshire schools have increased the levels of affluence (SES) in those communities. Schooling is a long-term proposition. Research needs to reflect that fact, and to gather longitudinal data that intertwines and iterates school effectiveness and SES.

SUMMARY

Lewis Thomas (1979) noted that the history of medical research contained no great reasons for rejoicing until researchers realized that most of their "science" had been bunk. That discovery led the way to the current extraordinary state of medical science. During the last fifteen years, educational effects research has gone through a similar owning of its history. We believe that research on teacher and school effects is now moving, slowly, toward a shared understanding of how effective schooling, by which we mean effective teaching within schools, works. Such knowledge, if applied in ways that reach the large numbers of school districts, schools, and classrooms that are operating far below their potential, may be a part of the "miracle drug" needed to improve America's educational health.

REFERENCES

Bridges, Edwin. *The Incompetent Teacher*. Philadelphia: Falmer, 1986.

Brookover, Wilbur; Beady, C.; Flood, P.; Schweitzer, J.; and Wisenbaker, J. *Schools, Social Systems, and Student Achievement: Schools Can Make a Difference*. New York: Praeger, 1979.

Brophy, Jere. "Research on Teacher Effects: Uses and Abuses," *Elementary School Journal* 89, no. 1 (1988): 3–22.

Coleman, James; Campbell, Ernest; Hobson, Carol; McPartland, James; Mood, Alexander; Weinfield, Frederick; and York, Robert. *Equality of Educational Opportunity*. Washington, D.C.: U.S. Government Printing Office, 1966.

Cuban, Larry. *How Teachers Taught*. New York: Longman, 1983.

deCaluwe, Leon; Marx, E.; and Petri, M. *School Development: Models and Change*. Technical Report, International School Improvement Project. Leuren, Belgium: ACCO, 1987.

Gage, N. L., and Needels, Margaret. "Process-Product Research on Teaching: A Review of Criticisms," *Elementary School Journal* 89, no. 3 (1989): 253–300.

Geske, Tom, and Teddlie, Charles. "Research on School Productivity: Where Do We Stand?" In *Employee Commitment: Performance and Productivity in Educational Organizations*, ed. P. Reyes. Beverly Hills, Calif. Sage, forthcoming.

Good, Thomas, and Brophy, Jere. "School Effects." In *Handbook of Research on Teaching*, 3d ed., edited by Merlin Wittrock. New York: Macmillan, 1986.

Hallinger, Philip, and Murphy, Joseph. "The Social Context of Effective Schools," *American Journal of Education* 94 (1986): 328–355.

Mortimore, Peter; Sammons, Pam; Stoll, Louise; Lewis, David; and Ecob, Russell. *School Matters: The Junior Years*. London: Open Books, 1988.

Peters, Ton, ed. *School Effectiveness and School Improvement*. Amsterdam: Swets and Zeitlinger, 1990.

Purkey, Stewart, and Smith, Marshall. "Effective Schools: A Review," *Elementary School Journal* 83 (1983): 427–452.

Rosenshine, Barak. "Teaching Functions in Instructional Programs," *Elementary School Journal* 83 (1983): 335–351.

Rosenshine, Barak, and Furst, Norma. "The Use of Direct Observation to Study Teaching." In *Second Handbook of Research on Teaching*, edited by Robert Travers. Chicago: Rand McNally, 1973.

Rosenthal, Robert, and Jacobson, Lenore. *Pygmalion in the Classroom*. New York: Holt, Rinehart, and Winston, 1968.

Rutter, Michael. "School Effects on Pupil Progress: Research Findings and Policy Implications." In *Handbook of Teaching and Policy*, edited by Lee Shulman and Gary Sykes. New York: Longman, 1983.

Rutter, Michael; Maughan, Barbara; Mortimore, Peter; Ouston, Janet; and Smith, Alan. *Fifteen Thousand Hours: Secondary Schools and Their Effects on Children*. Cambridge, Mass.: Harvard University Press, 1979.

Stallings, Jane. "Allocated Learning Time Revisited, or Beyond Time on Task," *Educational Researcher* 9, no. 10 (1980): 11–16.

Stringfield, Sam, and Teddlie, Charles. "Qualitative Results from the Louisiana

School Effectiveness Study." Paper presented at the Annual Meeting of the American Educational Research Association, San Francisco, 1986.

Stringfield, Sam, and Teddlie, Charles. "A Time to Summarize: Six Years and Three Phases of the Louisiana School Effectiveness Study," *Educational Leadership* 46, no. 1 (1988): 43–49.

Stringfield, Sam; Teddlie, Charles; and Suarez, Sandra. "Classroom Interaction in Effective and Ineffective Schools: Preliminary Results from Phase III of the Louisiana School Effectiveness Study," *Journal of Classroom Interaction* 20, no. 2 (1985): 31–37.

Stringfield, Sam: Teddlie, Charles; Wimpelberg, Robert; and Kirby, Peggy. "Design and First Analyses from a Five-year Follow-up of More and Less Effective Schools in the Louisiana School Effectiveness Study." Paper presented at the International Congress for School Effectiveness, Jerusalem, 1990.

Teddlie, Charles; Falkowski, Carol; Stringfield, Sam; Desselle, Stephanie; and Garvue, Robert. *The Louisiana School Effectiveness Study: Phase Two, 1982–1984*. Baton Rouge: Louisiana State Department of Education, 1984.

Teddlie, Charles; Kirby, Peggy; and Stringfield, Sam. "Effective versus Ineffective Schools: Observable Differences in the Classroom," *American Journal of Education* 97, no. 5 (1989): 221–236.

Teddlie, Charles, and Stringfield, Sam. "A Differential Analysis of Effectiveness in Middle and Low Socioeconomic Status Schools," *Journal of Classroom Interaction* 20, no. 2 (1985): 38–43.

Teddlie, Charles, and Virgilio, Irene. "An Examination of the Relationship among School Effectiveness, Time-on-Task, and Teacher Effectiveness in Elementary and Junior High Schools." Paper presented at the Annual Meeting of the American Educational Research Association, New Orleans, 1988.

Teddlie, Charles; Virgilio, Irene; and Oescher, Jeffrey. "Development and Validation of the Virgilio Teacher Behavior Instrument," *Educational and Psychological Measurement*, in press.

Thomas, Lewis. "Medical Lessons from History." In Lewis Thomas, *The Medusa and the Snail*. New York: Viking, 1979.

Part III

Research on Teachers

8

Second-Generation Research on Teachers' Planning, Intentions, and Routines

Christopher M. Clark and Saundra Dunn

INTRODUCTION

This analytic review summarizes the current research on teachers' planning, intentions, and routines. It also outlines a new direction for educational research in which planning is viewed and studied in contexts, as one important but not dominant focus of inquiry. This type of study has already begun, modestly and somewhat indirectly, in recent studies of teachers' thinking, knowledge, and actions.

As practical and conceptual aids in pursuing such questions, this

This work was sponsored by the Institute for Research on Teaching, College of Education, Michigan State University. The Institute for Research on Teaching is funded primarily by the Office of Educational Research and Improvement, United States Department of Education. The opinions expressed in this publication do not necessarily reflect the position, policy, or endorsement of the Office of Educational Research and Improvement.

review includes a theoretical section on teacher planning and its roles in schooling and a summary of the findings of direct and indirect research on teacher planning. The chapter concludes with a call for incorporating into future research on education explicit and context-sensitive attention to teaching and teachers' intentions.

The Importance of Teacher Planning

The importance of attending to teacher planning cannot be denied. Virtually everyone involved with education agrees that planning is a real phenomenon; that is, for better or for worse, all teachers at times do something they call planning. Yet those who began to do research on teacher planning in the mid 1970s did not anticipate that their work had the potential for connecting with the concerns of so many audiences. It has only been in hindsight that researchers on teacher thinking have come to see that to understand teacher planning is to understand a great deal about teaching; that the study of how teachers prepare for instruction can reveal much about which features of subject matter, students, and the physical, psychological, administrative, and political environments actually influence classroom instruction. One can theorize with the best of intentions about how teaching and school learning could be improved, but the finest ideas and proposals must still pass through the funnel of teacher planning.

Many now see teacher planning as the instrumental linking process between curriculum on the one hand and the particulars of instruction on the other. From a psychological perspective, to understand teacher planning is to understand how teachers transform and interpret knowledge, formulate intentions, and act from that knowledge and those intentions. From the curriculum theorist's point of view, the study of teacher planning can help explain why and how curriculum materials are understood or misunderstood, used, distorted, ignored, or transcended in classroom instruction.

In the political and administrative veins, to influence teacher planning is to influence in large measure the content, pace, emphasis, and process of instruction. For the student of the social context and of communication patterns, to study plans and their transformation in action provides a window through which to view the norms that govern teaching and school learning and can make visible the ways that teachers and students "negotiate the curriculum" (both what is taught and how it is taught, learned, and accounted for).

And, for the teacher, the study of teacher planning can enhance appreciation of the genuinely professional (as distinct from technical) aspects of teaching. That is, the study of teacher planning can document and has documented the many heretofore unappreciated ways in which the practice of teaching can be as complex and cognitively demanding as are the practices of medicine, law, or architecture.

Theoretical Issues

Conceptually, most of the extant research on teacher planning views the process as one of practical and pedagogical problem solving. Teachers are faced (day after day and year after year) with a problem of the general form "How should my students and I spend our time together?" Many constraints and competing priorities impinge on the process of answering this general question, ranging from class size and the physical limits of the classroom to school and district policies and goals, available curriculum materials, student characteristics, personal history, and tradition. Paradoxically, this welter of competing and conflicting priorities, demands, and constraints makes the planning task more open and free than it otherwise might be, because reasonable people recognize that there can be no optimal solution— not all of these demands can be simultaneously satisfied. Teachers must choose, decide, cope, and live with the consequences of the limitations.

Researchers have conceptualized teacher planning in two ways. First, they have thought of planning as a set of basic psychological processes in which a person visualizes the future, inventories means and ends, and constructs a framework to guide future action. This conception of planning draws heavily on the theories and methods of cognitive psychology. Second, researchers have defined planning as the things that teachers do when they say that they are planning. This definition suggests a phenomenological or descriptive approach to research on teacher planning in which the teacher takes on an important role as informant or even as research collaborator.

Both of these views of teacher planning are represented in the research literature either explicitly or implicitly. These two different starting points for the study of teacher planning probably account for the variety of methods of inquiry in use and for the challenge that reviewers of this literature face in pulling together a coherent summary of what has been learned. Planning is challenging to study because it is both a psychological process and a practical activity.

Implicitly or explicitly, teacher planning is thought to be motivated by the teacher's need or desire to attain educational ends or goals. Researchers, curricularists, teacher educators, and school administrators are most concerned with planning in relation to relatively short-range measurable changes in student performance on academic tasks. Specifying these "learning outcomes" is the first step in various rationalistic models of planning. This narrows the conception of the planning task to an ends-means analysis of how one might best increase prespecified indexes of student achievement. Measurable student achievement is indeed one concern of teachers (McLeod, 1981). But, logical and justifiable as academic ends-means models of teacher planning may be, they seriously underestimate the range of legitimate ends that teachers pursue as well as the complex ways in which these ends or priorities interact and compete. Ends-means models have been made to work in training novices and in simplified experimental situations, but they do not fare so well against the demands and complexities of classroom teaching. Development of more valid conceptualizations of teacher planning, then, requires realistic and practical explorations of ends and intentions as held by teachers. We cannot hope to understand fully why teachers act as they do until we learn more about their own intentions and goals.

Much of the research on teacher planning has taken the "instructional episode" as the unit of analysis. That is, researchers have studied planning as preparation for a teacher-directed activity, lesson, or unit. While this choice of research context makes sense to those interested in the dynamics of planning for instructional ends, it also has the effect of exaggerating the degree to which teaching is, day in and day out, a thoroughly and precisely planful set of activities. While teachers may entertain general intentions about how the flow of classroom activity should proceed throughout a day or week, it is primarily the novel, complex, problematic, and outcomes-driven events of schooling that warrant explicit planning. The salience of teacher planning, then, may be an indicator of anticipated change, uncertainty, or consequentiality in teaching.

SUMMARY OF THE RESEARCH

Clark and Peterson's (1986) comprehensive review of research on teacher thinking published in the *Handbook of Research on Teaching*, 3rd edition (Wittrock, 1986), includes a major section on research on teacher planning. The brief summary included here concentrates on the findings of that research rather than on the details of particular studies. The research has shown that experienced teachers do several different types of planning in the course of the school year (Clark and Yinger, 1979). Teacher education programs concentrate almost exclusively on lesson planning (with some attention to unit planning), but in-service teachers also do yearly planning, unit planning, term planning, daily planning, and weekly planning.

Research has also shown that the time-honored rational model (moving from learning objectives, through generating alternatives, to choice of an optimal alternative) is not used regularly by experienced teachers (Morine-Dershimer and Vallance, 1976; Yinger, 1977), although experienced teachers do claim that the rational model ought to be taught to novices (Neale, Case, and Pace, 1983). Experienced teachers work from sketchy plans rather than the detailed plans developed by (and required of) neophytes. In working through lessons, veteran teachers are guided more by images of what the lesson will be like and how it should proceed (based on past experience) than by specific written plans. Good planning is marked by thoroughness but not rigidity. Teachers who make overly rigid and detailed plans sometimes concentrate too much on presenting the content and not enough on responding to the students' needs, and they may fail to take advantage of the "teachable moments" that arise when students ask questions or make unanticipated responses (Institute for Research on Teaching, 1986, p. 51).

Teachers do attend to learning outcomes, sometimes prior to teaching (while planning), sometimes during teaching, and sometimes only after interactive teaching is over (McLeod, 1981). In planning, teachers also attend to goals, issues, and concerns other than learning outcomes. And the planning process serves immediate personal purposes for teachers, such as study of content, anxiety reduction, and confidence building, as well as longer-range instrumental purposes, such as determining the content and structure of classroom interaction (Hill, Yinger, and Robbins, 1981; Carnahan,

1980; Peterson, Marx, and Clark, 1978).

Psychological models of the planning process have been proposed and, to some degree, tested against the realities of practice (e.g., Yinger, 1977; Clark and Yinger, 1979). And styles of planning used by experienced teachers, such as "incremental planning" and "comprehensive planning" (Clark and Yinger, 1979), have been described. Curriculum planning has been shown to vary with the subject matter under consideration and with the degree of novelty or familiarity of the material, students, and teaching setting (Clark and Elmore, 1981). American elementary teachers report spending relatively large amounts of time planning (ten to twenty hours per week), but also report that relatively little time or support for planning are officially sanctioned or encouraged (Clark and Yinger, 1979).Important products of the planning process are routines (Yinger, 1979) or structured patterns of teacher and student behavior. The first weeks of the school year are particularly important for teacher planning, inasmuch as many of the routines, rules, relationships, and expectations that influence classroom interaction during the remainder of the year are planned, negotiated, replanned, and established during that time (Anderson and Evertson, 1978; Buckley and Cooper, 1978; Clark and Elmore, 1979; Schultz and Florio, 1979; Tikunoff and Ward, 1978).

Newer Research on Teacher Planning

The first phase of research on teacher planning began to taper off in about 1979. As we have seen, this work was largely descriptive and involved conceptual separation or even isolation of planning from other related aspects of teaching. As the reports of this early work began to influence the educational research community, a second generation of research began. Scholars in the area of curriculum theory began to appreciate the potential of research on teacher planning in furthering their understanding of the dynamics of curriculum implementation and interpretation. Planning research began to become incorporated into studies of knowledge transformation, of experts and novices, of conceptual change, and of the determinants of opportunity to learn, and into subject-matter-specific field studies of teaching and learning. It is to this second generation of research that we now turn.

Knowledge Transformation. One of the approaches to understanding teaching by attending, in part, to teachers' plans and intentions is reflected in research on teachers' knowledge of academic content and the ways in which that knowledge is transformed. Working with preservice (post-bachelors) and first-year teachers of high school English, mathematics, history, and science, the longitudinal "Knowledge Growth in a Profession" project (Wilson, Shulman, and Richert, 1987) starts with a model of the structure of academic disciplines (after Schwab, 1964), rather than with a psychological model of planning and design. The hypothesis driving this work is that secondary school teachers' knowledge of the particulars of the disciplines that they teach changes over time and influences the quality of instruction. Of central interest in this work is the transformation of subject matter knowledge acquired in university courses into forms of "pedagogical content knowledge" useful for engaging and instructing adolescents. At this early stage of the research process, it appears that the knowledge transformations of interest take place as a consequence of teaching itself (most dramatically in the first year on the job). Teachers' plans, interpretations of student responses to instruction, articulation of changes in their own understanding of what they are teaching, and revisions of plans after teaching constitute much of the data base of this descriptive research program.

Routines. Classrooms are complicated places. The complexity and unpredictability that characterize the teaching environment impose many demands on the teacher, and it is therefore necessary to find methods to decrease the amount of information to be processed at any one time. To cope with these demands, teachers develop routines. The routinization of action fixes certain aspects of behavior and thus reduces the amount of information that must be evaluated, decided on, and manipulated. The use of routines reduces the amount of time and energy expended for planning, thus freeing time and energy for other activities (Clark and Yinger, 1980).

Routines are particularly important in the first few weeks of school, when the social and instructional organization of a classroom is established rapidly. Establishing the basic classroom organization, rules, procedures, and routines constitutes the business of the first weeks of September and forms a framework within which the work of the remainder of the school year is planned, organized, experienced, and evaluated (Clark and Elmore, 1979; Shultz and Florio, 1979; Tikunoff and Ward, 1978).

One approach to understanding the nature of planning, in general, and the use of routines, in particular, has been to examine differences between the planning of experienced teachers and that of novices.[1] May (1986) has argued that the "ways in which persons plan reflect not only a recognition of (the) complexity (of life in classrooms) but a reduction of it in order to adequately cope. . . . Experienced teachers will have a better sense of how to be selective and reduce such dissonance for themselves and their pupils than will neophyte planners" (p. 7).

Experienced teachers interviewed by Borko and Niles (1987) reported that knowing what you are going to teach, the entering knowledge of those you are going to teach, and where you are headed are three of the most important variables in the planning process. Novice teachers experience much more uncertainty about these factors than do experienced teachers. Based in part on these interviews and Feiman-Nemser's (1983) work, Borko and Niles (1987) have outlined a developmental model of teacher planning. They claim that direct imitation of routines developed and incorporated successfully into experienced teachers' planning may be unhelpful, if not confusing, to novice teachers.

Another line of investigation has focused on the use of routines by experienced teachers in subject-matter-specific teaching. Leinhardt and her colleagues (Leinhardt, 1983; Leinhardt, Weidman, and Hammond, 1984) have examined "complete educational episodes" in the teaching of particular mathematics content (such as the teaching of subtraction with regrouping). They have described in detail a number of time-saving routines used by experienced teachers during mathematics lessons, contrasting this with the less efficient use of instructional time by novice teachers. When new material was to be presented, experienced teachers preplanned part of the lesson to fit into existing routines (such as the "how to do boardwork" routine). During actual instruction, these teachers were free to focus on dy-

---

[1]This type of inquiry is often referred to as the study of expert-novice differences. We have chosen to use the less evaluative term "experienced teacher," rather than "expert," because in most of these studies experience is the only criterion for being considered an expert teacher.

namic aspects of the material and feedback from students about how the lesson was progressing.

Routines Change Over Time

Research on teacher planning confirms that routines are an important outcome of teachers' plans and of the ensuing negotiations between teacher and students. A strong case has been made in this literature that the routines that are put in place during the first weeks of the school year are particularly consequential, because they are thought to persist for the remainder of the school year, setting patterns, limits, expectations, and boundaries within which subsequent teaching and learning take place. Also implicit in this research is the idea that "negotiation" is a quasi-adversarial process between teacher and students that takes place when a new task, routine, or set of proposed demands is being introduced and clarified. Usually, the teacher is depicted as advocating higher standards of performance, a shorter time line, and greater accountability, while students attempt to negotiate these downward (Doyle, 1985).

Rosaen's study of seven weeks of evolutionary development of an American History unit in an elementary classroom (Rosaen, 1987) both confirms and challenges the conventional wisdom of the literature of research on teaching summarized above. Her detailed and painstaking observation of participants confirms that routines developed early in the school year were indeed incorporated into the structure of the American History unit (which took place during March and April, near the end of the school year). But the concept of "negotiation" that applies here is different from Doyle's (1985). Rather than being a struggle between labor and management over work rules, the kind of "negotiation" Rosaen depicts is that of "negotiating a trail." That is, the structure, demands, and forms of accountability applied across the American History unit were adjusted by the teachers as they judged how the unit was going. The two team teachers involved in this study were engaged in what Schon (1983) calls a "conversation with the situation." Participants in this conversation included the two teachers, the students, the researcher, and, to some extent, parents of the students. Some of the adjustments to the unit involved raising performance standards and creating more learning opportunities in response to student pressures to read more, or to read faster. Other adjustments involved "opening up" the student self-monitoring system (various forms of checklists) to encourage and enable students to transcend the limits of routines that had served them (and their teachers) well early in the unit and earlier in the school year. One could claim that the first and last weeks of the unit had much in common (e.g., both involved working from a checklist). But the radically revised form of the checklist and the consequent changes in cognitive, social, and managerial demands and opportunities that the revised checklist entailed for the students made week seven seem importantly different (and a much richer learning environment) from week one.

In describing and explaining these evolutionary changes in routines and their consequences for teachers and students, Rosaen implicates several actors and factors. The teachers' shared sense of an ideal level of self-regulation by students competed with their own felt need to make visible progress each week in the coverage of academic content (and, less explicitly, with their practical need to "keep the flock together," that is, to avoid allowing individual differences among students to magnify the heterogeneity of progress and performance). The nature of the subject matter also played a part in the evolution of the unit: as students moved from studying the abstract and distant past (1600s, 1700s, 1800s) to consideration of the twentieth century, they had more (and more divergent) resources to draw on, including their own life experiences and those of their parents and grandparents. The American History unit began to look like a Mississippi River tour from St. Louis to the Gulf of Mexico. The early part of the voyage was predictably constrained by the banks of the great river, but when the vessel reached the Mississippi Delta, it encountered many, many possible competing routes to the Gulf. And, as the nature of the subject matter changed, so did the level of "student pull"—children began to bring in relevant magazine articles from home, and to urge the teachers to find a way to make it possible for all of them to read all of the teacher-provided resource readings. This the teachers did by changing the reading routine from individual silent reading to a small-group activity in which both students who read aloud and those who listened received credit for having read the resource materials.

In summary, Rosaen's study extends and enriches our understanding of the roles that routines play in teaching and learning, how they evolve and change, and how opportunity to learn changes as a consequence. A richer conception of negotiation of school tasks emerges from this study, as does a more positive view of the roles that teachers and students play as they work around the inevitable dilemmas and competing priorities that they encounter in the course of their work. And this study provides one of the few detailed expositions of how the nature of a subject can influence the ways in which it is taught, learned, and integrated with other subjects and with the lives of teachers and students.

The Role of Published Curriculum Materials. Teachers have many resources available to them as they begin to plan for instruction (e.g., other teachers, professional readings, past experiences). But published curriculum materials, particularly the student texts currently in use, exert considerable influence on instruction (Clark and Elmore, 1979; Roth, Anderson, and Smith, 1983; Putnam and Leinhardt, 1986). Examination of the role of published curriculum materials in content-specific instruction is another way to increase understanding of teachers' planning. We briefly describe here two important lines of work in this area.

In a series of studies, researchers Smith, Anderson, and Roth (Smith and Sendelbach, 1979; Roth, Anderson, and Smith, 1983; Smith and Anderson, 1984; Roth, 1985, in press) found that although textbook-centered instruction characterized most middle school science teaching they observed, students did not seem to be learning and understanding important scientific concepts from such instruction. These researchers, among others (G. Erickson, 1980; McCloskey, 1983; Posner et al., 1982), began to examine the central role that students' naive theories, or misconceptions, about phenomena play in their learning from science instruction. They found that despite a growing body of research on students' misconceptions, textbook writers and curriculum developers appeared to be unaware of students' potential misconceptions (Eaton, Anderson, and Smith, 1984). Teachers who followed traditional teaching guides met with little success in helping students understand fundamental scientific explanations of phenomena. To address this need, an experimental text was written to challenge and change students' common misconceptions about how plants get food (Roth, 1985).

The work of Roth, Anderson, and Smith (1983) has produced detailed case studies of classrooms in which the use of published curriculum materials was quite varied (e.g., following a traditional textbook, supplementing the text with transparencies that addressed students' misconceptions, using the experimental text, using no text). They conclude that textbooks and curriculum materials written to address students' misconceptions and induce conceptual change in learners can be important tools in helping teachers give explanations that are appropriate for their students and in helping teachers guide student thinking during verbal interactions. When using traditional texts, teachers must anticipate those concepts about which students may have powerful misconceptions and focus on eliciting students' misconceptions and on confronting students with the shortcomings of these misconceptions, as well as demonstrating the greater explanatory power of the correct scientific explanation. Such instruction requires an in-depth understanding of the subject matter to be taught and of students' potential difficulties with the material, as well as an on-going monitoring of each student's growing understanding of the material.

Putnam and Leinhardt (1986) have introduced the notion of a curriculum script, or a "predetermined ordered set of goals and actions for teaching a particular topic" (p. 27). They note that although this notion contrasts with an emphasis on diagnosis and individualization, the characterization of teaching as a series of curriculum scripts better describes their observations of teaching than does the characterization of teaching as driven by teachers' specific knowledge about individual students.

In this work, Putnam and Leinhardt contrast the curriculum scripts developed by experienced and novice teachers. Over time, curriculum scripts become more secure, or more scriptlike, than they were during the first few teaching episodes where the teacher followed the same script. While modifications to the script are made over time, the textbook is an important influence on the initial development of teachers' scripts, as it can be a source of "examples, explanations, and modes of representation" (Putnam and Leinhardt, 1986, p. 8).

Like Roth, Anderson, and Smith, Putnam and Leinhardt recognize the importance of a teacher's knowledge of the subject matter content to be taught, including specific knowledge about how the content can be taught and about potential student difficulties. Adjustments of the curriculum script made during teaching occur within the overall structure provided by the curriculum script. These adjustments are of two kinds. Microadjustments occur when the teacher deals with a response or cue from a particular student, but they do not affect the overall course of the lesson. Macroadjustments occur when the teacher makes a change in the pace or content of the lesson, such as changes in topic sequence or deletion of a portion of the curriculum script (Putnam and Leinhardt, 1986).

These two lines of work make important contributions to our understanding of the role of published curriculum materials in teacher planning as well as in subsequent teacher-student interactions in the classroom.

Teacher Planning in the Context of Other Studies of Teaching

Almost every project of the Michigan State University Institute for Research Teaching (IRT) for the years 1981–1986 noted something about teacher planning. (See IRT, 1986, for a summary of the reports' general findings.) For example, consistent with the Clark and Elmore (1981) finding that during yearly planning, individual teachers make consequential decisions about what content to teach or to emphasize, the Content Determinants Project concluded that

> most teachers would readily make changes in the content of their instruction when such changes are consistent with their repertoires. A great many teachers would even make changes that are inconsistent with their repertoires, provided that pressures for such changes came from persons perceived as having legal or expert authority and that the teachers received ample training and other help in making the changes. [IRT, 1986, pp. 31–32]

Another example of findings consistent with explicit work on teacher planning comes from a study of writing instruction. The finding that teachers tend to work from sketchy plans and images of what the lesson should be like was replicated by the Written Literacy Project. As summarized in their final report, "Rather than move students through lockstep sequences of skill drills, experienced teachers tend to develop loosely framed, long-range plans for writing and to emphasize flexible, activity-based plans for individual lessons" (IRT, 1986, p. 37).

Several important differences also arise, however, when one begins to compare across projects with respect to the issue of planning. Planning seems to differ significantly across grade levels. For example, the High School Standards Project reports that the sheer number of students that high school teachers face daily affects the types of lessons teachers plan (IRT, 1986, p. 50). Teachers also plan differently for different types of students. For example, the Classroom Strategies

Project found that different strategies appear to be appropriate for dealing with different types of problem students (IRT, 1986, p. 42). Teachers differ in the goals they hold for instruction, and not all goals are "learning outcomes" in the narrow sense. These differences in goals result in important differences in teacher practices and in what is accomplished with students.

Another important and interesting point of these research projects is that planning differs across subject matters in elementary school teaching. The picture that emerges from this work is one of important differences in the teaching of reading, mathematics, science, and writing. For example, time allocated for instruction varies considerably across subjects. Elementary school teachers allocate much more time to teaching reading than to any other subject (from 30 percent to 45 percent of their total instructional time). Although mathematics is a distant second, there is still a regularly scheduled time for it (typically each day for a period ranging from thirty minutes to an hour). In contrast, science is rarely if ever taught in many elementary school classrooms and writing is generally not taught at a regularly scheduled time (IRT, 1986, p. 18).

The role of instructional materials as an aid to planning also varies considerably across subject areas. Several IRT projects came to understand more about teacher planning through their examination of instructional materials. For example, studies of science teaching found that the teachers observed focused primarily on the activities to be carried out:

> [Many elementary school teachers] try to follow the recommendations in the teacher's guide, assuming or hoping that student learning will result, but they often are unsure about how the activities are supposed to contribute to learning. Frequently they do not understand the rationale for suggested activities, and they often unknowingly modify or delete crucial parts of the program. [IRT, 1986, p. 40]

In contrast, studies of elementary school teachers' planning for writing instruction looked quite different from the planning described for the science classes. As these researchers conclude:

> Teachers generally have been left on their own with respect to writing instruction. In contrast to the situation in other subject matter areas, teachers tend to plan and teach writing with neither the limitations nor the guidance of district policies, published materials, or professional training in theories of the writing

process. Most teachers are not experienced or confident as writers themselves, and they are unprepared to act as curriculum developers (which is in effect what is expected of them in the absence of clear policies or organized materials and programs). [IRT, 1986, p. 37]

In the field of research on teaching, there is an increasing interest in what happens to curriculum as it is enacted in classrooms (F. Erickson, 1982; Good, 1983). The study of planning is a central component to an understanding of what Doyle (1985) has called content representations, or "the ways in which the curriculum is made concrete in the classroom tasks teachers define for students" (p. 1). He goes on to argue that "the classroom tasks a teacher designs, often with managerial and pedagogical purposes in mind, have powerful effects on the way curriculum is represented to students" (p. 12).

CONCLUSION

The above examples illustrate, we hope, the ubiquity of teacher planning as an explanatory construct in any comprehensive program of research on teaching. Subject-matter-specific classroom studies have discovered, however unintentionally at times, much about the nature of planning. We argue that more explicit attention to teachers' (and students') intentions and planning ought to be included in the design of new research initiatives. A revived interest in studying pedagogical influences on student achievement is also compatible with attention to teacher planning as a determiner of instructional pacing, grouping patterns, and content decisions affecting opportunity to learn. And the study of teacher planning will provide practical, realistic, and relatively unthreatening opportunities for learning about teachers' knowledge in practice. Natural experiments abound as teachers grapple with new curricula, novice teachers enter the classroom, and experienced teachers are assigned to different schools or new grade levels and subjects. The perennial questions about the merits of teacher-made materials and tests compared to published materials could be asked and answered in more sophisticated ways with teacher planning and intentions as the conceptual organizers. And the cognitive skill of planning itself, as an outcome of schooling for both teachers and students, could receive long-overdue attention.

One could conclude from this analytic review that the time of studying teacher planning, as a direct and primary subject of inquiry, has passed. Rather, we have made a case for including attention to teachers' planning, intentions, and routines in every study of teaching. Planning is demonstrably a critical element in teaching and in school learning. But, we have also come to believe that the larger task of understanding and improving the teaching of school subjects demands that researchers transcend reductionistic, component-by-component analysis of teachers' thoughts and actions. The field of educational research has reached a stage of development at which more comprehensive studies are possible and desirable, and in which attention to teachers' planning, to teachers' intentions, and to classroom routines is essential. Our hope is that as researchers design and interpret studies of schooling they will include questions about the intentions of teachers and students; how those intentions are formulated, expressed, modified, and pursued; and how plans and intentions affect the process and consequences of classroom teaching.

REFERENCES

Anderson, Linda M., and Evertson, Carolyn M. "Classroom Organization at the Beginning of School: Two Case Studies." Paper presented at the meeting of the American Association of Colleges for Teacher Education, Chicago, 1978.

Borko, Hilda, and Niles, Jerome A. "Descriptions of Teacher Planning: Ideas for Teachers and Researchers." In *The Educator's Handbook: Research into Practice*, edited by Virginia Koehler. New York: Longman, 1987.

Buckley, Pamela K., and Cooper, James M. "An Ethnographic Study of an Elementary School Teacher's Establishment and Maintenance of Group Norms." Paper presented at the Annual Meeting of the American Educational Research Association, Toronto, 1978.

Carnahan, Richard S. *The Effects of Teacher Planning on Classroom Processes*, Technical Report No. 541. Madison, Wisc.: R & D Center for Individualized Schooling, 1980.

Clark, Christopher M., and Elmore, Janis L. *Teacher Planning in the First Weeks of School*, Research Series No. 56. E. Lansing: Institute for Research on Teaching, Michigan State University, 1979.

Clark, Christopher M., and Elmore, Janis L. *Transforming Curriculum in Mathematics, Science, and Writing: A Case Study of Teacher Yearly Planning*, Research Series No. 99. E. Lansing: Institute for Research on Teaching, Michigan State University, 1981.

Clark, Christopher M., and Peterson, Penelope L. "Teachers' Thought Processes. In *Handbook of Research on Teaching*, 3d ed., edited by Merlin C. Wittrock. New York: Macmillan, 1986.

Clark, Christopher M., and Yinger, Robert J. *Three Studies of Teacher Planning*. Research Series No. 55. E. Lansing: Institute for Research on Teaching, Michigan State University, 1979.

Clark, Christopher M., and Yinger, Robert J. *The Hidden World of Teaching: Implications of Research on Teacher Thinking*, Research Series No. 77. E. Lansing: Institute for Research on Teaching, Michigan State University, 1980.

Doyle, Walter. *Content Representation in Teachers' Definitions of Academic Work*, R & D Report No. 6161. Austin: Research and Development Center for Teacher Education, University of Texas at Austin, 1985.

Eaton, Janet F.; Anderson, Charles W.; and Smith, Edward L. "Student Misconceptions Interfere with Science Learning: Case Studies of Fifth-grade Students," *Elementary School Journal* 84, no. 4 (1984): 365–379.

Erickson, Frederick. "Taught Cognitive Learning in Its Immediate Environments: A Neglected Topic in Anthropology of Education," *Anthropology and Education Quarterly* 13, no. 2 (1982): 149–180.

Erickson, Gaalen L. "Children's Viewpoints about Heat: A Second Look," *Science Education* 63, no. 2 (1980): 221–230.

Feiman-Nemser, Sharon. "Learning to Teach." In *Handbook of Teaching and Policy*, edited by Lee S. Shulman and Gary Sykes. New York: Longman, 1983.

Good, Thomas L. "Classroom Research: A Decade of Progress," *Educational Psychologist* 18 (1983): 127–144.

Hill, Jane; Yinger, Robert J.; and Robbins, Debbie. "Instructional Planning in a Developmental Preschool." Paper presented at the Annual Meeting of the American Educational Research Association, Los Angeles, 1981.

Institute for Research on Teaching. *Final Report*. E. Lansing: Institute for Research on Teaching, Michigan State University, 1986.

Leinhardt, Gaea. "Routines in Expert Math Teachers' Thoughts and Actions." Paper presented at the Annual Meeting of the American Educational Research Association, Montreal, 1983.

Leinhardt, Gaea; Weidman, Carla; and Hammond, Katherine M. "Introduction and Integration of Classroom Routines by Expert Teachers." Paper presented at the Annual Meeting of the American Educational Research Association, New Orleans, 1984.

McCloskey, M. "Intuitive Physics," *Scientific American* 284, no. 4 (1983): 122–130.

McLeod, Marjorie A. "The Identification of Intended Learning Outcomes by Early Childhood Teachers: An Explanatory Study." Doctoral dissertation, University of Alberta, 1981.

May, Wanda T. "Teaching Students How to Plan: The Dominant Model and Alternatives," *Journal of Teacher Education* 37, no. 6 (1986): 6–11.

Morine-Dershimer, Greta, and Vallance, Elizabeth. *Teacher Planning*, Beginning Teacher Evaluation Study, Special Report C. San Francisco: Far West Laboratory, 1976.

Neale, Daniel C.; Pace, Ann J.; and Case, Angela B. "The Influence of Training, Experience, and Organizational Environment on Teachers' Use of the Systematic Planning Model." Paper presented at the Annual Meeting of the American Educational Research Association, 1983.

Peterson, Penelope L.; Marx, Ronald W.; and Clark, Christopher M. "Teacher Planning, Teacher Behavior, and Student Achievement," *American Educational Research Journal* 15 (1978): 417–432.

Posner, George J.; Strike, Kenneth A.; Hewson, Peter W.; and Gertzog, William A. "Accommodation of a Scientific Concept: Toward a Theory of Conceptual Change," *Science Education* 66, no. 2 (1982): 211–227.

Putnam, Ralph T., and Leinhardt, Gaea. "Curriculum Scripts and the Adjustment of Content in Lessons." Paper presented at the Annual Meeting of the American Educational Research Association, San Francisco, 1986.

Rosaen, Cheryl L. "Children as Researchers: A Descriptive Study of Intentions, Interpretations, and Social Interactions in an Elementary Classroom." Doctoral dissertation, Michigan State University, 1987.

Roth, Kathleen J. "Conceptual Change Learning and Student Processing of Science Texts." Doctoral dissertation, Michigan State University, 1985.

Roth, Kathleen J. "Learning to Be Comfortable in the Neighborhood of Science: An Analysis of Three Approaches to Elementary Science Teaching." In *Vital Connections: Children, Science, and Books*, edited by Wendy Saul. Washington, D.C.: Library of Congress, in press.

Roth, Kathleen J.; Anderson, Charles W., and Smith, Edward L. "Teacher Explanatory Talk during Content Area Reading." Paper presented at the Annual Meeting of the National Reading Conference, Austin, Texas, 1983.

Schon, Donald. *The Reflective Practitioner: How Professionals Think in Action.* New York: Basic Books, 1983.

Schultz, Jeffrey, and Florio, Susan. "Stop and Freeze: The Negotiation of Social and Physical Space in a Kindergarten/First-Grade Classroom," *Anthropology and Education Quarterly* 10 (1979): 166–181.

Schwab, Joseph J. "The Structures of the Disciplines: Meanings and Significance." In *The Structure of Knowledge and the Curriculum*, edited by Gervais W. Ford and Lawrence Pugno. Chicago: Rand McNally, 1964.

Smith, Edward L., and Anderson, Charles W. *The Planning and Teaching of Intermediate Science Study: Final Report*, Research Series No. 147. E. Lansing: Institute for Research on Teaching, Michigan State University, 1984.

Smith, Edward L., and Sendelbach, Neil B. "Teacher Intentions for Science Instruction and Their Antecedents in Program Materials." Paper presented at the Annual Meeting of the American Educational Research Association, San Francisco, 1979.

Tikunoff, William J., and Ward, Beatrice A. *A Naturalistic Study of the Initiation of Students into Three Classroom Social Systems*, Report A–78–11. San Francisco: Far West Laboratory, 1978.

Wilson, Suzanne; Shulman, Lee S.; and Richert, Anna E. "'150 Different Ways' of Knowing: Representations of Knowledge in Teaching." *In Exploring Teachers' Thinking*, edited by James Calderhead, pp. 104–124. London: Cassell, 1987.

Wittrock, Merlin C., ed. *Handbook of Research on Teaching*, 3d ed. New York: Macmillan, 1986.

Yinger, Robert J. "A Study of Teacher Planning: Description and Theory Development Using Ethnographic and Information Processing Methods." Doctoral dissertation, Michigan State University, 1977.

Yinger, Robert J. "Routines in Teacher Planning," *Theory Into Practice* 18 (1979): 163–169.

9

Mapping the Terrain: Knowledge Growth in Teaching

Pamela Grossman

While teachers need to know many things in order to teach, knowledge of the subject to be taught seems particularly salient; after all, can teachers teach what they do not know themselves? Yet all teachers confront the challenge of teaching material that is new to them. In secondary schools, English teachers find themselves teaching literature they have never read; biology teachers end up teaching a section or two of chemistry or earth science. Not uncommonly, teachers are asked to teach subjects that are entirely outside their speciality, as when a home economics teacher is assigned to teach mathematics. In elementary and middle schools, teachers must teach a range of different subjects, only a few of which they may have studied in any depth since they were themselves in elementary school. Does a teacher's knowledge of a subject really matter to good teaching?

While subject matter knowledge seems intuitively important to good teaching, early research in this area uncovered little evidence of a correlation between teachers' knowledge of a subject, as measured by the number of college units taken or by performance on standardized tests, and measures of student achievement. Because the research failed to develop a theoretical model concerning the particular aspects of teachers' subject matter knowledge that might be expected to affect student learning, this line of research may have been premature. More recently, a number of related research projects have returned to the issue of teachers' subject matter knowledge, focusing on the link between teachers' knowledge of particular content, as assessed in a wide variety of ways, and teachers' planning and classroom practices. These studies suggest that what teachers know, and do not know, about the content they teach influences how they represent that content to students.

SUBJECT MATTER KNOWLEDGE AND THE REPRESENTATION OF CONTENT IN TEACHING

Teachers represent content to students in a variety of ways. Perhaps most important, teachers represent the nature of knowing a subject—for example, what it means to know science, or to understand literature. In addition, teachers represent content to students through their selection of explanatory concepts and through their organization of content.

A number of studies suggest that teachers' own background knowledge in a subject affects how they represent the nature of knowing to their students. In her work in mathematics, Ball (1988) illustrates how prospective teachers who are weak in their own understanding of mathematics are likely to represent the nature of knowing in mathematics as arbitrary and rule-governed. These teachers represented concepts, such as division by zero, as arbitrary rules rather than as logically derivable concepts. Ball argues that these teachers essentially misrepresented the nature of knowing in mathematics. In studies of beginning secondary school mathematics teachers, researchers found that the teacher with the most background in higher mathematics encouraged students to find different ways of solving problems and then to discover why particular approaches did or did not work; in the classroom, the teacher emphasized mathematical thinking rather than the correct answer. In contrast, the teacher with a meager background in mathematics represented mathematics as a collection of arbitrary algorithms that had to be followed precisely; in her classroom, knowing mathematics meant getting the right answer (Steinberg, Marks, and Haymore, 1985). The ways in which the two teachers represented the nature of mathematical knowing in their classrooms paralleled their own understandings of mathematics. In studies of beginning social studies teachers, researchers also found that how teachers represented the nature of knowing in a subject related to their own background in and understanding of the content.

In a discussion of the ways in which four beginning social studies teachers understood and represented history, Wilson and Wineburg (1988) illustrate how the teachers' disciplinary backgrounds influenced how they represented the nature of knowing in history. The teachers with college majors in areas other than history, anthropology, and political science represented the knowledge of history as the knowledge of dates and facts; that is, they presented historical knowledge as more or less cut and dried. In contrast, the teachers with undergraduate majors in history represented the uncertain nature of historical knowing, and emphasized the role of alternative interpretations in the construction of historical knowledge.

Teachers also represent subjects through their selection of explanatory concepts to emphasize to students. In the same studies of beginning social studies teachers, for example, researchers found that teachers used strikingly different explanatory concepts and structured the content differently depending on their own disciplinary backgrounds. One teacher, with a major in physical anthropology and a special interest in archeology, focused her ninth-grade social studies class on the geographical features of countries that affected the development of culture. Wanting students to appreciate the value of archeological evidence in understanding different cultures, she brought artifacts to class and asked students to speculate on the cultures that produced them. A cultural anthropology major who taught a similar social studies course engaged students in ethnographic interviews and cross-cultural simulations to introduce students to the importance of an "endemic" or insiders' view of culture. He tried to teach apartheid from both black and Afrikaaner perspectives. Both teachers relied on the frameworks and explanatory concepts from their college majors in representing the nature of "social studies" to their students.

Teachers also represent content to students through classroom presentation of material and explanations. As Leinhardt and Smith (1985) suggest:

> It is in the context of presentation that teachers introduce new concepts, present new algorithms, review learned material, and offer explanations. It is

also in the context of a presentation that teachers must draw most heavily on
their subject matter knowledge. [P. 249]

In order to inform explanations and presentation of material,
subject matter knowledge must be explicit. Teachers who have procedural knowledge of an area (who can, for example, divide fractions)
but lack conceptual knowledge (such as knowing why it is necessary
to invert and multiply the fractions) may find themselves handicapped in their efforts to explain the content to students. In a number
of studies, researchers found that teachers had procedural knowledge
of a content area but lacked the conceptual knowledge necessary for
representing the content in different ways (Ball, 1988; Leinhardt and
Smith, 1985). Sometimes, the procedural knowledge involving a
particular skill is part of a teacher's tacit understanding. Without
more explicit knowledge of the subject, however, teachers find it
difficult to explain material to students. A beginning English teacher
explained that her intuitive sense of grammar, which had stood her in
good stead in her own writing, failed her in teaching: "I've always
been really good at grammar. I can do all the stuff, but I can't give the
reasons. And I can't teach it" (Grossman, 1987). Teaching students
involves giving reasons and providing explanations, which in turn rest
upon knowing the subject. In analyses of classroom instruction in
elementary science, the researchers reported that the teacher with the
most secure subject matter knowledge was best able to construct
activities and representations to facilitate children's understanding of
the concepts (Smith and Neale, forthcoming). Teachers' understanding of subject matter also affects classroom curriculum, both what gets
taught and how it is taught.

One strategy for dealing with unfamiliar content is avoidance.
When teachers have the discretion to do so, they may simply skip over
topics they do not understand well themselves. In their study of
elementary science teachers, for example, Smith and Neale (forthcoming) discuss how teachers' understanding of physical phenomena
informed their instructional practice: "Teachers admitted that they
avoided teaching science, and physics in particular, because of their
own lack of knowledge" (Smith and Neale, forthcoming, p. 20). A
similar finding occurred in studies of beginning secondary English
teachers, who avoided teaching grammar whenever possible due to
their own lack of understanding (Grossman, 1987). Conversely,
teachers may spend more time on topics or subjects about which they

are most knowledgeable; Carlsen (1988) found this to be true in his study of secondary school science teachers.

Teachers also control what gets taught through their selection of instructional methods or strategies. Carlsen also found that when teachers knew the material well, they were more likely to use whole-group instruction; when they were less familiar with the material, they more often selected student-centered activities such as group work. In instances of whole-group instruction, however, when teachers knew the material well, they allowed for more student talk; in teaching topics they were less familiar with, they tended to dominate the discussions. When teachers do not know the content well, they may be unconsciously following the rule of thumb for trial lawyers: Never ask a question to which you do not already know the answer. While this adage gives lawyers and teachers alike greater control over the direction of a cross-examination or a classroom discussion, it limits opportunities for students to raise their own questions about the content.

Subject matter knowledge also influences the nature of teachers' questions. Carlsen found that teachers asked more low-level questions when they did not know the topics well, and more higher-level questions when they were more knowledgeable about the material. A similar finding occurred in a study of experienced science teachers (Hashweh, 1987); in this study, biology and physics teachers were asked to think about teaching topics from both fields. When teachers designed examination questions in topics outside their area of expertise, they asked more recall questions; within their area of expertise, they were more likely to ask higher-level questions.

This discussion, however, is not meant to suggest that subject matter knowledge remains static. Teachers may develop their understanding of subjects as they encounter and teach new material. A number of beginning secondary teachers commented on the fact that as they prepared to teach new courses they were learning material, sometimes for the first time. As one beginning science teacher commented, "This is almost learning for the first time. I mean this is stuff that I probably didn't even learn in college." As teachers prepare to teach new material and teach the same material over time, they also acquire content knowledge. Very experienced teachers may have amassed deep knowledge of the content through years of teaching (Wilson, 1988). What teachers are able to learn about new content, however, is likely to be shaped by their prior knowledge (Grossman, Wilson, and Shulman, 1989). While teachers are likely to acquire new knowledge of facts or concepts within a subject during the course of teaching, they are less likely to acquire ways of thinking about how new knowledge enters a field. Studies of experienced elementary teachers learning about physics remind us of the conceptual change required by teachers, as well as students, as they grapple with new concepts (Smith and Neale, forthcoming).

This discussion illustrates the role of prior subject matter knowledge in teaching. As undergraduates, prospective teachers not only learn facts and concepts in different subjects, but also develop understandings about what it means to know a subject and how new knowledge is generated in different disciplines. In the best instances, when the match between the teachers' own knowledge and the content they will teach is a close one, knowledge of the subject provides teachers with a detailed road map of the content terrain, helping them understand important destinations, the relationships between different destinations, and the main roadways as well as alternative routes for getting where one wants to go. When the match is less close—for example, when an anthropologist tries to teach history—teachers may still rely on the map they know best, transposing it onto a different content terrain. In this instance, the destinations may become less historical than cross-cultural. Without the appropriate map, teachers may miss the central destinations completely, spending their time on uninteresting sideroads or driving long distances only to reach a dead end. As the researcher most responsible for the resurgence of interest in subject matter reminds us, in teaching as in sales, "you've got to know the territory" (Shulman, 1988).

Teachers need to know the territory in specifically pedagogical ways, however—ways that go beyond the understanding of experts in the subject. For teachers serve as guides, leading novices into unfamiliar territory. They must understand what makes a particular climb they themselves find easy difficult for inexperienced climbers and must know potential obstacles on specific journeys. This type of knowledge has been called pedagogical content knowledge.

PEDAGOGICAL CONTENT KNOWLEDGE

Subject matter knowledge alone is necessary but insufficient for the work of teachers. Teachers need to possess subject matter knowledge that differs from the knowledge of experts on the subject matter (Shulman, 1986; Wilson, 1988), because teachers are most concerned with the need to help others *understand* particular content. Knowledge of the subject, then, must be supplemented with knowledge of students and of learning, and with knowledge of curriculum and school context. Shulman (1986) called this specialized body of knowledge for teachers "pedagogical content knowledge":

> Within the category of pedagogical content knowledge I include, for the most regularly taught topics in one's subject area, the most useful forms of representation of those ideas, the most powerful analogies, illustrations, examples, explanations, and demonstrations—in a word, the ways of formulating the subject that make it comprehensible to others. Pedagogical content knowledge also includes an understanding of what makes the learning of specific topics easy or difficult; the conceptions and preconceptions that students of different ages and backgrounds bring with them to the learning of those most frequently taught topics and lessons. [Pp. 9–10]

The concept of pedagogical content knowledge is related to Dewey's notions of the need to "psychologize" subject matter for students. Teachers serve as mediators between the world of the discipline, on one side, and the world of the students, on the other. Beginning teachers may understand their content well, but may lack insight into what makes that content difficult for students (Grossman, 1988). In order to help students learn, teachers must rethink their subjects from the perspective of students.

One model of pedagogical content knowledge emerged from the studies of knowledge growth among beginning secondary teachers. This model included at least four components: conceptions of the purposes for teaching particular subjects; knowledge and beliefs regarding student understanding; curricular knowledge; and knowledge of instructional strategies and representations for teaching specific topics (Grossman, 1988). Since the term was introduced, a number of studies have looked at teachers' pedagogical content knowledge in different subject areas.

Conceptions of the purposes for teaching a particular subject include teachers' beliefs about what is most important for students to know, understand, and appreciate about specific content, and their understanding of the interrelationship of topics within a subject. These conceptions act as a template for teachers' decision making about what to teach, what texts to use, and what to emphasize within a course. In English, teachers hold conceptions of the purposes for teaching literature and writing, and of the relationship between teaching literature, language, and writing. In most subjects, alternative frameworks exist for thinking about the purposes for teaching the particular subjects and the relationships among topics and concepts.

Research on experienced teachers' pedagogical content knowledge has illustrated the organizing models or imagery that secondary teachers use to conceptualize the teaching of particular subjects (Grant, 1987; Gudmundsdottir, 1989). These studies suggest that secondary school teachers' conceptions of the purposes for teaching a subject are organized into pedagogical modes or imagery; these models in turn inform instructional decision making. Other research on beginning secondary school teachers suggests that teachers acquire a model of the purposes for teaching their subject during teacher education; when teacher education coursework failed to provide a clear subject-specific framework, a few beginning teachers constructed their own subject-specific frameworks for thinking about the purposes for teaching a subject area (Grossman and Richert, 1988).

Knowledge of students' understanding includes what teachers know about students' prior knowledge and understanding in a particular domain, the misconceptions and preconceptions students bring to the study of a topic, and an understanding of the concepts, topics, or skills that prove especially difficult for students to understand and acquire. In science, for example, teachers may know about the kinds of misconceptions students hold regarding physical phenomena. In studies of beginning secondary school teachers, researchers found that during the course of student teaching, teachers began to develop an understanding of what made particular topics difficult for students. As one beginning mathematics teacher commented, "Now I think more in terms of my students. When I look at a problem, I try to think of where they are going to have difficulty, whereas last summer, everything was easy and everything seemed easy" (Haymore, 1987).

Research on teaching elementary mathematics has focused particularly on teachers' knowledge of students' understanding in arithmetic (Carpenter et al., 1988). These researchers used a research-based taxonomy of problem types and students' problem-solving strategies in their study of experienced teachers' pedagogical content knowledge. This research suggests one way in which research on teachers' knowledge can build upon earlier research on learning in particular content areas. One caution, however, may be that teachers' knowledge, developed through classroom experience, may differ from taxonomies derived from research.

Curricular knowledge includes knowledge of the curricular materials and guidelines available for teaching particular subjects, and knowledge of the vertical curriculum for a particular subject. Finally, knowledge of instructional representations refers to the subject-specific instructional repertoire teachers acquire for teaching content.

If pedagogical content knowledge is important to teaching, how do teachers construct this knowledge? A number of researchers have suggested the logical link between courses on subject-specific methods and the acquisition of pedagogical content knowledge (McDiarmid, Ball, and Anderson, 1989; Grossman, 1988). Ideally, methods courses could help beginning teachers learn about the purposes for teaching a subject, confront student misconceptions and difficulties, and develop instructional representations of content.

Teachers also acquire pedagogical content knowledge from classroom experiences; there is nothing like an unexpected student question to help a teacher rethink the relative difficulty of a topic. Textbooks provide another source of pedagogical content knowledge, as they provide teachers with representations of content and some guidelines regarding potential student difficulties.

If subject matter knowledge provides teachers with a detailed road map, pedagogical content knowledge is analogous to a topographical map of specific terrain, which a guide would annotate for an expedition by novices. These maps include less territory but magnify the particular features of the landscape for those who intend to explore it. Topographical maps indicate the difficulty or ease of particular routes by the rise in elevation and potential obstacles ahead. The guide's annotations might include routes that help inexperienced hikers learn to ford a treacherous river and suggestions for worthwhile sidetrips for panoramic views or spectacular wildflowers. Like the detailed topographical map, pedagogical content knowledge is good for only a particular terrain; generic topographical maps do not exist.

IMPLICATIONS OF RESEARCH ON TEACHER KNOWLEDGE

If what teachers know about their content and about how to teach that content is central to instructional practice, issues concerning teachers' knowledge raise a number of implications for teacher education, including both preservice programs and professional development, and for further research on teaching.

One implication is that we need to take teachers' prior knowledge of a subject more seriously in teacher education programs. It has been too easy for teacher educators to assume that teachers acquire the content knowledge they need as part of their undergraduate major or in general education courses. Part of teaching teachers to teach content in different ways may involve first engaging them in the content as learners. Earlier curriculum projects that attempted to represent more sophisticated notions of disciplinary knowledge tried to bypass the teacher entirely; current efforts acknowledge the need for teachers to develop new understandings of the subject for themselves before they can help their students engage in conceptual change in science or mathematical thinking. A number of projects in mathematics, science, and writing have begun to incorporate this feature into in-service education. As teachers are encouraged to explore topics from the perspective of learners, they may be able to develop the more explicit conceptual knowledge of the content we have argued is necessary for teaching, while also developing an understanding of what makes the topic difficult for learners.

Teacher education coursework will also need to grapple with students' prior knowledge of content. As research in mathematics has suggested, just because a teacher has an undergraduate major in mathematics does not necessarily ensure that he or she has the explicit subject matter knowledge necessary for representing division by fractions appropriately (Ball, 1988). The match between the college curriculum and the content covered in K–12 education is imperfect at best. Courses on subject-specific methods can help bridge these gaps by incorporating substantive discussions about central topics in the field.

Recognition of the importance of subject matter knowledge also poses implications for curricular changes in schools. Requiring teachers to ask more higher-level questions in history or to teach the conceptual basis underlying mathematical algorithms without attending to their own understanding of the content may be futile. If we are to take the role of content knowledge seriously, we will need to rethink policies and institutional structures that require teachers to teach across a wide variety of subjects or that assign teachers to teach content outside their areas of preparation. This poses the most far-reaching implications for the organization of elementary and middle schools, in which teachers are regarded as generalists. As we restructure schools to include team-teaching, we should explore the potential for building different subject matter expertise into these teams.

The next step in research on teachers' subject matter knowledge will be to investigate the connection between teachers' knowledge and students' learning. Most current studies have focused on the connection between teachers' knowledge and the preactive and interactive aspects of teaching; only a few have made the connection to student learning. In order for these studies to be meaningful, however, we will need better assessments of student learning. Many of the distinctions we are trying to make might not be captured by standardized tests that assess computational skills or recall of factual information. The differences in student learning are more likely to revolve around students' conceptual understanding of topics, or their understanding of the nature of mathematical or historical studies. In an early study of the relationship of teacher knowledge to student achievement in mathematics, Begle (1972) found tentative evidence of a relationship between teachers' conceptual understanding of the algebra of the real number system and students' conceptual understanding of algebra; this relationship did not emerge in relation to students' computational skill in algebra. As we construct a more sophisticated understanding of the theoretical relationship between teachers' subject matter knowledge and instructional practice, we should also be able to create better ways of studying the relationship between teachers' knowledge and students' learning.

If teachers are to guide students in their journey into unfamiliar territory, they need to know the terrain well. Both knowledge of the content and knowledge of the best ways to teach that content to students help teachers construct meaningful representations for students, representations that reflect both the nature of the subject matter and the realities of students' prior knowledge and skill. Preparing teachers to teach content means first engaging them in their own explorations of the territory and helping them to construct their own conceptual understanding of the material. Teachers also need pedagogical maps of content, the understanding of the subject from an explicitly pedagogical perspective that enables teachers to track students' misunderstandings and guide them toward new conceptions.

REFERENCES

Ball, Deborah. "Knowledge and Reasoning in Mathematical Pedagogy: Examining What Prospective Teachers Bring to Teacher Education." Doctoral dissertation, Michigan State University, 1988.

Begle, Edward. *Teacher Knowledge and Pupil Achievement in Algebra*, Technical Report No. 9. Stanford, Calif.: School Mathematics Study Group, Stanford University, 1972.

Carlsen, William. "The Effects of Science Teacher Subject-Matter Knowledge on Teacher Questioning and Classroom Discourse." Doctoral dissertation, Stanford University, 1988.

Carpenter, Thomas; Fennema, Elizabeth; Peterson, Penelope; and Carey, Deborah. "Teachers' Pedagogical Content Knowledge of Students' Problem Solving in Elementary Arithmetic," *Journal for Research in Mathematics Education* 19 (1988): 385–401.

Grant, Grace. "Pedagogical Content Knowledge: A Case Study of Four Secondary Teachers." Paper presented at the Annual Meeting of the American Educational Research Association, Washington, D.C., 1987.

Grossman, Pamela. *A Passion for Language: The Case Study of Colleen, a Beginning English Teacher*. Knowledge Growth in a Profession Technical Report. Stanford, Calif.: School of Education, Stanford University, 1987.

Grossman, Pamela. "A Study in Contrast: Sources of Pedagogical Content Knowledge for Secondary English." Doctoral dissertation, Stanford University, 1988.

Grossman, Pamela, and Richert, Anna. "Unacknowledged Knowledge Growth: A Re-examination of the Effects of Teacher Education," *Teaching and Teacher Education* 4 (1988): 53–62.

Grossman, Pamela; Wilson, Suzanne; and Shulman Lee. "Teachers of Substance: Subject Matter Knowledge for Teaching." In *Knowledge Base for the Beginning Teacher*, edited by Maynard Reynolds. Oxford: Pergamon Press, 1989.

Gudmundsdottir, Sigrun. "Knowledge Use among Experienced Teachers: Four Case Studies of High School Teaching." Doctoral dissertation, Stanford University, 1989.

Hashweh, Maher. "Effects of Subject Matter Knowledge in Teaching Biology and Physics," *Teaching and Teacher Education* 3 (1987): 109–120.

Haymore, Judith. *From Successful Student to Frustrated Teacher: The Case Study of Sharon, a Beginning Math Teacher*. Knowledge Growth in a Profession Technical Report. Stanford, Calif.: School of Education, Stanford University, 1987.

Leinhardt, Gaea, and Smith, Donald. "Expertise in Mathematics Instruction: Subject Matter Knowledge," *Journal of Educational Psychology* 77 (1985): 247–271.

McDiarmid, William; Ball, Deborah; and Anderson, Charles. "Why Staying One Chapter Ahead Doesn't Really Work: Subject-Specific Pedagogy." In *Knowledge Base for the Beginning Teacher*, edited by Maynard Reynolds. Oxford: Pergamon Press, 1989.

Shulman, Lee. "Those Who Understand: Knowledge Growth in Teaching," *Educational Researcher* 15 (1986): 4–14.

Shulman, Lee. Address to the American Association of Colleges of Teacher Education, New Orleans, Louisiana, 1988.

Smith, Deborah, and Neale, Daniel. "The Construction of Subject Matter Knowledge in Primary Science Teaching." In *Advances in Research on Teaching: Subject Matter Knowledge*, edited by Jere Brophy. Greenwich, Conn.: JAI Press, forthcoming.

Steinberg, Ruth; Marks, Rick; and Haymore, Judith. "Teachers' Knowledge and Structuring of Content in Mathematics." Paper presented at the Annual Meeting of the American Educational Research Association, Chicago, 1985.

Wilson, Suzanne. "Understanding Historical Understanding: Subject Matter Knowledge and the Teaching of U.S. History." Doctoral dissertation, Stanford University, Stanford, Calif., 1988.

Wilson, Suzanne, and Wineburg, Samuel. "Peering at History Through Different Lenses: The Role of Disciplinary Perspectives in Teaching History," *Teachers College Record* 89 (1988): 525–539.

——— 10 ———

Learning from Exemplary Teachers

Kenneth Tobin and Barry J. Fraser

Much of the research that has been conducted in science and mathematics classrooms has identified serious shortcomings which suggest that teaching strategies need to be changed in order to build and maintain environments conducive to learning with understanding. As a consequence, it is important that alternative models of effective teaching and learning are available to guide practitioners and teacher educators in their endeavors to improve the quality of science and mathematics education. Investigations of exemplary teachers are an appealing source for models of effective classroom practices. David Berliner (1986) strongly advocated the study of expert teachers because such investigations provide extremely useful case material from which we can learn. Because prospective and beginning teachers in particular are likely to benefit from an expert's performance, both Berliner and Lee Shulman (1986) advocate that case studies of expert teachers should form a part of teacher education programs. However, what is an exemplary teacher? And what can be learned from investigations of exemplary practices? These questions are addressed through a description and synthesis of the findings of the Exemplary Practice in Science and Mathematics Education study (Tobin and Fraser, 1987), discussions of a follow-up study of an exemplary science teacher (Tobin et al., 1988), and other studies of teachers identified as exemplary (Tobin, Kahle, and Fraser, forthcoming).

BACKGROUND

A major problem facing high school science and mathematics teachers in the United States and in other countries around the world is how to facilitate high-level cognitive learning among students. Research suggests that the tasks in which high school students engage in science and mathematics classes have low cognitive demand. The emphasis is on learning facts and memorizing algorithms to solve problems without necessarily understanding why the algorithms lead to satisfactory solutions. The dominant teaching procedure is lecturing; there is a lack of student-student interactions, small-group learning, or any attempt at alternative approaches; the similarities between schools are striking; and the emphasis is on recall of science and mathematics facts. In science education, most teachers teach basic facts and definitions from textbooks; relatively little emphasis is placed on applications of knowledge in daily life or on the development of higher-order thinking skills; and, even though many programs purport to be inquiry-based, most classrooms show little evidence of inquiry on the part of students and teachers. A similar situation is evident in mathematics education.

The culture of science and mathematics classrooms seems to promote environments that lead to low-level cognitive learning. As Julie Sanford (1987) has indicated, on occasions when teachers emphasized high-level cognitive outcomes, teachers and students interacted to reduce the cognitive demands of academic tasks. Students attempted to renegotiate assigned tasks, students in small groups copied from one another, and, in open book tests, students were able to use information that had been previously copied from another source (e.g., the chalkboard or another student's writing). Other examples of "safety nets" (i.e., strategies used to reduce the risks of students' feeling embarrassed as a result of performing poorly on tasks) included group assignments; peer assistance; using easy or familiar content on tests; assigning more credit for the memorization or procedural components of a task than for its high-level cognitive components; allowing students to revise products after they had submitted them; peer review of products prior to submission; teacher assistance, prompts, and cues; extra-credit assignments; less exacting grading for low-achieving students; grading on completion rather than accuracy; and last-minute review of key content prior to a test.

Cries for reform have been common in the past seven years. Indeed, since publication of *A Nation at Risk* in 1983 (National Commission on Excellence in Education, 1983), more than three hundred reports have urged major restructuring of science and mathematics education. There appears to be a consensus on the need for change, and among professional educators at least, there is a consistent demand for learning with understanding as distinct from rote memorization of facts. What is not clear is whether teachers will be able to change classroom practices in the manner needed to implement the structural reforms that are demanded. Studies of what teachers do and why they do what they do suggest that teachers' beliefs about teaching, learning, and the curriculum underlie classroom practices. How should teachers change? It is possible that investigations of exemplary teachers might reveal practices and conceptualizations that could serve as models for teachers who want to make changes in their classroom practices.

John Penick and Robert Yager (1983) advocated studies in science education with a focus on academic excellence. They stated that

> what we wanted were case studies of excellence in science education that would guide and provide support for innovative efforts. By heeding such case studies, we thought that much of the trial and error associated with educational innovation could be eliminated and school programs could begin building on what was known to work. [P. 621]

These ideas were incorporated into a project known as the Search for Excellence, which began in 1982 in the United States under the sponsorship of the National Science Teachers Association, the Council of State Supervisors, the National Science Supervisors Association, and the National Science Board. Because the focus of the Search for Excellence project was on programs (instead of on teachers, as in our Exemplary Practice in Science and Mathematics Education study), the initial output from the Search for Excellence project included case studies of over fifty excellent science programs published as several volumes by the National Science Teachers Association. For the Search for Excellence project, criteria for excellence were derived from "Project Synthesis," which involved twenty-three science educators reviewing research and National Science Foundation reports in order to identify discrepancies between the actual and desired state of science education. After leading science educators nominated outstanding science programs in each state, review committees assessed nomination papers (and sometimes made site visits) in order to evaluate proposals against the criteria for excellence.

From the large number of programs chosen in the Search for Excellence project, six of the best were identified as "Centers of Excellence" and studied more intensively through site visits. In particular, information was sought about the critical ingredients of the program, the salient factors in the emergence of the program, and the major forces required for its maintenance. Among other common characteristics at these Centers of Excellence, there were administrative support for the program (especially from the school principal); the existence of a person operating as a leader within the program; community/parental involvement and support for the program; ties between the school and universities/colleges; exceptionally active professional involvement among teachers at the local, state, and national levels; and little reliance on textbooks.

Because the Search for Excellence project and other studies based on a similar philosophy caused considerable excitement, optimism, and motivation among teachers, our group of researchers decided to conduct a similar research effort in Western Australia. Our study, the Exemplary Practice in Science and Mathematics Education project, was based on an assumption that much could be learned from case studies of the best science teachers. Also, we believed that case studies of exemplary practice could lead to improvements in science teaching by motivating and guiding teachers' attempts to improve their practice. In contrast to the Search for Excellence project, however, researchers involved in the Exemplary Practice in Science and Mathematics Education study were committed to intensive classroom observation of the exemplary teachers involved in the project.

METHOD

Eleven case studies involved thirteen exemplary science teachers and seven exemplary mathematics teachers from schools in the metropolitan area of Perth, Western Australia. The participants were identified through a nomination process: Key educators in Western Australia, including teachers, State Education Department personnel, and university faculty were asked to nominate outstanding science teachers. Not surprisingly, those approached were somewhat reluctant to nominate anyone as outstanding or exemplary. Consequently, the request for an outstanding teacher was changed to a request for an "above-average" teacher. The educators felt more comfortable with this request, and readily submitted names; lists of nominees were then drawn up. Teachers with the most nominations were invited to participate in the study.

The study made use of an interpretive research methodology in which the data were primarily qualitative and were obtained by participant observers who directly observed at least eight lessons, interviews with the teachers and students, and examination of curriculum materials, tests, and student work. At regular intervals during the data-collecting phase, observers discussed their field notes, and assertions consistent with the observations were formulated. Subsequent observations were used as a basis for refuting, revising, and/or accepting assertions. The criterion for acceptance of assertions was a decisive balance of probabilities favoring the assertions. Throughout the study, team meetings were held to facilitate discussion of administrative matters and substantive issues related to interpretation.

Student perceptions of the psychosocial learning environment were measured using a variety of questionnaires selected from those that have been extensively described by Barry Fraser (1986). The measures provided a quantified picture of life in the classrooms of exemplary teachers as perceived by students, and they enabled comparisons between learning environments in the classes of exemplary teachers and learning environments in classes taught by nonexemplary teachers.

THE CONSTRUCTIVIST CLASSROOM

The personal epistemologies of researchers influence what they see, perceive to be important, and decide to write in their reports of research. Accordingly, we felt it important to explain the constructivist perspectives that underlie this chapter.

Ernst von Glasersfeld (1987) described radical constructivism as an epistemology that views knowledge as existing in the minds and bodies of cognizing beings only. The important aspect of constructivism is that learning involves the construction of knowledge as sensory experiences are given meaning in terms of prior knowledge. Because observation involves making interpretations based on one's prior knowledge and beliefs, humans do not have access to the external reality that exists. Their only access to the world outside their bodies is through constructed images of reality. Knowledge construction occurs within individuals who themselves are a part of a community that shares knowledge via verbal and nonverbal means. The social construction of knowledge in a culture involves negotiation and consensus building among the members of the culture.

A classroom structured on a constructivist epistemology would emphasize students' making sense of what they are to learn. The focus would be on student learning and meaning-making, and the most salient teaching role would be to facilitate student learning. Rather than provide students with correct answers and algorithms to calculate correct answers, teachers should provide cues to focus students' thinking and should provide students with opportunities to use their senses to experience events and phenomena, and also with ample time to reflect on what they have experienced, to connect their observations to prior knowledge, and to contemplate puzzles that emerge. A key to meaning making is to enable students to interact with the teacher and peers so that they engage in verbal and cognitive strategies that describe, clarify, elaborate, justify, evaluate, speculate, synthesize, analyze, question, compromise, reconsider, and form consensuses. Opportunities to negotiate meanings with peers and build consensuses are important components of the social construction of knowledge in science classrooms. Teachers, other students, films, books, and laboratory activities are not regarded as sources of knowledge but are considered important resources to be used by students as they construct knowledge.

THE EXEMPLARY PRACTICE IN SCIENCE AND MATHEMATICS EDUCATION STUDY

The major findings of the Exemplary Practice in Science and Mathematics Education study are represented next as four assertions.

Assertion 1: Exemplary Teachers Used Management Strategies That Facilitated Sustained Student Engagement

A distinctive feature of the classes of the exemplary teachers was the high level of managerial efficiency. The teachers maintained control-at-a-distance over the entire class and actively monitored student behavior by moving around the room and speaking with individual students from time to time. Little evidence of student misbehavior was noted. Students were able to work independently and cooperatively in groups. Interestingly, many of the teachers listed the development of autonomy and independence as one of their curriculum goals. Although our observations indicated that a rule structure was firmly in place in these classes and that students worked within the rules, there was no need for constant enforcement of the rules. Students knew what to do and appeared to enjoy working in the classroom.

In order for teachers to monitor understanding successfully, they needed students to be well-behaved and cooperative. In most classes, students demonstrated a capacity to work together if problems arose, to seek help from a peer, or to wait for the teacher to provide assistance. Consequently, teachers were not under pressure to maintain order, nor were they rushing from one student to another at the behest of students who were experiencing difficulties. Rather, the teachers had time to consider what to do next and to reflect on the lesson as it progressed. The evidence suggests that most teachers monitored student engagement and understanding in a thoughtful, systematic, and routine manner.

One key to teachers' successful monitoring strategies was to establish routines that enabled the teachers to cope with a relatively large number of students with diverse learning needs. In all cases, teachers emphasized an active student role in the learning process. Activities were prescribed to ensure that students were active mentally. When students encountered difficulties, they were encouraged to try to work them out for themselves and to consult resources such as textbooks and peers.

Although different teachers used different styles to establish and maintain an environment conducive to learning, in all case studies the crucial link between management, teaching, and learning was highlighted. For example, an investigation of the science teaching practices of two biology teachers revealed that the first exemplary teacher used a teacher-centered approach that emphasized whole-class activities and also used some small-group and individualized activities. In contrast, the second exemplary teacher emphasized small-group activities but also used some whole-class and individualized activities.

In each exemplary biology teacher's class, there was an easy flow from one activity to the next, little time was lost in transitions, and there were few instances of student misbehavior or time off task. Both classes were extremely well managed. The students in each class appeared to know what to do and how to do it. This situation might be attributable directly to the care taken by each teacher to explain task requirements. During class time, the teachers monitored student engagement, and when a student exhibited off-task behavior, they quickly and quietly spoke to him or her in a manner that did not disrupt the work of others in the class.

Most of the exemplary teachers did not focus unduly on management. The role that appeared most salient to them was that of facilitating the learning of students. Whereas many of their nonexemplary counterparts were preoccupied with management, the managerial strategies of the exemplary teachers facilitated learning. It might be argued that this was possible because exemplary teachers were able to deal with management in a routine manner. However, it is plausible that their beliefs about teaching were such that they assigned greater value, and hence priority, to facilitating student learning. What advice should we provide to a teacher who is having problems controlling students? Should the teacher focus on improving management or is a high incidence of student misbehavior symptomatic of other problems that ought to be addressed? At the very least, the practices adopted by exemplary teachers might serve as foci for the reflections of teachers who are experiencing problems with classroom management. Furthermore, it is possible that teachers can be assisted to improve their classroom practices by reflecting on the value assigned to each teaching role (e.g., facilitating learning, assessing students, controlling misbehavior) and the associated belief sets.

Assertion 2: Exemplary Teachers Used Strategies That Encouraged Students to Participate in Learning Activities

Julie Sanford (1987) explained how teachers used safety nets to allow students to circumvent the cognitive demands of a task. However, safety nets that allow students to participate without undue embarrassment in front of their peers can be beneficial.

A case study of an eighth-grade mathematics teacher provides illustrative examples of this assertion. The exemplary mathematics teacher was successful in involving students in whole-class interactions because of her debating style of teaching, which was non-threatening and encouraging. She held eye contact with students and avoided a tendency to call on the same three to five students. Before students could respond to a question from the teacher, they needed to raise a hand and be selected to respond. The teacher was sensitive to students not wanting to risk being wrong in the public forum of the whole-class activity. Consequently, she did not coerce, intimidate, or condemn. Occasionally she used "safety nets" that encouraged students to get involved in whole-class interactions without fear of the embarrassment of being wrong. The teacher used positive feedback to reward and reinforce pupil behavior. Positive feedback usually was verbal and was given during most types of activity and during social interactions as well. On occasions, the teacher motivated students to learn by using extrinsic rewards such as allocating house points and offering chocolates for quick and accurate work.

In the classes of most of the twenty exemplary teachers, the environment in which students learned was safe in the sense that teachers did not embarrass students who incorrectly responded to questions. In public interactions, the teachers used "safety nets" to encourage involvement from all students in the class. Involvement was maximized, and at the same time, the cognitive aspect of the work was maintained at an appropriately high level. Teachers appeared to be able to make it safe for students to engage in whole-class, small-group, and individualized activities and maintain a focus on meaningful learning. The practices employed by teachers were sensitive to the needs and feelings of students and encouraged participation in learning tasks. Not surprisingly, this tendency was accompanied by teachers' endeavors to follow up and ensure that students learn with understanding and perceive the learning environment favorably.

Assertion 3: Exemplary Teachers Used Strategies Designed to Increase Student Understanding of Science and Mathematics

Most of the exemplary teachers wanted to assist students to learn with understanding. As a consequence, the teachers set up activities in which students had overt involvement in the academic subjects. In elementary grades, the activities were based on the use of materials to solve problems, and the key to teaching for understanding was verbal interaction, which enabled teachers to monitor student understanding of the content to be learned. At the high school level, laboratory activities were used less frequently, but small-group discussions often enabled students to benefit from interactions with peers. At all levels, the exemplary teachers were effective in a range of verbal strategies, which included asking questions to stimulate thinking, probing student responses for clarification and elaboration, and providing explanations to students.

For example, two exemplary chemistry teachers were effective because of their strong content knowledge, a concern for meaningful learning, and the extent to which they monitored student understanding of chemistry concepts. Learning was facilitated in the classes taught by the exemplary chemistry teachers because they were concerned about each student's learning and because of their strong content knowledge, which enabled these teachers to probe for misunderstandings, to clarify, and to elaborate.

One exemplary upper-elementary mathematics teacher was in the process of changing from a traditional teaching approach that emphasized rote learning of arithmetic to an approach that valued and emphasized learning mathematical concepts. His approach to teaching reflected the changes occurring in his beliefs about what students should learn and how they learn. At times, the teacher emphasized activities that provided concrete experiences and opportunities to develop understandings of mathematical concepts, and at other times, he emphasized activities in which students listened to the teacher and participated in drill-and-practice exercises. In contrast, the other exemplary teacher was committed to a problem-solving approach to learning about mathematics. As a consequence, he allowed students to have direct materials-centered experiences and assisted them to develop mathematical knowledge from these experiences. This teacher highlighted the importance of systematic monitoring of student understanding during mathematics lessons.

The most successful teachers in the Exemplary Practice in Science and Mathematics Education study had obviously strong pedagogical content knowledge. They used questions skillfully to focus student engagement and to probe for misunderstandings; their explanations were clear and appropriate. They often used concrete examples, often from outside the classroom, to illustrate abstract concepts and analogies and to facilitate understanding. In addition, teachers appeared to anticipate areas of content that were likely to give students problems. At the conclusion of a lesson, the main points were highlighted in some manner so that they were reinforced prior to the close of the lesson. Quite clearly, these teachers had extensive knowledge of how students learned as well as what to teach and how best to teach it. An assertion that needs further investigation is that exemplary teachers are effective because they have sufficient pedagogical and content knowledge to teach in a routine manner. Further research also is needed on the question of how best to teach for meaningful high-level cognitive learning in science and mathematics.

Even in this study of exemplary teachers, the important role of content knowledge was supported, but in a negative sense. When teachers taught out of their field of expertise in general science classes in the secondary school and in some elementary science classes, there was evidence of nonexemplary practice. Because teachers did not have the content knowledge, errors of fact were made and opportunities to elaborate on student understandings and to diagnose misunderstandings were missed. In some instances, flaws were evident in attempts to explain concepts with which students were having difficulty and, in other cases, analogies were selected that compounded student problems in understanding the concepts. The net result of teachers' lack of content knowledge in high school classes was an emphasis on learning facts, and the lack of knowledge sowed the seeds for the development or reinforcement of misconceptions. These instances of teachers having less than optimal backgrounds in the content to be taught occurred in classes of teachers who had been nominated as exemplary. Such problems are likely to be of greater significance in the classes of nonexemplary science and mathematics teachers. There is considerable need for greater research into the extent to which mathematics and science teachers have the knowledge needed to teach their subjects effectively.

Assertion 4: Exemplary Teachers Maintained a Favorable Classroom Learning Environment

In an attempt to make meaningful interpretations of the learning environment data provided by exemplary teachers' students, the perceived environments of exemplary teachers' classes were compared, first, with the perceived environment of comparison groups of classes from past research; second, with the class environment preferred by the exemplary teachers' students; and, third, with the perceived classroom environment of nonexemplary teachers of the same grade levels within the same school. Overall, the results provide considerable evidence suggesting that, first, exemplary and nonexemplary science teachers can be differentiated in terms of the psychosocial environments of their classrooms as seen through their students' eyes and, second, that exemplary teachers typically create classroom environments that are markedly more favorable than those of nonexemplary teachers.

From pupil perceptions (measured with the My Class Inventory [MCI]), the classroom environment of an exemplary first-grade mathematics teacher was found superior to the average environment perceived by students in a large comparison group of one hundred classes. Although similar levels of Competitiveness were perceived by students in the exemplary teacher's classroom and by those in the comparison group of classrooms, large differences of approximately two standard deviations were found for each of the other four scales of the MCI. Moreover, three of these four results are readily interpretable in that the classroom climate of the exemplary teacher's class clearly was more favorable than the comparison group's; students in the exemplary teacher's class perceived greater Satisfaction, less Friction, and more Cohesiveness.

For the Difficulty scale, however, it is noteworthy that the exemplary teacher's class was perceived to be more difficult than the comparison group's. Although this could be interpreted as less favorable, the difference can be explained in part by the fact that students found the exemplary teacher's class especially challenging (as distinct from only very hard), and it is important to note, too, that the level of class Satisfaction in the exemplary teacher's class was very high despite the perceived high Difficulty of the class.

Past research evidence from both science and nonscience classes clearly indicates a pattern in which students' preferred classroom environment is consistently more positive than the environment perceived by the students. However, in the exemplary practice study, we found an unusually high congruence between perceived and preferred environment on most environment dimensions (as measured by the Classroom Environment Scale [Fraser, 1986]) in classes taught by an exemplary biology teacher. The levels of perceived and preferred Task Orientation, Order and Organization, and Rule Clarity were surprisingly similar, although students preferred somewhat more In-volvement, Affiliation, and Teacher Support. The comparison of perceived and preferred environment measures of students in the exemplary teacher's classes provides evidence about the favorableness of the classroom environments created by this exemplary biology teacher.

In another study, students in an exemplary mathematics teacher's class perceived their classroom environment more favorably than did students in four comparison eighth-grade classes on the majority of the learning environment dimensions assessed. A consideration of the standard deviations for class means obtained with previous comparison groups found sizable differences of approximately one standard deviation between the exemplary teacher's class and the other mathematics classes on the dimensions Teacher Control, Personalization, Participation, and Differentiation. The largest difference between exemplary and nonexemplary teachers' classes was approximately two standard deviations on the Order and Organization scale.

WHAT IS AN EXEMPLARY TEACHER?

What is exemplary practice? Whose definition of exemplary should be used to identify exemplary teachers? In the Exemplary Practice in Science and Mathematics Education study, we asked for nominations from a group within which there appeared to be a consensus on what constituted exemplary practice. However, in the community at large, such a consensus is not likely to be obtained. The problems of alternative perspectives on what constitutes exemplary practice were highlighted in a study undertaken by Kenneth Tobin and several of his colleagues (1988) soon after completion of the Exemplary Practice in Science and Mathematics Education study.

Mr. Hoskin, a high school science teacher from a southern U.S. state, was recommended as an outstanding teacher who was likely to agree to participate in a study of science teaching and learning. A university science educator nominated Mr. Hoskin based on his fine reputation among fellow teachers and district-level educators. When approached, Mr. Hoskin readily agreed to be involved in a study in which his five science classes would be observed over a period of about six weeks. The classes involved were one tenth-grade general science class, one twelfth-grade physics class, and three chemistry classes containing students from grades ten, eleven, and twelve.

When he taught, Mr. Hoskin emphasized the learning of science facts and algorithms and procedures that could be used to obtain correct answers to questions on tests and examinations. Homework activities also tended to have low cognitive demands. Mr. Hoskin's procedure was to assign a homework activity as the last in-class activity. Typically, this required students to complete problems from the text or a worksheet. In most cases, students applied a formula to a number of problems that had similar form. The work was routine and required little thinking that could be validly classified as "scientific." The purpose of this type of engagement appeared to be solely to perform well on tests and exams or to obtain a good grade.

Mr. Hoskin disagreed with the need to teach high-level cognitive objectives rather than algorithms and procedures. He also noted that he had a responsibility to prepare students for further education, and since student performance was the criterion on which his effectiveness would be judged, he had to ensure that students passed.

A common activity in all science classes was for students to copy notes that were summarized on the board by the teacher. One frequent problem with this strategy was that the teacher elaborated on the notes and clarified what was meant as the students copied them from the chalkboard. As a consequence, students were effectively required to engage in two tasks at one time. Because of the importance of having good notes to prepare for tests and examinations, students would most likely concentrate their efforts on copying the notes and not attend to the oral presentation as closely as they should in order to gain the most benefit from it.

Mr. Hoskin indicated that he believed students could do more than one thing at a time. His comments reflected a concern for getting the work done, but did not take account of what students would learn as a result of completing the work.

The laboratory activities that were undertaken in Mr. Hoskin's class tended to be of a cookbook type whereby students followed a recipe in a laboratory workbook or from a worksheet in order to obtain a predetermined answer. Also, there was little interpretation of the results. The main involvement of students was in collecting data, and in most groups one or two students monopolized the use of equipment and produced a laboratory report. The other group members tended to watch data collection, and they copied the laboratory report. Since so many of the schools' objectives related to process skills, and because laboratory activities were regularly scheduled, the research team felt that engagement in laboratories should have provided students with opportunities to plan and interpret investigations.

Tests provided a focus for the academic work in each of the observed classes. During activities, the teacher made specific note of the content and procedures that needed to be learned for the test. This practice, which was adopted in each class, together with the bi-weekly testing schedule, focused student attention on aspects of the course likely to be tested. It was apparent that the assessment was used to ensure that certain activities were regarded as important. During the class, the teacher routinely identified the content likely to be tested.

There was little doubt that the gulf was wide between Mr. Hoskin's perspectives on teaching and learning and those of the research team members. However, other parties also had strong views of Mr. Hoskin's teaching performance. Soon after the study was completed, the research team was stunned to observe this headline in the local newspaper: "Hoskin Named Teacher of the Year by Science Group." Although members of the research team were pleased at the recognition given to a hard-working teacher they had come to know and respect over a period of six weeks of intensive observation and interviews, they were at the same time perplexed. Why would one set of educators regard this teacher as exemplary, and another set of educators have serious concerns about the quality of science education in his classes?

The findings concerning the analysis of Mr. Hoskin's teaching suggest that exemplary teaching is in the eye of the beholder. Such an interpretation assumes that observations are theory laden. Personal epistemologies, values, and beliefs determine what one takes account of and decides to note and emphasize in an analysis and report on teaching and learning. Practices regarded as exemplary from one perspective might not be regarded as exemplary from another. From a constructivist perspective, Mr. Hoskin was not exemplary, and many of the activities in which students engaged were not optimal for learning science with understanding.

The study of teaching and learning in Mr. Hoskin's class highlighted the subjectivity of classroom research and the importance of epistemologies, beliefs, and values in describing teaching and learning practices. Researchers ought to make explicit the cognitive frames used to describe and interpret classroom processes. Furthermore, the

findings are a salient reminder that all teachers should be encouraged
to raise questions on what they are doing and why they continue to
teach the way they do. Mr. Hoskin was a hard worker and a dedicated
teacher. Given the rewards he received for his teaching efforts, there is
considerable doubt that he would be likely to make significant
changes to his "winning formula." However, reflection on the relationships between his stated objectives and the activities in which
students engaged might have produced dissonance in Mr. Hoskin's
mind that could have resulted in changed practices.

MODELS FOR IMPROVING TEACHING

A diversity of teaching approaches was very apparent during our
studies of exemplary practices. We can learn a great deal from such
diversity. Researchers should resist the temptation to search for
particular strategies that might be adopted by most successful teachers. Such a search appears to be based on a false premise, that is, that
there is an optimal way to structure learning environments. A more
fruitful direction for research might be to examine well a chosen case
(e.g., an exemplary teacher) to find out what he or she does in the
classroom, explore why he or she adopts the practices that are
identified, and contemplate the implications for that teacher's changing in a given direction. Grounded theories to guide teachers and
teacher educators in their endeavors to enhance the learning of
mathematics and science can emerge from such investigations.

What is clear from our investigations of exemplary teachers over
the past five years is the overly simplistic nature of the images conveyed
by those who advocate studying exemplary teachers as role models to
be emulated by novices. There is no doubt that videotapes of any of
these teachers in action could provide a context in which a change
process could begin. Critical instances from a videotaped lesson could
be identified and used as a basis for discussion and for stimulating
reflection on a teacher's personal teaching style. According to Donald
Schon (1987), reflective practices can initiate an intention to change,
which appears to be an essential ingredient for improvement of
teaching. Studies of teachers identified as exemplary are fertile
grounds for learning about teaching and learning. Even when these
teachers do not appear to be effective, the questions that arise and the

answers that are obtained represent invaluable contributions to the accumulating knowledge about teaching and teachers. But what should be the foci for reflections on teaching?

Since our study of Mr. Hoskin's teaching was completed we have undertaken other studies, some of which have involved the study of teachers identified as exemplary. Invariably the studies have not turned out as we expected. For example, we undertook an intensive study of two high school science teachers in an endeavor to understand how self-paced learning and associated teaching strategies facilitated student learning of high-level cognitive concepts (e.g., Tobin, Kahle, and Fraser, forthcoming). For a variety of reasons, the two teachers in the study did not build and maintain environments conducive to learning high-level cognitive concepts. Instead the activities resembled those described in Mr. Hoskin's classes. As we grappled to make sense of why the classes were implemented as we perceived them to be, we learned how beliefs and metaphors were used by teachers to make sense of their teaching roles. And we gained insights into the manner in which teachers' cognitive characteristics influenced what they did as they implemented the science curriculum. Those insights proved to be a key in follow-up studies of teacher change and enhancement of teaching and learning (Tobin, in press).

The idea that metaphors could be used as a "master switch" to change belief sets came in a study conducted in Australia (Tobin, Kahle, and Fraser, forthcoming). One teacher in this study, Peter, conceptualized his management role as his being "captain of the ship." When the context was right, Peter became the captain of the ship and his students were regarded as the crew. As captain of the ship, Peter was assertive and businesslike. He was in charge of the class and emphasized whole-class activities in order to maintain control of a teacher-centered and teacher-paced learning environment. Peter was particularly severe on students who stepped out of line and often scolded them in a strong voice. In this mode, he called on nonvolunteers and ensured that all students listened and participated in an appropriate manner. The teacher defined the students' and his own expected behavior in activities in terms of the metaphor he used to understand management. The metaphor (and associated images) became a filter for formulating beliefs associated with management in the context in which Peter thought it was relevant to manage the class in this way. He did not believe it was always appropriate to be captain of the ship; some contexts required different management styles. In another context, Peter believed he should be an "entertainer."

When Peter was entertaining the class, he was humorous, interactive, and amenable to student noise and risque behavior. Whole-class activities were appropriate for both metaphors. The captain of the ship gave orders and explanations to the entire crew and the entertainer performed to the whole audience. In both contexts the teacher was in charge, just as the captain manages the ship and the entertainer manages the show.

What was so interesting in Peter's teaching was the quite distinct teaching style associated with each metaphor for managing student behavior. As Peter switched metaphors a great many variables changed as well. This finding suggests that teachers might be assisted to construct new metaphors for specific teaching roles as a possible means of assisting them to improve their classroom learning environment.

Tobin (in press) described how identification of salient teaching roles and the metaphors used to conceptualize them offers the possibility of changing what teachers do in the classroom. The metaphor used to make sense of a role is a master switch for teachers' associated belief sets. If a switch is thrown (i.e., the metaphor is changed), a host of changes follow (i.e., as new beliefs are deemed relevant to the role) in the classroom. Reconceptualizing a role in terms of a new metaphor appears to switch an entirely different set of beliefs into operation. Organizing roles, metaphors, and belief sets in this way highlights the importance of the teacher's framing of the context in determining whether or not particular actions are taken in the classroom. It is possible for teachers to have a variety of context-specific conceptualizations for a given role. Whether or not specific teacher beliefs will influence classroom practices depends on the perceived relevance or utility of the role to the circumstances that apply in the classroom. The teacher's framing of the context in which learning is to occur is an important factor in determining what is done in the classroom. For example, a teacher might believe that in certain circumstances it is desirable to be a gardener (i.e., a teacher) nourishing the seedlings (i.e., the children). However, in the circumstances that prevail on another day, a teacher might decide that it is more appropriate to be a police officer.

The metaphors used to make sense of the roles and the belief sets associated with particular actions are important factors that might be productive foci for reflection. Teachers can identify the salient metaphors for specific teaching roles and consider whether or not alternatives would lead to improvements in the classroom. If teachers decide to alter the metaphors they use to understand particular roles, beliefs previously associated with the role might be perceived to be no longer relevant to that role. Beliefs consistent with the new metaphor can then be deemed relevant and influence what teachers do as they plan and implement the curriculum.

CONCLUSIONS

The idea that exemplary teaching practices could be cataloged to provide a basis for teacher education was appealing, but oversimplified. However, investigations of teachers regarded as exemplary have led to the development of rich descriptions of teaching and learning and of models for what teachers do and why they do what they do. These models provide insights into the conditions associated with teacher change and provide a rationale for the practices of teacher educators. Further studies of teachers regarded as exemplary promise a context in which theoretical models for teaching and teacher change can be further explicated.

REFERENCES

Berliner, David C. "In Pursuit of the Expert Pedagogue," *Educational Researcher* 15, no. 7 (1986): 5–13.

Fraser, Barry J. *Classroom Environment*. London: Croom Helm, 1986.

National Commission on Excellence in Education. *A Nation at Risk: The Imperative for Educational Reform*. Washington, D.C.: U. S. Government Printing Office, 1983.

Penick, John E., and Yager, Robert E. "The Search for Excellence in Science Education," *Phi Delta Kappan* 64 (1983): 621–623.

Sanford, Julie P. "Management of Science Classroom Tasks and Effects on Students' Learning Opportunities," *Journal of Research in Science Teaching* 24 (1987): 249–265.

Schon, Donald A. *Educating the Reflective Practitioner*. San Francisco: Jossey-Bass, 1987.

Shulman, Lee S. "Those Who Understand: Knowledge Growth in Teaching," *Educational Researcher* 15, no. 2 (1986): 4–14.

Tobin, Kenneth. "Changing Metaphors and Beliefs: A Master Switch for Teaching," *Theory Into Practice*, in press.

Tobin, Kenneth; Espinet, Mariona; Byrd, Stephen E.; and Adams, Darryl. "Alternative Perspectives of Effective Science Teaching," *Science Education* 72 (1988): 433–451.

Tobin, Kenneth, and Fraser, Barry J., eds. *Exemplary Practice in Science and Mathematics Education.* Perth: Curtin University of Technology, 1987.

Tobin, Kenneth; Kahle, Jane B.; and Fraser, Barry J., eds. *Opening Windows into Science Classrooms: Teaching for High Level Cognitive Learning.* London: Falmer Press, forthcoming.

von Glasersfeld, Ernst. *The Construction of Knowledge.* Seaside, Calif.: Systems Inquiry Series, Intersystems Publication, 1987.

Part IV

Cognition, Engagement, Cooperation, and Motivation

— 11 —

Students' Cognition and Classroom Instruction

Stephanie L. Knight and Hersholt C. Waxman

Traditionally, studies of classroom instruction have investigated the relationship between teacher behaviors and student achievement, assuming a direct relationship between the two. Recently, however, the role of students' thought processes as mediators between teaching and learning has been emphasized. This new approach has resulted in changes both in the questions researchers ask and in the methodology they employ to attempt to answer these questions. This new paradigm enables both teachers and researchers to examine teaching and learning through the eyes of students in the classroom. The results can be used to understand and, ultimately, improve classroom instruction.

This chapter will focus on classroom instruction from a student cognition perspective. In particular, we summarize the results of selected studies that examine the relations among students' perceptions of their use of cognitive strategies, students' perceptions of specific instruction and generic teacher behaviors related to these strategies, students' perceptions of classroom environment, and students' academic achievement.

The chapter contains three main parts. First, a brief introduction will provide background information on the student mediating paradigm in order to establish a frame of reference for discussion of selected studies of students' perceptions of classroom processes. The rationale for investigating instruction from the point of view of its recipients will be presented in this section. Next, the findings of selected studies of students' perceptions will be summarized. In the last section, the implications of this approach for classroom instruction will be examined.

STUDENT MEDIATING PARADIGM

Most of the information to date on behaviors associated with effective classroom instruction has been accumulated through studies conducted within the process-product paradigm. (See, e.g., the review of process-product research by Needels and Gage in this volume). In general, trained observers used low-inference coding instruments to quantify types and frequencies of individual teacher behaviors, which were then correlated with student outcomes. Through the use of a descriptive-correlational-experimental research approach (Gage, 1985), sets of instructional behaviors were identified that have become synonymous with the term "effective teaching" (e.g., Brophy and Good, 1986; Rosenshine and Stevens, 1986). For the most part, however, the student outcomes used as indicators of effective teaching were limited to the results of standardized achievement tests that focused on basic skills attainment. And when these teaching behaviors have been used to help students acquire higher-order thinking skills, mixed results have occurred. In fact, there is some evidence that the use of certain types of teacher behaviors found to be effective for teaching basic skills may actually hinder acquisition of critical thinking skills (Knight and Waxman, 1989).

Although the observation methods typically employed within the process-product paradigm have been useful for acquiring certain types of information, they may not provide adequate knowledge about instructional behaviors for developing other types of outcomes. For example, they have not proven to be very effective in gathering information about teaching and learning strategies for promoting the higher-level thinking that may be embedded in mental events or interaction patterns that are not readily observable. Furthermore, they assume a direct relationship between teacher behaviors and student outcomes.

The student mediating paradigm extends the teaching-learning connection assumed by the process-product paradigm by suggesting that the link is mediated by student cognitions that may not always be readily observable. This extension reflects a change in perspective of the teaching and learning process from a behaviorist to an information-processing point of view. From a behaviorist perspective, teaching is viewed as the stimulus that elicits a direct learning response from students. In contrast, Information-processing theory views students as active interpreters or mediators of teacher behaviors, instead of passive recipients of informational input (Wittrock, 1974, 1978, 1986). This emphasis on internal cognitive processes has resulted in a movement away from a total reliance on assessments of overt behavior and a move toward examining mental processes and perceptions that previously were not considered to be amenable to study.

Student perceptions, from this perspective, function as mediators of student behaviors and outcomes. These behaviors may include overt actions that can be recognized by outside observers, such as time on task or student question-response patterns. However, they may also include covert mental processes that cannot be detected by observation, such as the use of certain cognitive and metacognitive strategies. Students first selectively perceive and interpret classroom processes. Their interpretation cues or reinforces cognitive processes (which may be covert or result in overt behaviors), which in turn influence achievement. This mediation may explain certain inconsistencies in the findings of other research studies on instruction. When students interpret instruction in a manner consistent with the intentions of the instructor, the relationship between instruction and student learning appears to be direct. However, when student interpretation and teacher intention do not match, the expected or desired outcomes are not achieved. In this manner, a teacher's instructional behaviors may be effective for some students and not for others or may be affected by other classroom process variables that impact student perceptions.

The challenge, then, appears to be for researchers to bring students' covert mental processes to the surface so that their relationship to student outcomes can be investigated. Once these covert processes are made overt, they can presumably be recognized and classified. This, in fact, is the approach that many researchers have taken by eliciting and analyzing verbal protocols or "think-aloud" interviews. In this manner, researchers can investigate what students actually do, not what they think or say they do. Despite problems with methodology, this approach has yielded a great deal of information, particularly in the area of problem solving by experts and novices (Tuma and Reif, 1980).

Although what both students and teachers actually do, according to unbiased observers, is important, another equally important approach can be taken within the student mediating-process paradigm. Recent research has begun to examine the critical role that students' perceptions of classroom instruction play in teaching and influencing achievement (Wittrock, 1986). This research assumes that better understanding and improvement of teaching can emerge by knowing the effects of teaching on students' thought processes that mediate achievement. Classroom teachers have long been aware that students do not always respond to instruction in the manner in which it is intended. Since students are active interpreters of teacher behaviors, instruction as experienced by the student may be different from the intended instruction. Furthermore, cultural, ethnic, and linguistic differences may influence student interpretations of instruction (Padron and Knight, 1989).

Student responses during interviews or on self-report instruments have been found to be realistic and reliable measures of classroom environment, processes, and teacher behaviors that may not be easily detected by use of observation instruments (Fraser, 1986; Walberg, 1976). Studies, for example, that compared students' and classroom observers' reports of classroom processes have found that students' perceptions agreed significantly with the measures collected from experienced classroom observers (Fox et al., 1983; Stallings, Needels, and Stayrook, 1979). Although this finding is interesting, contrary findings would not necessarily invalidate the use of student perception data when the issues at question involve differential student interpretation of classroom processes or the match between teacher intention and student interpretation. Student perception data have been criticized because there may be a discrepancy between what students say and what they do (Doyle, 1977). However, student perception methodology also provides us with a vehicle for understanding why this mismatch occurs. Perhaps more relevant to the focus of this chapter are the findings documented by Fraser and Walberg (1981) and Rosenshine (1971). They report that student perception measures have typically explained more variance in students' postachievement than has classroom observation data. Students' perceptions, whether valid or not, affect their performance and therefore merit investigation.

In summary, the student mediating paradigm suggests that how students perceive and react to instruction, learning tasks, and classroom environment is essential to their academic achievement. This paradigm also assumes that classroom processes experienced by the student may be quite different from the observed or intended processes. Therefore, it is of great importance for us to understand what students think about classroom instruction and environment and how these perceptions affect their cognitive processes and academic achievement. Likewise, it is of great importance for us to understand how these perceptions differ among various groups in the classroom and how these perceptions explain differences in academic achievement within and across groups. If the connections between students' perceptions of their cognitions in response to their perceptions of classroom instruction can be uncovered and eventually tied to achievement, the match between teaching and learning for all students can ultimately be improved.

RESEARCH ON STUDENT PERCEPTIONS

Historically, there has been a great deal of research involving student perceptions. This research has investigated questions concerning students' attitudes, motivation, perceptions of classroom processes including learning environment and classroom climate, and, more recently, cognitive thought processes. Although it is beyond the scope of this chapter to review each of these areas, brief overviews will be provided in the following sections in order to place in context current research that investigates student perceptions in relation to classroom instruction. Findings of selected research that examines classroom instruction from a student cognition perspective will be presented. The final part of this section will focus on the ways the current research differs from traditional approaches that examine classroom instruction.

Student Cognitions

Wittrock (1986) provides a current review of the research on student cognitions in his chapter in the third edition of the *Handbook of Research on Teaching*. He defines student cognitions as "the student perceptions, expectations, attentional processes, motivations, attributions, memories, generations, understandings, beliefs, attitudes, learning strategies, and metacognitive processes that mediate achievement" (p. 297). He describes the findings of research in the following areas: students' perceptions and expectations, attention, motivation, learning and memory, comprehension and knowledge acquisition, learning strategies, and metacognitive processes.

In general, the findings provide support for the study of instruction using student perceptions and imply that students' mediating processes can help explain results that may be difficult to understand from a process-product view of the relationship between teaching and student achievement. Furthermore, the research provides support for the use of the individual student and the teacher-student dyad as appropriate units of statistical analyses, since the interpretation of instruction may differ among pupils within the same classroom.

Wittrock's review of cognitive and metacognitive strategies perhaps provides the link between the affective and cognitive dimensions of students' thought processes. Learning or cognitive strategies, as defined by Weinstein and Mayer (1986), are the actions and thoughts that occur during learning and influence students' motivation to learn and their subsequent learning outcomes. Metacognitive strategies, so closely linked to cognitive strategies that they are often difficult to separate, compose an individual's knowledge about his or her own cognitive processes and refer to the monitoring and regulation of these cognitive processes (Flavell, 1976). Wittrock briefly summarizes the research in this area and concludes, although the findings are still tentative, that students can be taught cognitive and metacognitive strategies that will help them achieve in several content areas. However, recent research has documented mixed, and often disappointing, results involving students' strategy maintenance and transfer of these strategies after specific instruction (Pressley et al., 1989). Perhaps further investigation of the conditions surrounding strategy training needs to be conducted to determine the role that student perceptions of strategy instruction play in the acquisition, durability, and generalizability of students' strategies.

Perceptions of Cognitive Strategy Use

One of the first steps in determining the relationship between students' cognitions and their perceptions of classroom instruction is to examine students' cognitions. Researchers need to determine the kinds of strategies that students are currently using, since there may be interference between existing strategies and those that may be most effective for the task at hand or that the teacher wants to introduce.

Another question involves whether different individuals and different ethnic, linguistic, or cultural groups exhibit differences in patterns of use or in preferences for certain types of strategies that might influence their academic achievement. For example, strategies that enable students to link new information to prior knowledge may exhibit age- or culture-related differences and therefore may be an important source of variation for strategy use and outcomes (Steffenson, Joag-Dev, and Anderson, 1979). In addition, certain populations, especially young, low-ability, or culturally different students, may not be able to tap in on necessary prior knowledge without help or may not possess the knowledge required to establish the linkage.

In a series of studies designed to investigate the cognitive strategies that elementary and junior high school students use during higher-level thinking tasks in a variety of content areas, we have obtained findings that are generally consistent with the findings of other studies on students' learning strategies (e.g., see Pressley et al., 1989). These studies investigate in some detail individual differences in reports of strategy use. Our results indicate that higher-ability and older students use more strategies during higher-level tasks than lower-ability or younger students. The differences have been primarily quantitative, with some indication that higher-ability and older students also employ more strategies classified as strong by previous research. Although gender differences have emerged in students' strategy use (Knight and Padron, 1986; Waxman, 1987), these findings have not revealed a consistent pattern of differences. Monolingual and Anglo students reportedly use more strategies than bilingual or Hispanic students (Padron and Waxman, 1988; Padron, Knight, and Waxman, 1986). In general, minority students, low-ability students, and students in lower grade levels report relatively little strategy use during higher-level thinking activities in mathematics (Waxman, Knight, and Owens, 1990; Waxman et al., 1988); in reading (Knight, 1990; Knight and Padron, 1988); in social studies (Knight, Waxman, and Padron, 1989, 1987); and in science (Knight and Waxman, forthcoming). However, they can be taught to use effective strategies (Knight and Padron, 1988).

Perceptions of Classroom Processes

Classroom processes encompass several different components that are experienced by students in the classroom. These include the classroom learning environment, generic teacher behaviors identified by previous process-product research, and specific instruction tied to particular content within a subject area. Individual or group differences may play a role in interpretation of teacher behaviors and learning environment. For instance, students who share ethnic, cultural, or linguistic backgrounds may interpret events similarly and these interpretations may be very different from the interpretations of students from other backgrounds (Padron and Knight, 1989). The questions of interest involve students' perceptions of the type and frequency of processes in these three areas and the nature of individual differences in perceptions.

Specific Strategy Instruction. Specific strategy instruction refers to direct instruction provided by the teacher in specific cognitive strategies. In conjunction with some of the studies previously described that investigated students' cognitive strategy use, students were asked to describe the type and extent of specific strategy instruction they received in their classrooms (Knight, 1990; Knight, Waxman, and Padron, 1989; Knight and Waxman, forthcoming; Waxman, Knight, and Owens, 1990). Although students report that some strategy instruction occurs in mathematics, science, social studies, and reading, specific strategy instruction is relatively infrequent. For the most part, students reported using more strategies than they perceived were being taught by their teachers. Furthermore, Anglo students report receiving significantly more strategy instruction than their Hispanic counterparts reported (Waxman and Knight, 1987). At this point, however, there is very little information about individual differences in students' responses to strategy instruction (Pressley et al., 1989).

Generic Teacher Behaviors. Research on teacher effectiveness has identified certain behaviors as effective, with slight variations, for most content areas and contexts. These behaviors are referred to as "generic teacher behaviors" and include pacing, feedback, and modeling; they form the basis for many of the teacher evaluation measures used to make retention and promotion decisions in public schools. In contrast with instruction in specific strategies, students perceived that a high degree of instruction associated with generic teacher behaviors was used in basic skills instruction (Knight, 1990; Knight, Waxman, and Padron, 1989; Knight and Waxman, forthcoming; Waxman, Knight, and Owens, 1990). In general, means were higher and standard deviations were lower in this area of classroom processes. However, students perceived relatively few generic teacher behaviors that have been associated with higher-level outcomes (i.e., tolerance for divergent responses, emphasis on process as opposed to product, opportunity for higher-level thinking, etc.). Despite these similarities in perceptions, there is evidence of differences among ethnic groups in their perception of generic teacher behaviors. For example, in a study comparing over eight hundred urban black and Hispanic elementary students' perceptions of classroom instruction (Waxman, 1989), black students perceived their teachers to be more effective in the teacher behaviors of enthusiasm, pacing, feedback, and task orientation.

Classroom Learning Environment. One of the areas that has been extensively studied is the classroom learning environment or atmosphere that forms the context in which interactions between the teacher and students occur (e.g., see Fraser, 1986). Environment variables are generally categorized into Moos's (1974) three types of dimensions (see Fraser, 1986): relationship (teacher- student relationships, student-student relationships, and degree of involvement); personal development (directions of personal growth and enhancement); and system maintenance and change (environmental order and change, expectations, control).

Selected classroom environment dimensions have been found to be related to students' academic achievement (Fraser, 1986; Fraser and Fisher, 1982; Haertel, Walberg, and Haertel, 1981), and to improvement in school productivity (Walberg, 1983, 1984). Studies have recently found, however, that the learning environment in predominantly minority classrooms is significantly different than in classrooms of majority students (Waxman, forthcoming). In general, it has been found that black and Hispanic students perceive their learning environment to be significantly less favorable than do white students in the same classroom.

Classroom Processes and Student Strategy Use

The results of several studies reveal a direct relationship between students' perceptions of specific strategy instruction and their cognitive strategy use (Knight, 1990; Knight, Waxman, and Padron, 1989; Knight and Waxman, forthcoming; Waxman, Knight, and Owens, 1990). On the other hand, little direct relationship between student perceptions of generic teacher behaviors or their perceptions of classroom environment variables alone and students' reported cognitive strategy use emerges in any of the studies cited previously. However, when combined with students' perceptions of specific instruction in strategy use, perceptions of generic behaviors and classroom environment variables may cue students to use or dismiss specific strategies.

Although students can recognize specific instructional behaviors, the interpretation of sets of behaviors over time may actually cue students to use or abandon certain strategies during tasks. Students may actually perceive and respond to teacher behaviors and classroom processes in a hierarchical manner. More specifically, students may perceive instruction in a cognitive strategy, but the concurrent perception of another classroom process variable or a conflicting instructional behavior may take precedence. The student would recognize the instruction, but would not be able to adopt the cognitive strategy or would alter the response to instruction in a way not expected by the teacher. In a study that examined students' reported strategy use during problem-solving tasks in social studies and their perceptions of related instructional behaviors (Knight, Waxman, and Padron, 1989), students perceived instruction in the use of an organizing strategy, but they did not report actually using the strategy. Instead, they reported using two other strategies. Since they perceived this strategy instruction in conjunction with inappropriate instructional pacing, it is easy for us to visualize a classroom situation in which the teacher provides adequate strategy instruction, but then does not allow ample time during guided or independent practice for this strategy to actually be implemented by students. In other words, students respond to the limitations imposed by time allotment rather than to the direct instruction.

Similarly, students may choose to respond to instruction according to their perceptions of the importance the teacher assigns to the content being taught or to the task assigned. For example, in the study previously mentioned (Knight, Waxman, and Padron, 1989), students who perceived that their teachers taught strategies that did not involve deep processing of content (i.e., guessing or getting help from peers) also avoided use of time-consuming strategies that might result in deep processing of social studies content. The type of strategy specifically taught appeared to cue them to engage in the level of processing they perceived the teacher desired. Since students tend to expend effort in relation to the anticipated payoff (Doyle, 1983), they did not report going beyond the shallow processing they thought the teacher required, despite task demands of a different nature. Whether teacher intentions matched student interpretation in this case was not determined, but this would be an interesting question to pursue. Although the design and analysis used in this study does not allow causal inferences to be made, the findings suggest that students interpret and react to classroom instruction by selectively responding to what they perceive are the most salient or important of conflicting behaviors.

In general, when students perceive direct instruction in cognitive strategies without the existence of interfering or conflicting teacher behaviors, they respond by using the suggested strategy. However, they may spontaneously add other cognitive strategies that are cued by instruction but not perceived as being specifically mentioned by the teacher. For example, students may respond to perceived instruction in summarizing during a reading comprehension task by using a self-questioning strategy to aid in the summary even though they did not perceive specific instruction in self-questioning (Knight, 1990).

In conclusion, students appear to respond to specific instruction if they don't perceive conflicting behaviors that cue them to do otherwise. Student interpretation of cues may result in the tendency for students to engage in "invention" when exposed to either direct or indirect instruction (Doyle, 1983). The finding discussed previously—that students report using more strategies than they perceive being taught—can perhaps be explained by this tendency toward invention.

Relations Between Perceptions and Achievement

As previously discussed, student perceptions of classroom processes appear to exhibit both a direct and an indirect relationship to student achievement. One study investigated the relationship between students' reported use of a cognitive reading strategy, students' perceptions of classroom processes, and students' achievement on a variety of standardized basic skills and critical thinking tests and

tasks requiring higher-order skills (Knight, 1990). Although a relationship between the combination of students' reported use of the
strategies of Imaging and Changing Speed and success on the reading
task and metacognitive indicator emerged, the study did not document a direct relationship between students' perceptions of instructional behaviors and any of the outcome measures. However,
additional analyses revealed a strong relationship between students'
perceptions of instructional behaviors and their reported strategy use.
In this case, student perceptions of teacher behaviors appear to
function as mediators of their strategy use, which in turn influences
achievement.

However, another study investigated the impact of black and
Hispanic elementary students' perceptions of generic instructional
behaviors on their performance on a standardized achievement test,
and found that students' perceptions of instruction exhibited differential, but direct, effects on their reading achievement (Waxman, 1989).
Black students' perceptions of their teachers' use of instructional time
and structuring comments significantly explained their reading
achievement, while Hispanic students' perceptions of pacing affected
their reading achievement.

SUMMARY

The group of studies reviewed in each of the previous sections
differs from traditional studies of classroom instruction in several
ways. Perhaps the most obvious difference is the use of student
perceptions as the primary source of information about student
cognitions and classroom processes. Although this information may
not correspond to the "reality" documented by an unbiased observer,
it may better represent the range of reality for individual students and
subgroups within the classroom. This approach does not preclude
systematic, unbiased observation as a means of generating information about classroom instruction; the two approaches provide different
types of information.

Since the questions asked generally focus on individual and
subgroup perceptions, the unit of analysis is the individual student as
opposed to the class. Patterns of perceptions that focus on individual
differences such as age, grade level, gender, ability, and ethnicity can

be explored in this manner. However, since teachers must frequently deal with students combined in large and small groups, patterns across and within subgroups in the classrooms are also investigated. It is helpful to determine if ethnic, cultural, or linguistic minorities in the classroom tend to interpret instruction in ways that are different from other groups in the classroom, but researchers must still be alert to the possibility of greater differences within groups than across groups.

Another property of the research previously reviewed concerns the type of research question posed. The questions asked reflect a more complex view of the classroom than was often explored through observation of discrete behaviors that did not take differential student perceptions into consideration or explore patterns of influences on perceptions.

In short, research on classroom instruction conducted from a student cognition perspective complements and extends previous research on classroom instruction in several ways. The use of student perception methodology enables researchers to examine perceived instructional and environmental influences on students' thought processes and the influences of both of these on academic achievement. Furthermore, the relationship among various classroom processes can be investigated to reveal the effects of various patterns of combination of perceptions of generic and specific instruction with classroom environment variables.

IMPLICATIONS FOR CLASSROOM INSTRUCTION

Research on teaching from a student cognition perspective has the potential for providing both direct and indirect ways to improve classroom instruction. Information gained about students' perceptions of cognitive strategy instruction and their subsequent reported strategy use can be used to improve strategy instruction. The view that students can be successfully taught to use strategies that they would not necessarily adopt independently implies that "student failures to use strategies are often *instructional failures*" (Pressley et al., 1989). By documenting and examining the patterns of perception of instruction and strategy use, instructional decisions can be made that minimize the mismatch between teaching and learning and enable teachers to plan for more effective instruction.

Knowing students' existing strategy preference and use will also enable teachers to avoid problems that result from strategy interference or conflict. Additional research investigating students' strategy use and response to instruction may result in the identification of common response patterns similar to those uncovered through research on error analysis in mathematics (e.g., see Schoenfeld, 1985). Teachers could then use information about strategy "bugs"or common misinterpretations to plan instruction and to diagnose student difficulties. Information about individual and group differences influenced by cultural, ethnic, or linguistic differences may eventually enable the teacher to predict how particular students will react to the conditions of instruction. This research can also be done in the classroom by the individual teacher using self-report and "think-aloud" procedures to provide information specific to a particular class.

In a more global sense, findings from a student cognition approach to the study of classroom instruction foster a more complex interpretation of teaching and learning that enhances the roles of the participants in the process. Students do not always respond to instruction as intended. Their interpretation of the situation, not merely of the facts associated with the situation, determines their behavior (Stipek, 1986). Teachers need to be aware that their use of generic and specific instructional behaviors combine to influence students' interpretation of the situation and, ultimately, their cognitive processing and achievement. Effective teaching requires more than mere execution of individual skills such as wait time or modeling and extends beyond direct presentation of content. Effective teaching requires teachers to understand students' thought processes and then to facilitate their students' mediation of both content and instruction. In order to accomplish this, teachers will need to know how students interpret instruction as well as content and will base instructional decision making on knowledge of the relationships among subject matter, student characteristics and perceptions, and pedagogical principles.

REFERENCES

Brophy, Jere E., and Good, Thomas L. "Teacher Behavior and Student Achievement." in *Handbook of Research on Teaching*, 3d ed., edited by Merlin Wittrock, pp. 328–375. New York: Macmillan, 1986.

Doyle, Walter. "Paradigms for Research on Teacher Effectiveness." In *Review of Research in Education*, vol. 5, edited by Lee Shulman, pp. 163–195. Itasca, Ill.: Peacock, 1977.

Doyle, Walter. "Academic Work," *Review of Educational Research* 53 (1983): 159–199.

Flavell, John. "Meta-cognitive Aspects of Problem Solving." In *The Nature of Intelligence*, edited by Lauren Resnick, pp. 231–238. Hillsdale, N.J.: Erlbaum, 1976.

Fox, Ronald; Peck, Robert; Blattstein, Abraham; and Blattstein, Deborah. "Student Evaluation of Teacher as a Measure of Teacher Behavior and Teacher Impact on Students," *Journal of Educational Research* 77 (1983): 16–21.

Fraser, Barry J. "Two Decades of Research on Perceptions of Classroom Learning Environment." In *The Study of Learning Environments*, edited by Barry J. Fraser. Salem, Ore.: Assessment Research, 1986.

Fraser, Barry J., and Fisher, Darrell. "Predicting Students' Outcomes from Their Perceptions of Classroom Psychosocial Environment," *American Educational Research Journal* 19 (1982): 498–518.

Fraser, Barry J., and Walberg, Herbert J. "Psychosocial Learning Environment in Science Classrooms: A Review of Research," *Studies in Science Education* 8 (1981): 67–92.

Gage, Nathaniel. *Hard Gains in the Soft Sciences: The Case of Pedagogy*. Bloomington, Ind.: Phi Delta Kappa, 1985.

Haertel, Geneva; Walberg, Herbert J; and Haertel, Edward. "Socio-psychological Environments and Learning: A Quantitative Synthesis," *British Educational Research Journal* 7 (1981): 27–36.

Knight, Stephanie L. "The Effects of Cognitive Strategy Instruction on Elementary Students' Reading Outcomes." In *Cognitive and Social Perspectives for Literary Research and Instruction*, edited by Sandra McCormick and Jerry Zutell, pp. 241–251. Chicago: National Reading Conference, 1990.

Knight, Stephanie L., and Padron, Yolanda N. "Investigating Gender Differences in the Use of Cognitive Reading Strategies by Hispanic Students," *Journal of Educational Equity and Leadership* 6 (1986): 340–341.

Knight, Stephanie L., and Padron, Yolanda N. "Teaching Cognitive Reading Strategies to At-Risk Students." In *Teaching Strategies That Promote Higher-Level Thinking Skills for At-Risk Leaners*, edited by Hersholt C. Waxman, Stephanie L. Knight, and Yolanda N. Padron, pp. 8–17. La Marque, Tex.: Consortium for the Advancement of Professional Excellence, 1988.

Knight, Stephanie L., and Waxman, Hersholt C. "Effective Teaching of Critical Thinking Skills," *National Forum of Applied Educational Research Journal* 2, no. 1 (1989): 45–53.

Knight, Stephanie L., and Waxman, Hersholt C. "Analyzing Effective Teaching of Hispanic Students' Problem-solving Strategies in Science." In *National Association of Bilingual Education Annual*, edited by L. Malave. Fall River, Mass.: National Dissemination Center, forthcoming.

Knight, Stephanie L.; Waxman, Hersholt C.; and Padron, Yolanda N. "Investigating Hispanic Students' Cognitive Strategies in Social Studies," *Journal of Social Studies Research* 11 (1987): 15–19.

Knight, Stephanie, L.; Waxman, Hersholt C.; and Padron, Yolanda N. "Examining the Relationship between Classroom Instruction and Elementary Students'

Cognitive Strategies in Social Sciences." *Journal of Educational Research* 82 (1989): 270–276.

Moos, Rudy M. *The School Climate Scales: An Overview*. Palo Alto, Calif.: Consulting Psychologists Press, 1974.

Padron, Yolanda N., and Knight, Stephanie L. "Linguistic and Cultural Influences on Classroom Instruction." In *Leadership, Equity, and School Effectiveness*, edited by H. Prentice Baptiste, James Anderson, Judith Walker de Felix, and Hersholt C. Waxman, pp. 173–185. Newbury Park, Calif.: Sage, 1989.

Padron, Yolanda N.; Knight, Stephanie L.; and Waxman, Hersholt C. "Analyzing Bilingual and Monolingual Students' Perceptions of Their Reading Strategies," *Reading Teacher* 39 (1986): 430–435.

Padron, Yolanda N., and Waxman, Hersholt C. "Bilingual and Monolingual Students' Perceptions of Their Cognitive Reading Strategies," *Journal of Social Psychology* 128 (1988): 687–688.

Pressley, Michael; Goodchild, Fiona; Fleet, Joan; Zajchowski, Richard; and Evans, Ellis D. "The Challenges of Classroom Strategy Instruction," *Elementary School Journal* 89 (1989): 301–342.

Rosenshine, Barak. *Teaching Behaviors and Students' Achievement*. London: National Foundation for Educational Research, 1971.

Rosenshine, Barak, and Stevens, Robert. "Teaching Functions." In *Handbook of Research on Teaching*, 3d ed., edited by Merlin Wittrock, pp. 376–391. New York: Macmillan, 1986.

Schoenfeld, Alan H. *Mathematical Problem Solving*. Orlando, Florida: Academic Press, 1985.

Stallings, Jane; Needels, Margaret; and Stayrook, Nicholas. *The Teaching of Basic Reading Skills in Secondary Schools, Phase II and Phase III*. Menlo Park, Calif.: SRI International, 1979.

Steffenson, Margaret S.; Joag-Dev, Chitra; and Anderson, Richard. "A Cross-Cultural Perspective on Reading Comprehension," *Reading Research Quarterly* 15 (1979): 10–29.

Stipek, Deborah. "Children's Motivation to Learn." In *Academic Work and Educational Excellence*, edited by Tommy M. Tomlinson and Herbert J. Walberg, pp. 197–222. Berkeley, Calif.: McCutchan, 1986.

Tuma, David T., and Reif, Frederick, eds. *Problem Solving and Education: Issues in Teaching and Research*. Hillsdale, N.J.: Erlbaum, 1980.

Walberg, Herbert J. "Psychology of Learning Environments: Behavioral, Structural, or Perceptual?" In *Review of Research in Education*, vol. 4, edited by Lee Shulman, pp. 142–178. Itasca, Ill.: Peacock, 1976.

Walberg, Herbert J. "Education, Scientific Literacy, and Economic Productivity," *Daedalus* 112 (1983): 1–28.

Walberg, Herbert J. "Improving the Productivity of America's Schools," *Educational Leadership* 41, no. 8 (1984): 19–30.

Waxman, Hersholt C. "Investigating Sex-Related Differences in Mathematical Problem-Solving Strategies of Elementary School Students," *Perceptual and Motor Skills* 65 (1987): 825–926.

Waxman, Hersholt C. "Urban Black and Hispanic Elementary School Students' Perceptions of Classroom Instruction," *Journal of Research and Development in*

Education 22 (1989): 57–61.

Waxman, Hersholt C., ed. *The Study of Learning Environments*, vol. 5. Houston, Texas: University of Houston, forthcoming.

Waxman, Hersholt C., and Knight, Stephanie L. "Applying Research on Higher-Level Thinking to Classroom Instruction: Students' Perceptions of Cognitive Strategy Instruction in Mathematics," *Southwest Journal of Educational Research into Practice* 1 (1987): 40–43.

Waxman, Hersholt C.; Knight, Stephanie L.; and Owens, Emiel W. "The Relations between the Classroom Learning Environment and Students' Problem-Solving Strategies in Mathematics." In *The Study of Learning Environments*, vol. 4, edited by Hersholt C. Waxman and Chad D. Ellett, pp. 94–103. Houston, Texas: University of Houston, 1990.

Waxman, Hersholt C.; Knight, Stephanie L.; Owens, Emiel W.; Ebner, Kay; and Padron, Yolanda. "Effective Teaching of Math Problem-Solving Strategies to Elementary School Subjects," *Southwest Journal of Educational Research into Practice* 2 (1988): 35–42.

Weinstein, Claire, and Mayer, Richard. "The Teaching of Learning Strategies." In *Handbook of Research on Teaching*, 3d ed., edited by Merlin Wittrock, pp. 315–327. New York: Macmillan, 1986.

Wittrock, Merlin. "Learning as a Generative Process," *Educational Psychologist* 11 (1974): 87–95.

Wittrock, Merlin. "The Cognitive Movement in Instruction," *Educational Psychologist* 13: (1978): 15–30.

Wittrock, Merlin. "Students' Thought Processes." In *Handbook of Research on Teaching*, 3d ed., edited by Merlin Wittrock, pp. 214–229. New York: Macmillan, 1986.

——12——

Student Engagement:
When Recitation
Becomes Conversation

Martin Nystrand and Adam Gamoran

In the stream of critiques of American education that appeared during the 1980s, one persistent theme concerns the apathy and listlessness that seem to characterize secondary school classrooms. Life in schools is "emotionally flat"; neither students nor teachers get very excited about their work. In order to avoid conflicts, challenges, and other disruptions that might be emotionally or intellectually upsetting, teachers and students make bargains that allow both parties to get through their days satisfactorily. Teachers implicitly agree not to demand too much of students, and students acquiesce to the standards of conduct required by teachers. This gloomy picture is painted by several writers: National Commission on Excellence in

The authors appreciate the suggestions of Fred Newmann and Michael Smith. This paper was prepared at the National Center on Effective Secondary Schools, Wisconsin Center for Education Research, School of Education, University of Wisconsin-Madison, which is supported by a grant from the Office of Educational Research and Improvement (Grant No. G-008690007-89). Any opinions, findings, and conclusions or recommendations expressed in this publication are those of the authors and do not necessarily reflect the views of this agency or the U.S. Department of Education.

Education (1983); Sizer (1984); Goodlad (1984); Powell, Farrar, and Cohen (1985); and McNeil (1986).

What role do teachers play in these negotiations? The 1980s studies conclude that teachers are willing participants in the establishment of lifeless but orderly classrooms. McNeil (1986), in particular, describes the strategies teachers use to avoid disturbing the balance of order and control. By avoiding controversial topics, simplifying complex issues, and fragmenting tasks and information into small pieces that can be easily managed, teachers maintain control over students but at the same time eliminate enthusiasm and excitement in their classrooms. From these studies, one might conclude that many teachers have given up trying to engage students, and are just trying to get through the day.

Our research, however, suggests that most teachers seek something different. When asked what an ideal class session is like, many secondary-school teachers cited involved discussions, even arguments, in which students play a large role in directing the flow of topics and ideas. When asked what causes a class session to go exceptionally well, one eighth-grade English teacher put it this way:

> [The students] question you back. I give them a question, and they explain it, but then they go a little farther. And when they start asking me questions, that's when I think I know I've got them where I want them: where they're interested enough to want to find out more. Equal interaction; they can go away and I know we've both gotten something out of it.

These teachers were less clear on how one generates such lively class sessions. When asked, some spoke of particular students who instigated such discussions or of classes in which discussions just seemed to emerge. The teachers thought it was the *students'* contributions, not theirs, that made the difference.

In our view, the nature and extent of student engagement depends on contributions from both students and teachers. Instead of a "treaty" in which low academic demands are traded for good behavior, another kind of agreement is possible, one in which interesting challenges are met with willing participation. Although students admittedly play a key role in such bargains, as we were told, the teacher also plays a critical part in initiating activities that foster student engagement.

This chapter examines the nature of student engagement in the instructional activities of eighth- and ninth-grade English classes. It focuses on the teacher's pivotal role, while recognizing nonetheless that teachers cannot create student engagement all by themselves. Using examples from a study of eighth- and ninth-grade English classes, this chapter examines substantively engaging instruction to show how students become most profitably engaged and learn most in classrooms characterized by extensive interaction between students and teacher.

PROCEDURAL VERSUS SUBSTANTIVE ENGAGEMENT

As we explored the activities of junior and senior high classes, we noted two sorts of student engagement. The first, which we call "procedural engagement," characterizes the typical, lifeless classroom described in the studies noted at the beginning of this chapter. In such classes, students and teachers go through the motions of schooling: they ask and answer questions, assign and carry out homework, and maintain reasonable standards of comportment. Ordinarily, however, they do not grapple in depth with difficult or controversial academic work. Indeed, although most students are regularly engaged in school, they are less often engaged in their studies. Conformity to school procedures should not be confused with significant, ongoing engagement with challenging academic problems and issues. More than competence in school procedures, serious learning requires "substantive engagement," a sustained commitment to and involvement with academic work. Rather than a treaty between opposing sides, substantive engagement requires a contract between willing participants.

It is exceedingly difficult to distinguish between procedural and substantive engagement simply by observing students or asking them what they think about in class. From watching students, one can tell whether they are procedurally engaged or disengaged, but not whether they are seriously involved with the work. Substantively engaged students do not all look the same: some may appear to concentrate; others may gaze out the window. Student engagement depends on student effort, but indicators of this will vary with the nature of the curriculum and instructional activities in which students are involved. At the same time, we believe that some tasks and some patterns of interaction are inherently more substantively engaging. For these reasons, we study student engagement by examining the classroom activities in which students are involved.

To explore the relation between substantively engaging instruction and student learning, we studied eighth- and ninth-grade English instruction in eight midwestern communities. Sixteen middle schools, which fed into nine high schools, participated in the study. Of the eight communities, six were public school districts: three were in small-town or rural areas, with one junior high and one high school apiece; one was suburban, with three middle schools and one high school; and two were urban, adding five middle schools and three high schools to our sample. The other two communities contained Catholic high schools that drew students from a number of urban and suburban K-8 feeder schools. Over 1,100 students completed tests and questionnaires in the fall and spring of 1987–88 and 1988–89, and the teachers responded to questionnaires and interviews about classroom activities. Further details on the data collection are provided elsewhere (Nystrand and Gamoran, in press; Nystrand, forthcoming).

The following examples and general statements come from this sample of classes, as does the interview quotation presented above. We studied the discourse of instruction as evident in classroom talk and in reading and writing assignments. Our portrayal of procedural and substantive engagement, and their effects, is based on what we saw, and on what the teachers and students had to say.

QUALITY OF INSTRUCTIONAL DISCOURSE AS AN INDICATOR OF STUDENT ENGAGEMENT

Normally classroom discourse is recitation: the teacher asks a question to test recall, a student makes a response, and the teacher evaluates the answer and then moves on to the next question. Most of these exchanges occur at a fairly rapid clip of three or more questions a minute, and unless students fail to give acceptable answers, the teacher rarely follows up on a response. By contrast, other teachers engage their students in more probing and substantive discussions, and in the best of these classes, these exchanges resemble conversations in the extent and quality of their interaction.

To clarify some key distinctions between normal classroom discourse and high-quality, substantively engaging talk, we begin by analyzing two excerpts of classroom talk. In the first, a ninth-grade English teacher leads his class in a review of homework and study questions concerning Book I of *The Odyssey*:

Teacher: According to the poet, what is the subject of the Iliad?
Student: Achilles' anger.
Teacher: Where does the action of the first part of Book 1 take place when we enter the story?
Student: On the Achean ship?
Teacher: Well, they're not on their ships. Let's see if we can give you a little diagram. . . .
Student: Was it on the shore?
Teacher: Yes, it's on the shore. Let's see if we can kind of visualize where everything is here. [proceeds to draw on the board] . . . Remember that Troy is on the coast of Turkey—at the time called Asia Minor—so let's see if we can—okay—this is the scene, and all of the ships are anchored—a thousand ships are anchored here. . . . So the war has been going on now for how long?
Student: Ten years.
Teacher: "Ten years." You have to understand—the battle takes place only during the day time. . . . [draws some more on the board] So this is approximately what it looked like. . . . Now the city is immense—much larger probably than what we consider the [our own city]; it could be as large as all of [our own] county.
Student: There was a wall all the way around it?
Teacher: Oh, at least. Consider some of the walled cities of ancient times. . . .
Student: Didn't they put a wall up in Ireland?
Teacher: In Ireland? I'm not familiar with that. . . . So, let's take a look at some of the other questions. . . . What's the story behind the quarrel . . . it deals with Achilles and Briseis and Agamemnon and Chryses and Chryses' daughter Chryseis and how Agamemnon takes Briseis away from Achilles to replace the prize, Chryseis, who has gone back to her father. What is the result of the quarrel between Agamemnon and Achilles?
Student: He's not going to participate in the battle anymore.
Teacher: "He's not going to participate in the battle anymore." What's the common custom of Greek warfare and prizes?
Student: That the prizes that they get. . . .
[Recitation continues]

In this instructional episode, the teacher initiates nearly all the questions and neither picks up nor follows up on any student response. The teacher does no probing here, no working with responses that students make. One gets the impression that the teacher here follows a script, that he has planned the questions ahead of time, has asked them before, and, if he teaches this lesson again, will ask them again and in the same order regardless of who is in the class. And it is not just the questions that have been planned. For each question, the teacher has a particular answer in mind, as well: there are clearly right and wrong answers here. The purpose of this exchange is to test student knowledge.

This example of instructional discourse is recitation, which, as Mehan (1979) notes, typically consists of an *initiation* (the teacher's question), a *response* (a student's answer), and an *evaluation* (the teacher's response to the student's answer). Typically, teachers' evaluations of students' answers are a perfunctory "right" or "wrong," a "good" or an "okay," sometimes merely a nod, sometimes nothing (indicating a satisfactory student response). This three-part structure characterizes the normal procedures of classroom recitation, and students who regularly participate in such exchanges may be said to be procedurally engaged. Because recitation so completely typifies classroom discourse, we call it *normal classroom discourse*.

Now consider the teacher-student exchange which could not be more different from the previous one, in the following transcript from another ninth-grade English class studying *The Odyssey*:

Teacher: What does Odysseus do to the guys who eat the [lotus] flower?

First student: Drags them back by "main force" and ties them.

Teacher: What do they discover?

Second student: Don't they land on another island—is that the one?

Teacher: Actually, they go to two places in this chapter: the Land of the Lotus Eaters and the Cyclops. What does Odysseus want to do [there]?

Third student: Make friends and get food, provisions. . . .

Teacher: Why make friends?

Second student: What if they can't give it [provisions] to you?

Teacher: That's an important point—if they can't or won't; let's wait a minute on that. What does [Odysseus] want to do?

Fourth student: He's curious—wants to find out about the Cyclops, but the Cyclops goes against Zeus' laws.

Teacher: What would have happened if [Cyclops] had not violated Zeus' hospitality laws?

Fourth student: Odysseus' men wouldn't have been killed and Odysseus captured.

Teacher: Odysseus is so wise—why didn't he know?

First student: When they're going away, how come [Cyclops] is praying to the gods?

Second student: I thought all the Cyclops didn't believe in the gods.

Teacher: They don't, but Odysseus does. He still has to use his own wits—his wisdom—to get himself out of these scrapes, and, in the cave . . . it's interesting why a nonbeliever would pray. Where do we see Odysseus' cleverness in the cave?

[Discussion Continues]

This teacher-student exchange is noteworthy for the extent to which students as well as the teacher contribute to the discussion. Unlike the first teacher above, this teacher gauges her questions in terms of previous student answers. For example, when the teacher asks "Why make friends?" she is specifically querying the student who has explained that Odysseus visits the Land of the Lotus Eaters and the Cyclops to "[m]ake friends and get food, provisions. . . ." And when a student explains, "He's curious—wants to find out about the Cyclops, but the Cyclops goes against Zeus' laws," the teacher follows up by asking, "What would have happened if he [Cyclops] had *not* violated Zeus' hospitality laws?" The exchange here is a lot like conversation in that what each person says is largely determined by what has previously been said. Indeed, at the end of this brief excerpt, the discussion veers away from the standard initiation-response-evaluation sequence and moves toward something very conversational: after one student says, immediately following another student's comment, that she "thought all the Cyclops didn't believe in the gods," the teacher, rather than evaluating this response, simply contributes to the point the two students are seeking to articulate, saying, "They don't, but Odysseus does." Despite the apparent absence of a script, this teacher is very well prepared and is especially prepared to be flexible. We call this *high-quality classroom discourse*.

Here is another example of high-quality discourse from a ninth-grade class discussion of *Roll of Thunder, Hear My Cry*. Just prior to this exchange, a student (John) has just read his plot summary of chapter four aloud to the class, and the teacher has attempted to write his key points on the board.

Teacher [to the class as a whole]: Wow! What do you think about that?

Student: It was very thorough.

Teacher: Yeah, pretty thorough. I had a lot of trouble getting everything down [on the board], and I think I missed the part about trying to boycott. [Reads from the board]: ". . . and tries to organize a boycott." Did I get everything down, John, that you said?

John: What about the guy who didn't really think these kids were a pest?

Teacher: Yeah, okay. What's his name? Do you remember?

John: [indicates he can't remember]

Another student: Wasn't it Turner?

Teacher: Was it Turner?

Students: Yes.

Teacher: Okay, so Mr. Turner resisted white help. Why? Why would he want to keep shopping at that terrible store?

John: There was only one store to buy from because all the other ones were white.

Teacher: Well, the Wall Store was white too.

Another student [addressed to John]: Is it Mr. Holling's store? Is that it?

John: No. Here's the reason. They don't get paid till the cotton comes in. But throughout the year they still have to buy stuff—food, clothes, seed, and stuff like that. So the owner of the plantation will sign for what they buy at the store so that throughout the year they can still buy stuff on credit.

Teacher [writing on board]: So "he has to have credit in order to buy things, and this store is the only one that will give it to him."

John: [continues to explain]

Teacher: [continues to write on board]

Another student: I was just going to say, "It was the closest store."

Teacher [writing on board]: Okay—it's the closest store; it seems to be in the middle of the area; a lot of sharecroppers who don't get paid cash—they get credit at that store—and it's very hard to get credit at other stores. So it's going to be very hard for her to organize

that boycott; she needs to exist on credit. Yeah? [nods to another
student]
[Discussion continues]

This exchange is noteworthy for the seriousness with which the
teacher treats this student's ideas. Unlike the teacher in the first
transcript, who comes to class with a prepared list of questions with
prespecified answers, this teacher comes prepared to deal on the spot
with what this student has to say. Not only does she "give him the
floor" to express himself at some length, she also attempts to capture
his main points by summarizing them on the board and asking for
clarification when she is uncertain: "I think I missed the part about
trying to boycott. . . Did I get everything down, John, that you said?"
The teacher shows meticulous interest in this student's thinking, and,
as a result, there is a genuineness about this teacher's questions that
stands in sharp contrast to those in the first transcript ("What is the
subject of *The Iliad*?", "What's the common custom of Greek warfare
and prizes?", "What is Achilles' heritage?", etc.). This third teacher
operates on a need-to-know basis, asking each question not just to
move on to the next question but instead to draw out implications of
the previous response—not to find out what the student does not
know but instead to engage his thinking and to follow and promote
the line of inquiry that he initiated. She does more, however, than
merely encourage his expression. Specifically, she plays a key social-
izing role, modeling the kinds of questions and issues that are ger-
mane here to academic discussions of literature; she teaches him to
think as a literature scholar might. She asks either open-ended
questions (e.g., "What do you think about that?") or questions to
which she really doesn't know the answer (e.g., "What's his name?").
These questions, which in our study we call *authentic questions* to
distinguish them from *test questions*, signal to students the teacher's
interest in what they think and not just whether they know and can
report what someone else thinks or has said.

These three transcripts help clarify key differences between the
normal classroom discourse of recitation (and procedural engagement) on the one hand, and more extended, probing discussions that
are characteristic of high-quality instructional discourse (and substantive engagement), on the other hand. In normal classroom discourse, as we have noted, the teacher asks a question, gets an answer,
evaluates it, and then repeats the cycle with the next question. If

someone gives a wrong or inadequate answer, the teacher repeats or rephrases the question, yet most of the time, the questions the teacher asks depend little on the answers students give to previous questions. As a result, each teacher-question/student-response/teacher-evaluation units tends to be discrete and self-contained. This is why the first example here is so choppy: in just eight questions, the teacher asks first about the subject of *The Iliad,* then about length of the Trojan War, then the quarrel between Agammemnon and Achilles, and finally the relationship between the gods and men; no topic is covered in much depth. Perhaps this is why one lost student asks, "Didn't they put a wall up in Ireland?"

By contrast, in high-quality classroom discourse, such as the second and third transcripts, many of the teacher's questions are partly shaped by what immediately precedes them. This process of teachers' incorporating students' answers into subsequent questions is called *uptake* (Cazden, 1988; Collins, 1982, 1986), and it is an important way in which teachers engage students in probing discussion. As it so happens, the latter two discussions are noteworthy because the uptake goes both ways: students as well as the teacher inquire about each other's remarks. In the second class, for example, when one student explains that Odysseus wants to "make friends and get food, provisions," another student asks, "What if they can't give [provisions] to you?"

In the second transcript, even when a student brings up something important that the teacher is not quite ready to pursue, the teacher nonetheless puts it on the agenda for subsequent discussion. Hence, in response to the student who asks about provisions, the teacher says, "That's an important point . . . let's wait a minute on that." In our study we call this *high-level evaluation,* which occurs when the teacher ratifies the importance of a student's response ("That's an important point") and allows it to modify or affect the course of the discussion in some way. Another example of high-level evaluation occurs in the third transcript when the teacher acknowledges the main points of the student's paper by writing them on the board, an act that certifies their importance. Both uptake and high-level evaluation are substantively engaging because, like authentic questions, they are ways in which teachers take students seriously, not merely because they accept these responses as "correct' but rather because they encourage and build on what is noteworthy for future discussion and consideration.

In the first example of recitation, we noted a certain choppiness that resulted from the teacher's having prespecified answers to his questions and then checking off student knowledge, as it were, against a list of essential information and knowledge. This choppiness occurs because the teacher responds less to what the students actually say (as he might in a conversation) and more to what he expects them to say. By contrast, the second and third discussions are noteworthy for the very coherence the first one lacks: through both uptake and high-level evaluation, both the second and third teachers pick up on what students have said, in each case weighing its possibilities for discussion and weaving it into the fabric of an unfolding exchange. The first teacher apparently knows beforehand which questions he will ask and, as a result, can no doubt predict, for the most part, how the recitation will unfold; reenacting the recitation with another class is relatively straightforward. By contrast, the teachers in the second and third examples can neither predict before class how the discussion will proceed nor easily reenact the same discussion with another class because, as in conversation, exactly what these teachers say depends on what their students, in turn, have said. As discourse, both uptake and high-level evaluation function to "chain" together teacher questions and student responses, and it is this conversation-like quality—this chaining—that contributes to its coherence.

The extent to which classroom discourse resembles conversation is in fact an excellent criterion for judging both the instructional quality of the discourse and the extent of substantive student engagement. By this, we do not mean to suggest that instruction should be given over to idle chatter, but rather that students are most likely to be substantively engaged when the treatment of subject matter allows for extensive interaction in which both students and the teacher follow up on each other's statements. In short, students play essential roles in creating high-quality classroom discourse—the teacher cannot do it alone—and this is why it is so substantively engaging and productive. Just as the substance and conduct of student talk are "negotiated" in the process of conversing (Sacks, Schegloff, and Jefferson, 1974), substantively engaging instruction is created as teachers and students negotiate topics of instruction (Nystrand and Gamoran, 1988). This is why substantive student engagement is often prevalent in cooperative small-group work and discussion; why it is much less likely in lecture; and why it generally exists in question-and-answer exchange only to the extent that questions are authentic, teacher evaluations are high-level, and uptake is present.

By discussion, we mean turn taking among students and teachers that departs from the normal initiation-response-evaluation structure of classroom discourse and does not obligate students to wait for the teacher's evaluation before they respond themselves to another student's response; we also mean that their teacher, rather than evaluating a student's response, joins in and becomes a conversant. Discussions typically include relatively few questions, which most often are asked in order to clarify ideas and information ("By that do you mean?") and are consequently authentic because, rather than quiz each other, conversants exchange only that information they actually know. In addition, discussion displays regular uptake so long as the conversants listen and respond appropriately to each other.

By small-group work, we mean *real* small-group work, in which, as with discussion, students have some input into and control over the discourse; we do not mean small-group time that is used to complete worksheets, that is, "collaborative seatwork." In collaborative work among peers in small groups, all the exchanges are initiated by students, are authentic, and typically exhibit uptake in just the way that discussion and conversation do.

To sum up, high-quality instructional discourse is substantively engaging when teachers take students seriously, acknowledging and building on what students say. By contrast, recitation is rarely more than procedurally engaging, since the teacher typically asks a series of preplanned questions, initiates all the topics, and rarely interacts with the substance of students' answers except to evaluate them. Taken together, high-level evaluation, authentic questions, and uptake distinguish classroom discourse when teachers and students interact with each other in mind, and where, as a result, the course of classroom talk depends on what both teachers and students bring to the instructional encounter. When teachers ask authentic questions, they open the floor to what students have to say; when they engage in uptake, they build on what students have said; and when their evaluation of student responses is high, they certify new turns in the discussion occasioned by student answers. These aspects of classroom discourse, which lend *thematic coherence* to the talk by interweaving discussion topics as the teacher and student take turns speaking, serve to sustain student-initiated ideas and responses and consequently promote articulate thinking.

Procedural engagement is more or less obvious, we have noted, from the direct observation of individual students: they do their work, are not disruptive, pay attention in class, and so on. Though substantive engagement is more subtle and often cannot be directly ascertained by just observing individual students, it can be inferred from the quality of student-teacher and peer interactions where the conversants clearly consider each other as they work, as we have noted above, so that topics are sustained across conversation turns. If procedural engagement characterizes classes where the teacher carefully structures classroom activities, then substantive engagement, by contrast, requires instruction to which both teachers and students contribute.

We can think of the quality of instructional discourse as a continuum, with recitation—repeated cycles of initiation-response-evaluation—at one end and discussion/conversation at the other. As a given class session moves away from recitation toward conversation, authentic questions and uptake become increasingly common, and teacher evaluation is transformed into just another conversant turn. High-level evaluation seems to be a transitional form somewhere between initiation-response-evaluation and conversation.

As the two poles of the instructional discourse continuum, recitation and discussion entail sharply different social relationships between teachers and students. In recitation, the teacher initiates and dominates; students are passive and are expected to recall, when asked, what they have learned and to report other people's thinking. What students say affects the conduct of recitation (i.e., the sequence of questions) very little. In discussion, by contrast, the teacher leads but does not dominate. Students are required to be active, not just recalling what they have learned and what others have thought but also thinking themselves on the spot. For discussion to work, teacher and students alike must enter a partnership, observing reciprocity and thinking of each other as they work. Consequently what students say in a discussion can affect both the content and focus of instruction. Students are an essential factor in high-quality instructional discourse, which is why it is substantively so engaging.

Teachers who promote high-quality classroom discourse and students who become so engaged as a result are typically immersed in a dialogue that spans a variety of instructional activities; and classes devoting significant amounts of time to discussion and peer-group work typically exhibit authenticity, contiguity, and high levels of teacher evaluation in their reading and writing, as well as in their classroom talk; that is, in instruction across the board.

IMPLICATIONS FOR WRITING

Like classroom discourse, the potential of school writing for substantive engagement depends largely on the tasks and questions teachers pose for their students, and on how they respond to what students have to say. If they read student papers only to comment on spelling and punctuation and matters of form, student engagement is likely to be only procedural. Similarly, if the purpose of written assignments is mainly to report previously learned material, as on a test, student engagement will also be procedural.

In many English classes, students learn exposition by practicing a pedagogical form known as the five-paragraph theme, which requires an introductory paragraph, a three-paragraph body (each paragraph developing a main point or topic sentence), and a concluding paragraph. This format often precludes substantive student engagement because it assumes that all essays categorically have three main points regardless of the writer's purpose. This approach to teaching exposition trivializes essay writing as a recipe, with a particular procedure, and it too often promotes procedural engagement at the expense of substantive engagement, as do all types of writing instruction in which content, substance, and the writer's purpose are subjugated to form and procedure. Britton and colleagues (1975) call these writing tasks, which are endemic to schools, *dummy runs*.

For students to become substantively engaged in their writing, they must write for a reader who takes a serious interest in what they say, certainly someone who does more than judge exposition by the number of paragraphs. This does not mean that teachers must encourage and praise "any old thing" that students say; rather they respond to the content of student papers, asking questions where students are unclear and prompting them to develop points that seem important.

Substantive engagement in school writing is difficult to achieve. This is largely due to the situation in which the teacher, by definition, is an expert and the students are novices. Hence, when teachers ask their students to explain "if there are any examples of Scottish dialects in Burns's poems" or "the main features of Elizabethan sonnets," they do so not to find out about these things (as in authentic discourse) but rather to assess student knowledge of these things (cf. Applebee, 1982). Ideally, substantive engagement is fostered in school writing when the ostensible and actual purposes of the writing are the same, for example, when the teacher's requests for explanations are authentic.

One kind of writing that potentially promotes substantive engagement is the position paper that some social studies and English teachers ask their students to write, in which students must articulate their views on social issues that seem important to them. Such assignments are typically authentic because the teacher does not evaluate them looking for particular answers. Applebee and Langer have argued that such writing tasks promote student "ownership" because they afford students considerable flexibility concerning the content they cover and the views they express. (See Applebee and Langer, 1983; Langer and Applebee, 1984, 1986.) Sometimes these position papers are assigned at the end of an involved class discussion when students have staked out their positions. Alternatively, the teacher may ask students to articulate their views in writing before class in order to heighten engagement during the discussion itself. Either way, this conjunction of writing and discussion serves a purpose very much like uptake in classroom talk: it increases the coherence of instructional activities as they relate to each other.

Another related kind of writing that often promotes substantive engagement is student journal keeping. When teachers ask students to keep journals, they typically ask them to write once a day for fifteen to twenty minutes on topics of importance to them. Teachers usually do not mark these journals for punctuation, spelling, or content, and consequently do not grade them (though they often count them for credit), but rather respond to individual entries with conversational kinds of remarks (e.g., "Very interesting. I've never thought of that," "Why do you say that?", "When you thought about this the next day, how did it seem then?", "I can remember doing this," "I'm laughing"). The cumulative effect of journal entries and teacher responses is that of a written dialogue or conversation; indeed, keeping journals is sometimes called *dialogue-journal communication* (cf. Staton, et al., 1988) because students and teachers take turns speaking just as conversants do. Journals are often effective with reluctant learners, and although they probably do not teach students very much about other more formal kinds of school writing such as essays or tests, they nonetheless give students practice and help them feel comfortable with a medium that is often frustrating and difficult. More than this, journals allow each student to get to know the teacher as someone who is interested in the student's thoughts and listens to what the student has to say. In short, journal keeping promotes substantive engagement and an instructional tone that potentially benefits students when they do other sorts of writing.

Reading is authentic when it addresses questions that students deem important, teaching them new things that they value, and also to the extent that teachers help students relate their readings to their own experiences. Reading will contribute to instructional coherence when students discuss and write about their readings—in other words, to the extent that reading relates to talk and writing.

Of course, no given instructional activity categorically promotes either procedural or substantive engagement. The nature of student engagement always depends, in the final analysis, on the nature of the interaction between teacher and students. Hence, position papers tend to elicit substantive engagement but will not do so if students expect the teacher to mark them only for spelling or if the teacher does not respond at all. By contrast, five-paragraph themes tend to promote procedural engagement, but this engagement can be substantive if the teacher thoughtfully responds to what students say and allows students some latitude on just how many paragraphs their papers must have.

STUDENT ENGAGEMENT AND LITERATURE ACHIEVEMENT

Substantively engaging instruction fosters achievement more fully than does instruction that is merely procedurally engaging. Theoretical support for this proposition originates with the principle of reciprocity: instruction, like any other form of interaction, requires give and take between participants (Nystrand, 1986, 1990). When reciprocity is merely procedural, students concentrate on procedures. By contrast, when reciprocity is substantive, students become involved in the issues and problems required for mastery and understanding. In short, when reciprocity is substantive, teachers and students communicate more fully. Beyond this, when reciprocity is procedural, students have little stake in learning the material aside from extrinsic rewards and sanctions. By contrast, when teacher-student reciprocity concerns the substance of academic issues, students play an essential role in their own learning—experiencing "ownership," some would say (e.g., Applebee, 1986)—and as they grapple seriously with the academic content, their learning surpasses grade requirements.

Empirical support for our claim comes from analyses of the eighth-grade classes in our study. We administered a test of literature achievement, which contained questions about the literary selections used in each class. The questions were the same on each test—ranging from ones that required simple recall to others that called for in-depth understanding—but the selections they concerned varied, depending on the literature curriculum of each class. Higher scores thus indicated that students had greater mastery of the literature they studied. More information on the tests and analyses is available elsewhere (Nystrand and Gamoran, in press; Gamoran, 1989; Nystrand, forthcoming).

Not surprisingly, we found that disengaged students failed to learn much. Students who were off-task in class, and who did not turn in their work, were seriously impeded. A more interesting finding results from the comparison of procedural and substantive engagement. Procedural engagement had an ambiguous relation to achievement: students who spent more time on homework learned more, but those who asked questions in class and whose classes showed high rates of on-task behavior did *not* learn more than other students. Such measures of student behavior, we believe, conflate procedural and substantive engagement, and this is why their relation to achievement is unclear.

By contrast, several measures of substantive engagement showed clear effects on achievement. Students whose teachers posed higher proportions of authentic questions and used uptake achieved significantly higher scores. Coherent lessons, in which activities are related to one another rather than fragmented, also resulted in higher scores on the literature test.

When we divided the test results into separate scores for recall of information and depth of understanding, we found that both recall and depth require procedural engagement and uptake, but that depth requires authentic discourse as well. Last, we discovered that the effects of writing frequency depend on the type of writing: more frequent essays promote higher achievement, whereas more frequent short-answer assignments do not.

CONCLUSION

One can think of student engagement as a cognitive phenomenon essentially having to do with the extent to which students are mentally involved with the issues and problems of academic study. Hence, it may be considered in terms of sustained mental concentration, focus, and habits of thoughtfulness (Newmann, Onosko, and Stevenson, 1988). But like most aspects of cognition, student engagement has a social foundation. Substantive student engagement occurs only in certain contexts and involves more than individual students: more precisely, it involves the interaction of students and teachers. This requirement for interaction clearly underlies the social nature of instruction.

Student engagement poses some puzzles for both teachers and researchers. On the one hand, it underscores the importance of individual student effort and commitment to schooling. And clearly, when we speak of student engagement, we have in mind individual students, not classes. Yet despite the fact that student engagement refers to the cognition of individual students, we seem unable to detect it or adequately describe its manifestations except in relation to the interactions of students with their teachers or with other students. When we attempt to describe what individually engaged students do or look like, we inevitably limit ourselves to describing procedural engagement: as noted, we speak of students who appear to be paying attention, who do their work, who ask questions in class, and so on. By contrast, in order to describe substantively engaging instruction, we must turn to the particular conditions of the class and its discourse. Some relevant questions are: When students respond to the teacher's questions, does the teacher follow up on their responses? How much latitude do students have in answering their teacher's questions? Do these questions mainly test their knowledge of what other people have thought and said, or do they respectfully elicit and follow up on actual thinking? Does classroom discourse tend more toward recitation or more toward conversation?

Substantive engagement requires, on the one hand, more of teachers than transmitting important knowledge and presenting good lessons, and, on the other hand, more of students than paying attention, taking in information, and doing their work. More fundamentally, substantive student engagement depends on what teachers and students do together and how they work in terms of each other; neither can do it alone. Nonetheless, teachers are key to creating classrooms where students become engaged in challenging issues and interesting topics. In the classroom, certain discourse practices elicit substantive student engagement. When they ask authentic questions, teachers open the floor to students and establish ground rules of classroom talk that prize student opinion and thinking. Through uptake, teachers help students develop a train of thought, and through high-level teacher evaluation, teachers publicly demonstrate their regard for this thinking. Each of these practices moves classroom discourse away from recitation toward conversation; the result is coherent instruction and learning, as shared understandings are elaborated, built upon, and revised.

REFERENCES

Applebee, Arthur. "Writing and Learning in School Settings." In *What Writers Know: The Language, Process, and Structure of Written Discourse*, edited by Martin Nystrand. New York and London: Academic Press, 1982.

Applebee, Arthur. "Problems in Process Approaches: Toward a Reconceptualization of Process Instruction." In *The Teaching of Writing*, edited by Anthony Petrosky and David Bartholomae, Eighty-fifth Yearbook of the National Society for the Study of Education, Part 2. Chicago: University of Chicago Press, 1986.

Applebee, Arthur, and Langer, Judith. "Instructional Scaffolding: Reading and Writing as Natural Language Activities," *Language Arts* 60, no. 2 (1983): 168–175.

Britton, James; Burgess, Tony; Martin, Nancy; McLeod, Alex; and Rosen, Harold. *The Development of Writing Abilities: 11–18.* London: Macmillan, 1975.

Cazden, Courtney. *Classroom Discourse: The Language of Teaching and Learning.* Portsmouth, N.H.: Heinemann, 1988.

Collins, James. "Discourse Style, Classroom Interaction and Differential Treatment," *Journal of Reading Behavior* 14 (1982): 429–437.

Collins, James. "Differential Instruction in Reading." In *The Social Construction of Literacy*, edited by Jenny Cook-Gumperz. Cambridge: Cambridge University Press, 1986.

Gamoran, Adam. "Schooling and Achievement: Additive versus Interactive Multilevel Models." Paper presented at the International Conference on Multilevel Methods in Educational Research, Edinburgh, Scotland, 1989.

Goodlad, John. *A Place Called School.* New York: McGraw-Hill, 1984.

Langer, Judith, and Applebee, Arthur. "Language, Learning and Interaction: A Framework for Improving Instruction." In *Contexts for Learning to Write: Studies of Secondary School Instruction*, edited by Arthur N. Applebee. Norwood, N.J.: ABLEX Publishing Corporation, 1984.

Langer, Judith, and Applebee, Arthur. "Reading and Writing Instruction: Toward a Theory of Teaching and Learning." In *Review of Research in Education*, vol. 13, edited by Ernst Z. Rothkopf. Washington, D.C.: American Educational Research Association, 1986.

McNeil, Linda. *Contradictions of Control: School Structure and School Knowledge*. London: Routledge and Kegan Paul, 1986.

Mehan, Hugh. *Learning Lessons*. Cambridge, Mass.: Harvard University Press, 1979.

National Commission on Excellence in Education. *A Nation at Risk: The Imperative for Educational Reform*. Washington, D.C.: U. S. Government Printing Office, 1983.

Newmann, Fred; Onosko, Joe, and Stevenson, Robert. *Higher-Order Thinking in High School Social Studies: An Analysis of Classrooms, Teachers, Students, and Leadership*. Madison, Wisc.: National Center on Effective Secondary Schools, 1988.

Nystrand, Martin. *The Structure of Written Communication: Studies in Reciprocity between Writers and Readers*. Orlando, Fla., and London: Academic Press, 1986.

Nystrand, Martin. "Sharing Words: The Effects of Readers on Developing Writers," *Written Communication* 7, no. 1 (1990): 3–24.

Nystrand, Martin. "Making It Hard: Curriculum and Instruction as Factors in the Difficulty of Literature." In *The Idea of Difficulty in Literature and Literature Learning: Joining Theory and Practice*, edited by Alan Purves. Albany: State University of New York Press, forthcoming.

Nystrand, Martin, and Gamoran, Adam. "A Study of Instruction as Discourse." Paper presented at the Annual Meeting of the American Educational Research Association, New Orleans, 1988.

Nystrand, Martin, and Gamoran, Adam. "Instructional Discourse, Student Engagement, and Literature Achievement," *Research in the Teaching of English*, in press.

Powell, Arthur; Farrar, Eleanor; and Cohen, David. *The Shopping Mall High School*. Boston: Houghton Mifflin, 1985.

Sacks, Harvey; Schegloff, E. A.; and Jefferson, Gail. "A Simplest Systematics for the Organization of Turn-taking in Conversation," *Language* 50 (1974): 696–735.

Sizer, Theodore. *Horace's Compromise*. Boston: Houghton Mifflin, 1984.

Staton, Jana; Shuy, Roger; Kreeft Peyton, Joy; and Reed, Leslie. *Dialogue Journal Communication: Classroom, Linguistic, Social, and Cognitive Views*, Writing Research Series, Vol. 10, edited by Marcia Farr. Norwood, N. J.: ABLEX Publishing Corporation, 1988.

——13——

Classroom Instruction and Cooperative Learning

David W. Johnson and Roger T. Johnson

THE NATURE OF SOCIAL INTERDEPENDENCE

Jim is sitting in the classroom, doing nothing. His book is open—to the wrong page. His sheet of printed questions has disappeared. He does not care. He is seventeen years old. His classmates ignore him. Within this class that primarily stresses competition, Jim is considered a loser to be shunned. Within this individualistic class, classmates considered Jim irrelevant to their own striving for personal success. When students are required to compete with each other for grades, they are taught to strive to be better than classmates ("Who can beat Jim in math?"), to work to deprive others ("You win, Jim loses."), to celebrate classmates' failures ("Jim did not do his homework, that puts you ahead."), to view resources such as grades as limited ("Remember, in a class of 30, only 5 people can get an A."), to recognize their negatively linked fate ("The more you gain, the less for me; the more I gain, the less for you."), and to believe that the more competent and hard-working individuals become "haves" and the less competent and deserving individuals become the "have nots" (only the strong prosper). When students are required to work individualistically on their own, they are expected and encouraged to

277

focus on their strict self-interest ("How well can I do?"), to value only their own efforts and own success ("If I study hard, I may get a high grade."), and to ignore as irrelevant the success or failure of others ("Whether Jim studies or not does not affect me.").

Cooperation is working together to accomplish shared goals. Within cooperative activities, individuals seek outcomes that are beneficial to themselves *and* to all other group members. Cooperative learning is the instructional use of small groups so that students work together to maximize their own and each other's learning. The idea is simple. Class members are split into groups of two to four members after receiving instruction from the teacher. The groups then work through the assignment until all group members have successfully understood and completed it. Day after day, they must resolve their personal differences and work together. Students realize they have a stake in each other's success. They become mutually responsible for each other's learning.

Consider again the case of Jim, who is sitting in the classroom doing nothing. The teacher assigns all students to cooperative learning groups. Jim finds himself sitting with three classmates. "Jim, where is your paper?" they immediately ask. "Don't know," Jim replies. "Here are the questions," the group members reply, "let's go over them and make sure you know the answers. Don't worry. We'll help you." Cooperative efforts result in participants' striving for mutual benefit so that all group members benefit from one's efforts ("Jim, your success benefits me and my success benefits you."), recognizing that all group members share a common fate ("We all sink or swim together here."), recognizing that one's performance is caused by both oneself and one's colleagues ("We cannot do it without you, Jim."), and feeling proud and jointly celebrating when a group member is recognized for achievement ("Jim, you got a B! That is terrific!").

An essential instructional skill that all teachers need is knowing how and when to structure students' learning goals competitively, individualistically, and cooperatively. By structuring positive, negative, or no interdependence, teachers can influence the pattern of interaction among students and the instructional outcomes that result (Deutsch, 1962; Johnson and Johnson, 1987, 1988; Johnson, Johnson, and Holubec, 1990). Cooperative learning is the most important of the three ways of structuring learning situations, yet it is currently the least used. In most schools, class sessions are structured cooperatively for only 7 to 20 percent of the time. In order to increase the use of cooperative learning, teachers need to understand the essential components of a well-conducted cooperative lesson, the research validating the use of cooperative learning, the different types of cooperative learning, and the approaches of implementing cooperative learning in a classroom, school, and school district.

ESSENTIAL COMPONENTS OF EFFECTIVE COOPERATIVE LEARNING

Simply placing students in groups and telling them to work together does not in and of itself create effective cooperation. There are many ways in which group efforts may go wrong (Johnson and Johnson, 1989a). Less able members sometimes "leave it to George" to complete the group's tasks, thus creating a "free rider" effect whereby group members expend decreasing amounts of effort and just go through the teamwork motions. At the same time, the more able group member may expend less effort to avoid the "sucker effect" of doing all the work. High-ability group members may be deferred to and may take over the important leadership roles in ways that benefit them at the expense of the other group members (the "rich-get-richer effect"). In a learning group, for example, the more able group member may give all the explanations of what is to be learned. Since the amount of time spent explaining correlates highly with the amount learned, the more able member learns a great deal while the less able members flounder as a captive audience. The time spent listening in group brainstorming can reduce the amount of time available for any individual to state an idea. Group efforts can be characterized by self-induced helplessness, diffusion of responsibility and social loafing, ganging up against a task, reactance, dysfunctional divisions of labor ("I'm the thinkist and you're the typist"), inappropriate dependence on authority, destructive conflict, and other patterns of behavior that debilitate group performance.

The barriers to effective cooperative learning are avoided when it is properly structured. Effective cooperative learning is based on the operationalization of the essential components within each cooperative lesson (Johnson and Johnson, 1989a). The first requirement for an effectively structured cooperative lesson is *positive interdependence,* which exists when a group member perceives that he or she is linked with others in a way such that he or she cannot succeed unless they do (and vice versa) and/or that he or she must coordinate his or her efforts with the efforts of others to complete a task. If individuals do not believe that they "sink or swim together," then the situation is not cooperative. Positive interdependence begins when learning groups are presented with a mutual goal, and has numerous effects on individuals' motivation and productivity, not the least of which is to highlight the fact that the efforts of *all* group members are needed for group success. When members of a group see their efforts as dispensable for the group's success, they may reduce their efforts. When group members perceive their potential contribution to the group as being unique (because of their role, resources, or task responsibilities), they increase their efforts. When positive interdependence is clearly understood, individuals realize that their efforts are required in order for the group to succeed (i.e., there can be no "free-riders").

The second element for an effective cooperative lesson is *face-to-face promotive interaction* among group members. Within cooperative lessons, teachers need to maximize the opportunity for students to promote each other's success by helping, assisting, supporting, encouraging, and praising each other's efforts to learn. Such promotive interaction has a number of effects. First, there are cognitive activities and interpersonal dynamics that occur only when students get involved in explaining to each other how the answers to assignments are derived. This includes orally explaining how to solve problems, discussing the nature of the concepts being learned, teaching one's knowledge to classmates, and connecting present with past learning. Second, it is within face-to-face interaction that the opportunity for a wide variety of social influences and patterns emerges. Helping and assisting take place. Accountability to peers, ability to influence each other's reasoning and conclusions, social modeling, social support, and interpersonal rewards all increase as the face-to-face interactions among group members increase. Third, the verbal and nonverbal responses of other group members provide important information concerning a student's performance. Fourth, it provides an opportunity for peers to pressure unmotivated group members to achieve.

The third element is *individual accountability*, which exists when the performance of each individual student is assessed and the results are given back to the group and the individual. It is important that the group knows who needs more assistance, support, and encouragement in completing the assignment. It is also important that group members know that they cannot "hitch-hike" on the work of others. When a group works on tasks where it is difficult to identify members' contributions, when there is an increased likelihood of redundant efforts, when there is a lack of group cohesiveness, and when there is lessened responsibility for the final outcome, group members tend *not* to contribute to goal achievement. If, however, there is high individual accountability and it is clear how much effort each member is contributing, if redundant efforts are avoided, if every member is responsible for the final outcome, and if the group is cohesive, then the "social loafing effect" vanishes. The smaller the size of the group, furthermore, the greater the individual accountability may be.

The fourth element is the appropriate use of *interpersonal and small-group skills*. Placing socially unskilled individuals in a group and telling them to cooperate does not guarantee that they are able to do so effectively. Persons must be taught the social skills for high-quality collaboration and be motivated to use them. Collaborative skills include leadership, decision-making, trust-building, communication, and conflict-management skills. (Johnson, 1986, 1987; Johnson, Johnson, and Holubec, 1986).

The fifth element of good cooperative learning is *group processing*, which exists when group members discuss how well they are achieving their goals and maintaining effective working relationships. Groups need to describe what member actions are helpful and unhelpful and make decisions about what behaviors to continue or change. Such small-group processing, usually at the end of a lesson, (a) enables learning groups to focus on group maintenance, (b) facilitates the learning of collaborative skills, (c) ensures that members receive feedback on their participation, and (d) reminds students to practice collaborative skills consistently.

WHAT DO WE KNOW ABOUT COOPERATIVE LEARNING?

The best answer to the question, "What is the most effective method of teaching?" is that it depends on the goal, the student, the content, and the teacher. But the next best answer is, "Students teaching other students." There is a wealth of evidence that peer teaching is extremely effective for a wide range of goals, content, and students of different levels and personalities.

W. J. McKeachie, *1988*

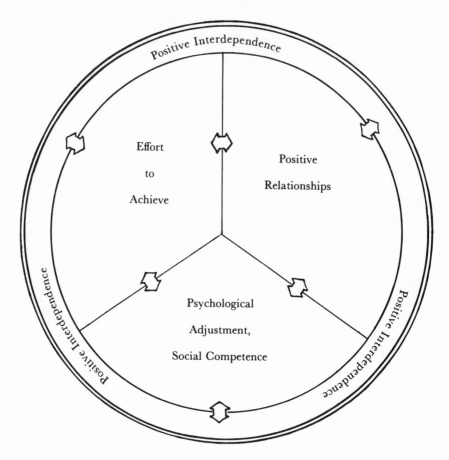

Figure 13-1
Outcomes of Cooperative Learning

Working together to get the job done can have profound effects. In trying to understand how cooperation works, and in continually refining our understanding of how to implement cooperation most effectively, we have (a) reviewed over 520 experimental and over 100 correlational research studies, conducted during the last ninety years, that compare cooperative, competitive, and individualistic efforts and (b) conducted a twenty-five-year program of research that has resulted in over eighty published studies. The numerous variables that are affected by cooperation may be subsumed within three broad and interrelated outcomes (see Figure 13-1): (1) effort exerted to achieve,

(2) quality of relationships among participants, and (3) participants' psychological adjustment and social competence (Johnson and Johnson, 1989a).

Effort to Achieve

When asked how a small country like Japan with almost no natural resources could become such an economic power, a Japanese businessman replied, "Our people's hard work is our most important resource." Achievement comes from hard, intense, persistent, long-term efforts. Productivity depends on the physical and psychological energy individuals are willing to commit toward achievement. Many students spend very little time studying, avoid hard subjects such as mathematics and science, and do far less than they are capable of doing. Some students do no schoolwork at all. No matter how intellectually capable or skilled individuals are, if they do not exert considerable effort and seek to achieve challenging goals, their productivity will be low.

Working together to achieve a common goal produces increased effort, higher achievement, and greater productivity than does working alone (Johnson and Johnson, 1989a). During the past ninety years, over 375 studies on the relative impact of cooperative, competitive, and individualistic efforts have been conducted. The overall effect size is 0.67 when cooperative and competitive efforts are compared, 0.66 when cooperative and individualistic efforts are compared, and 0.29 when competitive and individualistic efforts are compared. These effect sizes are weighted for the number of findings within each study and for effect-size variances. When only the methodologically high-quality studies are included, the effect sizes for the cooperative-competitive and the cooperative-individualistic comparisons go up to 0.86 and 0.88 respectively.

While cooperation tends to promote higher achievement on all school-related tasks, its superiority over competitive and individualistic learning is most clearly seen in conceptual learning and on problem-solving tasks. Cooperation, cognition, and metacognition are all intimately related. Cooperative learning provides the context within which cognition and metacognition best take place. The interpersonal exchange within cooperative learning groups, and especially the intellectual challenge resulting from conflicting ideas and conclusions (i.e., controversy), promotes critical thinking, higher-level reasoning, and metacognitive thought. The divergent thinking and inspiration that sparks creativity results from the oral explanations and elaboration required within cooperative learning groups. Explaining what one knows to the groupmates facilitates the understanding of how to apply one's knowledge and skills to work and community settings.

A number of the operationally conducted studies defined cooperation to include elements of competition and individualistic work. The original jigsaw studies, for example, operationalized cooperative learning as a combination of positive resource interdependence and an individualistic reward structure (Aronson, 1978). Teams-Games-Tournaments (TGT) (DeVries and Edwards, 1974) and Student-Team-Achievement-Divisions (STAD) (Slavin, 1986) operationalized cooperative learning as a combination of in-group cooperation and intergroup competition, and Team-Assisted Individualization (TAI) (Slavin, 1986) is a mixture of cooperative and individualistic learning. When such "mixed" operationalizations were compared with "pure" operationalizations, the effect sizes for the cooperative-competitive comparison were 0.45 and 0.74 respectively, $t(37) = 1.60$, $p<0.06$ (Johnson and Johnson, 1989a). The effect sizes for the cooperative-individualistic comparisons were 0.13 and 0.61 respectively, $t(10) = 1.64$, $p<0.07$.

Since the most credible studies (due to their high-quality methodologies) and the "pure" operationalizations of cooperative learning produced stronger effects, considerable confidence can be placed in the conclusion that cooperative efforts promote more positive cross-ethnic relationships than do competitive or individualistic efforts.

Quality of Relationships: Shelter Against the Cold

A faithful friend is a strong defense, and he that hath found him, hath found a treasure.

Ecclesiasticus 6:14

We are created not for isolation, but for relationships. At heart, we are not a thousand individual points of light, but, rather, part of a larger brightness. Within schools, caring and committed relationships are not a luxury. They are a necessity. Children who are poorly accepted by their peers were found to be more likely to drop out of school than children who are better accepted. Recent national surveys indicate that feeling valued, loved, wanted, and respected by others gives life meaning and purpose and that intimate relationships create happiness. This is as true within schools as it is in life in general.

Students care more about each other and are more committed to each other's success and well-being when they work together to get the job done than when they compete to see who is best or when they work independently from each other (Johnson and Johnson, 1989a). Especially when students are heterogeneous (i.e., when their intellectual ability, handicapping conditions, ethnicity, social class, and sex differ), cooperating on a task results in more realistic and positive views of each other than if they were to compete or work individualistically. Over 190 studies have been conducted on the relative impact of cooperative, competitive, and individualistic efforts on relationships among students. The weighted effect sizes for cooperation versus competition and for cooperation versus individualistic efforts are 0.65 and 0.64 respectively. When only the methodologically high-quality studies are examined, the effect sizes go up to 0.77 and 0.67. "Pure" cooperation results in greater effects than do mixtures of cooperative, competitive, and individualistic efforts (cooperative versus competitive, pure = 0.75 and mixed = 0.48; cooperative versus individualistic, pure = 0.67 and mixed = 0.36).

The more frequently cooperative learning is used, the more positive relationships become. Cooperation, compared with competitive and individualistic efforts, promotes greater liking, social support, caring, mutual commitment, and cohesion among group members. Within cooperative classrooms, every student can form friendships. As relationships become more positive, furthermore, there are corresponding increases in productivity, feelings of personal commitment and responsibility to do the assigned work, willingness to take on and persist in completing difficult tasks, higher morale, and greater commitment to peers' success and growth.

Psychological Adjustment and Social Competence

Psychological health is the ability to build, maintain, and appropriately modify interdependent relationships with others to succeed in achieving goals. Social competence is an essential aspect of psychological health, and self-esteem is often used as an index of how psychologically adjusted a person is. Working cooperatively with peers and valuing cooperation results in greater psychological health, higher self-esteem, and greater social competence than does competing with classmates or working independently (Johnson and Johnson 1989a). When students are graduated from school, they need enough psychological stability to build and maintain career, family, and community relationships, to establish a basic and meaningful interdependence with other people, and to participate effectively within society. Depression, anxiety, and anger, furthermore, interfere with classroom functioning. The more positively students see themselves, the greater their productivity, acceptance and support of others, and autonomy and independence.

Self-esteem is often used as an index of psychological health and adjustment. Over seventy-seven studies have been conducted on the relative impact of cooperative, competitive, and individualistic efforts on self-esteem (Johnson and Johnson, 1989a). The weighted effect sizes for cooperation versus competition and cooperation versus individualistic efforts are 0.60 and 0.44 respectively. When only the methodologically high-quality studies are examined, the effect sizes go up to 0.63 and 0.46. "Pure" cooperation results in greater effects than do mixtures of cooperative, competitive, and individualistic efforts (cooperative versus competitive, pure = 0.78 and mixed = 0.33; cooperative versus individualistic, pure = 0.51 and mixed = 0.22).

An important aspect of psychological health is social competence. Social skills and competencies tend to increase more within cooperative than in competitive or individualistic situations (Johnson and Johnson, 1989a). Working together to get the job done increases students' abilities to provide leadership, build and maintain trust, communicate effectively, and manage conflicts constructively. Employability and career success depend largely on such social skills. Most modern work occurs within teams. An individual's intelligence and technical expertise are of no use if he or she is not a skillful group member. The social skills learned within cooperative learning groups, furthermore, provide the basis for building and maintaining life-long friendships, loving and caring families, and cohesive neighborhoods.

Reciprocal Relationships Among the Three Outcomes

The reason we were so good, and continued to be so good, was because he (Joe Paterno) forces you to develop an inner love among the players. It is much harder to give up on your buddy, than it is to give up on your coach. I really believe that over the years the teams I played on were almost unbeatable in tight situations. When we needed to get that six inches we got it because of our love for each other. Our camaraderie existed because of the kind of coach and kind of person Joe was.

David Joyner

There are bidirectional relationships among efforts to achieve, quality of relationships, and psychological health (Johnson and Johnson, 1989a); that is, each influences the others. On the one hand, caring and committed friendships result from a sense of mutual accomplishment, mutual pride in joint work, and the bonding that results from joint efforts. The more students care about each other, on the other hand, the harder they will work to achieve mutual learning goals. Long-term and persistent efforts to achieve do not come from the head, they come from the heart (Johnson and Johnson, 1989b). Individuals seek out opportunities to work with those they care about. As caring increases, so do feelings of personal responsibility to do one's share of the work, willingness to take on difficult tasks, motivation and persistence in working toward goal achievement, and willingness to endure pain and frustration on behalf of the group.

Joint efforts to achieve mutual goals promote psychological health and social competence. The more successful the group, the higher the participants' self-esteem, self-efficacy, personal control, and confidence in their competencies. Contributing to others' success, furthermore, can cure the "blues." On the other hand, the healthier individuals are psychologically, the better able they are to work with others to achieve mutual goals. Joint efforts require coordination, effective communication, leadership, and conflict management. States of depression, anxiety, guilt, shame, and fear all interfere with one's ability to cooperate and decrease the amount of energy a person has to devote to a cooperative effort.

Psychological health is built on the internalization of the caring and respect received from loved ones. Friendships are developmental advantages that promote self-esteem, self-efficacy, and general psychological adjustment. The internalization of positive relationships, direct social support, shared intimacy, and expressions of caring can help to build psychological health and the ability to cope with stress. Destructive relationships and the absence of caring and committed relationships tend to increase psychological pathology. On the other hand, the healthier that persons are psychologically (i.e., free of psychological pathologies such as depression, paranoia, anxiety, fear of failure, repressed anger, and feelings of hopelessness and meaning-lessness), the more caring and committed are their relationships.

Since each outcome can induce the others, they are likely to be found together. Efforts to achieve, quality of relationships, and psychological health are a package, with each outcome a door into all three. And together they induce positive interdependence and promotive interaction.

TYPES OF COOPERATIVE LEARNING

Cooperative learning may be incorporated into courses through the use of *formal learning groups*, which are given an assignment to complete and typically stay together for several weeks; *informal learning groups*, which are given a short discussion task and stay together for a few minutes; and *base groups*, which are long-term groups whose purpose is primarily to provide peer support and accountability and stay together from at least one semester or year to optimally several years. When used in combination, these formal, informal, and base cooperative learning groups provide an overall structure to classroom life (Johnson, Johnson, and Holubec, 1988, 1990).

Formal cooperative learning groups may last from one class period to several weeks to complete a specific task or assignment (such as solving a set of problems, completing a unit, writing a report or theme, conducting an experiment, or reading and comprehending a story). Through the use of formal cooperative learning groups, any course requirement or assignment may be reformulated to be cooperative rather than competitive or individualistic. The teacher structures the learning groups (deciding on group size and how to assign students to groups); teaches the academic concepts, principles, and strategies that the students are to master and apply; assigns a task to be completed cooperatively; and then monitors the functioning of the learning groups and intervenes to (a) teach collaborative skills and (b) provide assistance in academic learning when it is needed. Students are taught to look to their peers for assistance, feedback, reinforcement, and support. Students are expected to interact with each other, share ideas and materials, support and encourage each other's academic achievement, orally explain and elaborate the concepts and strategies being learned, and hold each other accountable for completing the assignment. A criteria-referenced evaluation system is used.

Informal cooperative learning groups are temporary, ad hoc groups that last from a few minutes to one class period. Their purposes are to focus student attention on the material to be learned, set a mood conducive to learning, help organize in advance the material to be covered in a class session, ensure that students cognitively process the material being taught, and provide closure to an instructional session. They may be used at any time, but are especially useful during a lecture or movie. During direct teaching, the instructional challenge for the teacher is to ensure that students do the intellectual work of organizing material, explaining it, summarizing it, and integrating it into existing conceptual structures. This may be achieved by having students do the advance organizing of the lesson, do the cognitive processing of what they are learning, and provide the closure to the lesson. Informal cooperative learning groups are often organized so that students engage in focused discussions before and after a lecture and by interspersing "turn-to-your-partner" discussions throughout the lecture. Use of these groups helps counter what is proclaimed to be the main problem of lectures: The information passes from the notes of the professor to the notes of the student without passing through the mind of either one.

Base groups are long-term, heterogeneous cooperative learning groups (e.g., one might consist of three academically oriented students and one at-risk student), with stable membership. The purposes of the base group are to give the support, help, encouragement, and assistance members need to make academic progress, (e.g., attend, complete all assignments, and learn in all their classes) and develop cognitively and socially in healthy ways. Class schedules are arranged so that all members of the base group are assigned to as many of the same classes as possible. Members spend much of the day together and regularly work together to complete cooperative learning tasks. They formally meet twice a week to discuss the academic progress of each member, provide help and assistance to each other, and verify that each member is completing assignments and progressing satisfactorily through the academic program. Base groups may also be given the task of letting absent group members know what went on in the class. Informally, members interact everyday within and between classes, discussing assignments and helping each other with homework. The use of base groups tends to improve attendance, personalize both the required work and the school experience, and improve the quality and quantity of learning.

IMPLEMENTING COOPERATIVE LEARNING IN CLASSROOMS AND SCHOOLS

Approaches to implementing cooperative learning may be placed on a continuum, with conceptual applications at one end and direct applications at the other (Johnson, Johnson, and Holubec, 1990). *Conceptual applications* are based on an interaction among theory, research, and practice. Teachers are taught a general conceptual model of cooperative learning (based on the essential elements of positive interdependence, face-to-face interaction, individual accountability, social skills, and group processing—the *essential elements approach*), which they use to tailor cooperative learning specifically for their circumstances, students, and needs. In essence, teachers are taught an "expert system" of how to implement cooperative learning. The resulting expertise is based on a metacognitive understanding of cooperative learning.

Conceptual applications may be contrasted with *direct applications*, which consist of packaged lessons, curricula, and strategies that are used in a lock-step prescribed manner. The *direct approach* can be divided into three subcategories. Teachers can adopt a strategy (such as groups-of-four in intermediate mathematics) that is aimed at using cooperative learning in a specific subject area for a certain age student (the *strategy approach*), they can adopt a curriculum package that is aimed at a specific subject area and grade level (the *curriculum package approach*), or they can replicate a lesson they observed another instructor teach (the *lesson approach*).

While the conceptual and direct approaches are not contradictory, they differ in how workshop training transfers to the classroom and in the long-term implementation and survival of cooperative learning. Conceptual applications are theory-based, while direct applications are materials- and procedures-based. The conceptual approach trains teachers to be engineers who adapt cooperative learning strategies to their specific circumstances, students, and needs. Direct approaches train teachers to be technicians who use the cooperative learning curriculum or strategy without understanding how it works. When teachers engineer cooperative learning strategies to work within their specific situation, they become personally committed to cooperative learning; but teachers who technically conduct a cooperative learning lesson in a locked-step manner do not. The conceptual approach promotes research that tests theory which generalizes to many different situations. Direct approaches promote evaluation studies that are in essence case studies demonstrating how well the curriculum or strategy was implemented in a specific instance, but the results do not generalize to other situations and implementations. Conceptual approaches are dynamic in that they are modified as new research occurs and the theory is refined. Direct approaches are static in that they remain fixed no matter how the knowledge about cooperative learning changes.

When teachers gain expertise in cooperative learning through conceptual understanding, they become independent of outside experts and can generate new lessons and strategies as the need arises. They can also transfer their use of cooperative learning strategies to create more cooperative collegial relationships, staff meetings, relationships with parents, and committees. They become important figures in the staff-development process as they train their colleagues to use cooperative learning. Teachers trained in the direct approaches stay dependent on outside experts, cannot generate new lessons or strategies on their own, cannot transfer cooperation strategies from the classroom to the school, and cannot train their peers (except in a direct way). Finally, the conceptual approach requires ongoing support and assistance in gaining expertise in cooperative learning. Direct approaches do not.

Direct approaches have value within the context of a long-term implementation of a training program emphasizing conceptual understanding of the essential elements of well-structured cooperative lessons. Without the conceptual context, direct approaches are, in the long run, inadequate at best and counterproductive at worst. Simply presenting a theoretical framework, on the other hand, is also inadequate. A carefully crafted training program requires a combination of a clear conceptual understanding of the essential elements of cooperative learning, concrete examples of lessons and strategies, and continued implementation in classrooms and schools.

SUMMARY

The study of social interdependence requires a validated theory, validating research conducted to confirm or disconfirm the theory, and procedures for operationalizing social interdependence within the classroom and school. Each time teachers prepare a lesson, they must choose to use either of the two types of social interdependence (cooperative and competitive) or the absence of social interdependence (individualistic). Teachers may structure academic lessons so that students are (a) in a win-lose struggle to see who is best (competitive), (b) learning individually on their own without interacting with classmates (individualistic), or (c) learning cooperatively in small groups, helping each other master the assigned material (cooperative).

Cooperative learning is the instructional use of small groups so that students work together to maximize their own and each other's learning. The essential components of cooperative learning include students' perceiving that they sink or swim together (positive interdependence), must provide face-to-face help and support, must do their fair share of the work (individual accountability), must interact skillfully by providing leadership and resolving conflicts constructively, and must periodically process how to improve the effectiveness of the group. Doing so promotes efforts to achieve, positive and supportive interpersonal relationships, and the social competencies, self-esteem, and coping skills required for healthy psychological adjustment. These outcomes are bidirectional: (1) the harder students work to achieve mutual goals, the more they care about each other; the more students care about each other, the harder they will work to meet their responsibilities to the group; (2) the harder they work together to get the job done, the healthier students become psychologically; and the healthier students are psychologically, the harder and more productively they work; (3) the more positive and supportive the relationships among students are, the better their psychological health becomes; and the healthier students are psychologically, the more able they are to build and maintain positive relationships.

Teachers may use three types of cooperative learning groups: formal, informal, and base. Each has its purposes. Together they make up a comprehensive instructional program of cooperative learning and provide an overall structure to classroom life. When cooperative learning is implemented in a classroom, school, and school district, two major approaches can be used: conceptual and direct. The conceptual approach emphasizes teachers' understanding the essential components of cooperative learning and using that understanding to modify any lesson in any subject area using any curriculum so that the lesson is cooperative. The direct approach emphasizes teachers' knowing how to take a packaged lesson, strategy, or curriculum and implement it in a locked-step, technically correct manner. While expertise in using cooperative learning depends on a conceptual understanding of cooperation, the direct examples of cooperative learning can facilitate teachers' implementation efforts.

REFERENCES

Aronson, E. *The Jigsaw Classroom*. Beverly Hills, Calif.: Sage Publications, 1978.

Deutsch, Morton. "Cooperation and Trust: Some Theoretical Notes." In *Nebraska Symposium on Motivation*, edited by Marshall R. Jones, pp. 275–319. Lincoln: University of Nebraska Press, 1962.

Devries, David L., and Edwards, Keith J. "Cooperation in the Classroom: Toward a Theory of Alternative Reward-Task Classroom Structures." Paper presented at the Annual Meeting of the American Educational Research Association, Chicago, 1974.

Johnson, David W. *Reaching Out: Interpersonal Effectiveness and Self-Actualization*, 3d, 4th editions. Englewood Cliffs, N.J.: Prentice-Hall, 1986, 1990.

Johnson, David W. *Human Relations and Your Career*, 2d, 3d editions. Englewood Cliffs, N.J.: Prentice-Hall, 1987, 1991.

Johnson, David W., and Johnson, Roger T. *Learning Together and Alone: Cooperative, Competitive, and Individualistic Learning*. Englewood Cliffs, N.J.: Prentice-Hall, 1987.

Johnson, David W., and Johnson, Roger T. *Cooperation in the Classroom*. Edina, Minn.: Interaction Book Co., 1988.

Johnson, David W., and Johnson, Roger T. *Cooperation and Competition: Theory and Research*. Edina, Minn.: Interaction Book Co., 1989a.

Johnson, David W., and Johnson, Roger T. *Leading the Cooperative School*. Edina, Minn.: Interaction Book Co., 1989b.

Johnson, David W.; Johnson, Roger T.; and Holubec, Edythe. *Advanced Cooperative Learning*. Edina, Minn.: Interaction Book Co., 1988.

Johnson, David W.; Johnson, Roger T.; and Holubec, Edythe. *Circles of Learning*. Edina, Minn.: Interaction Book Co., 1986, 1990.

Slavin, Robert E. *Using Student Team Learning*. Baltimore: Center for Research on Elementary and Middle Schools, Johns Hopkins University, 1986.

——14——

Motivation and Teaching

Philip H. Winne

MOTIVATION HAS A NEW LOOK

The last four decades have been an era of revolution in psychology—the cognitive revolution. Repercussions from this revolution have been many. One, for instance, is that we now have quite solid evidence that students can be taught cognitive strategies that help them accomplish specific tasks and that create opportunities for learning. In a very important sense, a new curriculum is evolving, an overarching one whose domain is cognition rather than merely geography or mathematics.

Theory and research about motivation also have been deeply affected by the cognitive revolution. Instructional psychologists in particular have been engineering bridges to link yesteryear's separated realms of emotion, thought, and action, of "hot" and "cold" cognition. This new, cognitive view of motivation is the topic of my chapter.

A first step in explaining this new view is to describe a model of motivation. The model characterizes what motivation is and sketches in a general way how motivation meshes with other factors to influence students' emotion, thought, and action. With this as a backdrop, the second main section of the chapter surveys research. There, I synthesize guidelines about how to plan and provide instruction that develops and sustains positive motivation in classrooms. The last section recaps the first two and appeals for careful experimental applications.

A COGNITIVE MODEL OF MOTIVATION

Students Use Two Kinds of Knowledge to Learn

Answering questions on a history worksheet or balancing oxidation-reduction equations are tasks that call for knowledge of history and of chemistry. To carry out these activities, students also require reading skills and a knowledge of how to write answers, as well as metacognition for monitoring progress and repairing mistakes. My point is that when students work on academic exercises, they use knowledge and skills from multiple domains plus metacognitive strategies to work toward goals and to achieve them. I call this collection of information *task knowledge*. Task knowledge is the knowledge and skills that students use to carry out a task. Without task knowledge, no kind or amount of motivation will lead to achievement.

In addition to task knowledge, students have information about means they use to approach goals and about properties of what they actually achieve. Students "have" these thoughts in their minds. They "use" this information to guide thinking that we cannot observe as well as behavior that we can see and hear. I call this collection of information *motivational knowledge*, or just motives. Motivational knowledge colors and shapes students' involvement in learning and it stimulates feelings that students associate with these experiences (Winne, 1985). My choice of the word "associate" in the preceding sentence was deliberate. In a cognitive view, the mental links between a feeling and the information the student has about an event are the same kinds of links as those between bits of task knowledge and an event. Feelings are not the same kind of mental object as bits of task knowledge, but they break into consciousness and they are experienced and modified by the same mental apparatus as in the case of task knowledge. (Winne and Marx, 1989).

What Does Motivational Knowledge Affect?

All the kinds of motivational knowledge that I consider in this chapter are key elements in *goal-directed behavior*. Whenever students have a goal, there is something to achieve. Do not think of achievements narrowly, as just a grade on a literature quiz or a successful layup in basketball. A broad view of achievements is appropriate, one that embraces events as superficially different as persuading a peer to agree to a prank, avoiding having to answer a hard question in a discussion lesson, enticing a tutor to do the real work on a trigonometry problem, and having the best drawings in a science project.

Current theories of cognition view *every* thought and act as being directed by a goal. Some goals are difficult to bring to consciousness where they can be examined, but, on probing, people always seem able to identify one or several goals that govern how they are thinking and what they are doing. This is simply noting in a formal way that people are not aimless beings, acting randomly. It does not mean, however, that someone else's goals are ones we value or accept.

When students pursue goals, in what ways does motivational knowledge affect what they think, how they perform tasks, and how they feel about what they do? Three main kinds of effects can be distinguished. First, motivation influences which tasks students select to do. Different tasks can call for very different profiles of motivational knowledge. Second, motivation shapes qualities of students' involvement with a task, that is, students' observed temperament. Temperamental qualities that motivation influences include how much effort students put into their work and the degree of interest they show. Third, motivation affects how persistently students perform tasks. Persistence includes how long they work at a task and how quickly they return to it if work is interrupted. Thus, to decide how a student is motivated, we can observe (1) what they select to do, (2) what temperament they display when they do it, and (3) how persistent they are in doing it.

Students sometimes use these same three indicators to make inferences about their own motivational knowledge *after* they have begun a task or finished it. This is an important point. It means that motivational knowledge is not just a predictor of behavior. It can also be an outcome of involvement with a task. Students who stop to reconsider motivational knowledge may change it. If we were talking about task knowledge, we would say that they might have been unclear or even mistaken in what they thought they knew. The same holds for motivational knowledge.

What Kinds of Motivation Are There?

There are five main kinds of motivational knowledge. I use a memory aid—the five vowels, AEIOU—to organize the five categories of motivation by the first letter of each category: *a*ttribution, *e*fficacy, *i*ncentive, *o*utcomes, and *u*tility. In performing tasks, all five kinds are involved in shaping a student's selections, temperament, and persistence (Winne and Marx, 1989).

Attribution. An attribution is a thought that identifies a reason for why an event has the outcome that it does. Mike attributes his embarrassment to a belief that he was just unlucky on his guess about the date of Sputnik's launch. When she sees everyone else finishing the mathematics worksheet before she does, Sarah attributes her belief about why she needs to check each problem to her low aptitude for mathematics. People, in general, naturally seem to crave explanations.

Attributions can be categorized using a three-dimensional scheme: locus, stability, and controllability. Locus concerns whether the reason that explains an event's outcome is located within oneself or exists in the external world (e.g., ability vs. a teacher's help). Stability addresses whether the cause is always the same for this situation or whether it applies inconsistently (e.g., a teacher's tough standards vs. luck). Controllability is about whether the cause is governed by oneself or is beyond one's influence (e.g., studying vs. being ill).

Efficacy. Efficacy is a belief about one's competency, ability, and power to achieve goals. When a task is first posed for a student or when a student approaches a task, it is usual to make a prediction or *efficacy expectation* about being able to perform the task. When a task has just been completed and outcomes are precise and clear, students also reflect on how accurate their efficacy expectation was, that is, whether goals have been achieved.

A student's information about efficacy can derive from four sources. Perhaps the most common source of efficacy information is memories students have of their past experiences with similar tasks. A second source of information about efficacy is second hand, by observing how and how well another person, a peer or a teacher, achieves goals. A third source of information about efficacy is one's level of arousal. In conjunction with other information, high levels of arousal can suggest that efficacy is low, as in anxiety, or that efficacy is high, as in being "pumped up." The fourth and usually the least forceful source of efficacy information is persuasion or exhortation.

Incentive. An incentive is the value that a goal has if it can be achieved. It is what a student seeks from a task but does not yet have.

Some incentives reflect a biological imperative (satisfying thirst, avoiding pain). Almost all other incentives important in classrooms are learned values. These can be categorized according to a bewildering variety of systems, but I favor one that has just three categories.

Mastery incentives reflect a student's value of learning for learning's sake. When a student views a task as having mastery incentives, then acquiring facts, developing and extending skills, and simply involving oneself in the task are valued. This is probably because mastery incentives offer opportunities to expand on information about efficacy. *Performance incentives* refer to how much students value demonstrating, to themselves and to others, that they are able and how much they value avoiding the appearance of incompetence. Tasks and situations that have high performance incentives are ones that the student views primarily in terms of already established efficacy information. In other words, the task is viewed as one that validates an already held efficacy expectation, be it a positive or a negative expectation. Mastery and performance incentives highlight relations between a student and aspects of tasks. In contrast, *social incentives* focus mostly on values students hold about relations between themselves and other people in the context of a task. Social incentives generally involve balancing two potentially competing values. On one side is the value in being accepted by peers or accepting guidance from an authority. On the other side are values about having liberty to be oneself and autonomy to perform tasks in one's own preferred ways.

Outcomes. Every task has outcomes, the actual results of working on the task. Outcomes have some degree of value to students, including no value. Outcomes are immediate triggers for attributions.

When students lack a clearly specified goal or when external feedback is absent, it sometimes can be difficult for a student to judge what a finished task should look like or whether a task is finished. What are the defining features of a finished book report? Have I followed all the safety rules about the trampoline?

When the outcomes of tasks are obvious, as when all the worksheet exercises have something written in each answer space, outcomes usually are unambiguous, but not always. Is a teacher's "That's pretty good work" a message that there are no errors? That extra effort was applied? That there is room for personal improvement? (See Brophy, 1981.)

Utility. Every act has alternatives. Students can venture answers in discussions or wait for peers or the teacher to give the answers. Even if directly questioned, a student can bluff, say "I don't know," or try his best.

Different actions usually have different outcomes. Dissimilar outcomes invoke different attributions, invite students to reshape beliefs about efficacy, and may spawn revised incentives. Each alternative action thus has a profile involving the other four motivational thoughts. To choose among acts, students might inspect these profiles, judging the value of each relative to the others. This judgment yields the utility of each alternative within the set.

How Is Motivational Knowledge Activated?

Tell Students. One apparently obvious way to activate students' motivational AEIOUs is simply to tell them which motivational knowledge to think about. Persuasion, exhortation, and such are common in classrooms. Teachers often are heard to say things such as, "You know how to do that" (efficacy) or "It would be simpler if you looked up the formula," (utility) or "You didn't study enough, did you?" Telling students what motivational knowledge they cognitively process along with task information sometimes works, but not often enough (Bandura, 1986).

Prompt Students. Teachers also prompt students to think about motivational knowledge. Suppose students are just starting an in-class exercise in descriptive composition. The teacher might say, "Think carefully, now!" By this prompt, the teacher is, first, probably trying to remind students about a particular bit of task knowledge, perhaps the three-step method he taught yesterday about how to write clear descriptive paragraphs. This is a direct attempt to influence which method students will select to write their essays. The teacher implies that the three-step method has greatest utility. The teacher is also trying to influence temperamental qualities of how students write. Careful thinking implies that there are particular criteria to use in judging how the essay is developing (task knowledge) and that students should take care (apply effort) to monitor the match between these criteria and what they are writing. This is a foreshadowing about an attribution. Finally, because it is emphasized, the prompt might be considered to carry a weak injunction about persisting with the three-step method. The teacher most likely intends that students view the exercise as being associated with mastery incentives.

Prompts can fail (Winne, 1982) and when they do, teachers will likely infer that a student is not motivated. As a matter of fact, the student is motivated, is pursuing a goal. It is just not the same goal as the teacher intended.

Prompts can fail in four ways. First, some students do not notice prompts. Perhaps they are busy with the task. Or, they may be entirely off task. Listening to the teacher just then had no utility for them. Second, some students may misinterpret the prompt. They may not link a very general "Think carefully" with the three-step method. These students may have lower efficacy expectations because they are not clear about how to work through the task. Third, other students may know full well what was prompted, but they may believe they have not learned the three-step method well enough to use it (low efficacy expectation). They will probably substitute some other method to finish their essays, treating the exercise as having just performance incentives. Fourth, some students will not experience any of these three preceding problems but simply choose to do it their own way. Autonomy may have more social incentive for them.

Firsthand Experience. Finally, and probably most important, students themselves inevitably activate AEIOUs when they interpret teachers' directions, begin to process information about a task to work through it, observe their progress, receive external feedback and generate their own feedback, and examine the degree to which their outcomes meet standards. This thinking is a natural and intrinsic aspect of mentally processing information in instructional activities (Winne and Marx, 1989). I use another first-letter acronym— COPES—to help remember five important attributes of tasks: *c*onditions under which the task is performed, *o*perations that actually carry out the task, *p*roducts that result, *e*valuations that provide feedback about products, and *s*tandards by which achievement is measured. These five features affect how a student *copes* with every task.

Summary: Models for Examining Research About Motivation in Teaching

Motivational knowledge and task knowledge together affect the paths that students follow to reach goals and the perceptions students have about both means and ends. Whereas task knowledge determines what students are able to do, motivational knowledge determines what students select to do, their temperament while doing it, and their persistence. Students also use these three indicators to reflect on what they have done to revise their motivational knowledge. Motivational knowledge comes in five types, the AEIOUs: *attributions* explain performance, *efficacy* expresses competence, *incentives* gauge value, *outcomes* describe actual results, and *utility* weighs alternatives. All five AEIOUs can be told, prompted, or experienced firsthand when students work on tasks. A thorough account of a student's experience with a task addresses how task knowledge and motivational knowledge jointly determine how the student copes with the task's *conditions, operations, products, evaluations,* and *standards* (COPES).

RESEARCH FINDINGS

Linking Cognition, Motivation, and Affect

The cognitive view of motivation in achievement settings proposes that different patterns or schemata of motivational and task knowledge are associated in one's memory with particular feelings or emotions. As a student participates in instruction and experiences a pattern of motivational and task variables, memory automatically brings into the student's perception a set of affects associated with that kind of experience.

This view has an important implication. To promote or to lessen the chances that students experience particular feelings, instructional tasks and classroom environments need to be engineered so that they guide students toward remembering particular patterns of motivational and task knowledge. Well-planned, firsthand experiences that students have in lessons can facilitate their development of positive feelings about learning, subject matter, and activities. Of course, the opposite can happen when lessons are planned badly or led inexpertly.

The next sections sample highlights from recent research that is beginning to build toward guidelines for teaching effectiveness. (See C. Ames and R. Ames, 1985, 1989; R. Ames and C. Ames, 1984, for thorough reviews). The line of development I follow has two stages. In the first stage, instructional conditions that teachers design are treated as causal factors. Patterns of motivational knowledge that students develop are direct consequences of these instructional factors. In the second stage, after students have acquired motivational knowledge by participating in instructional events, motivational knowledge becomes a trigger for a second important set of student outcomes—feelings.

My discussion of these stages proceeds "backward." First, I review research that reveals links between patterns of motivational knowledge and feelings. Then, I review research about instructional conditions that promote or are associated with particular patterns of motivation. Putting the two pieces back together links feelings we would like to encourage in students with motivational knowledge that students learn as they participate in instruction that teachers plan. In short, positive feelings are ultimate objectives that can be approached by cultivating particular motivational knowledge through careful instructional design.

Links Between Motivation, Affects, and Affect-Related Frames of Mind

Satisfaction, Pride, Guilt, and Shame. A significant misconception is afield: that satisfaction requires a constant diet of successful outcomes. But failures too can be satisfying under proper conditions. Those conditions are that learners hold mastery incentives and, importantly, have a strategy they can apply to make a new experiment that offers an opportunity to learn more.

Success, especially when it is attributed to high effort, carries a potentially heavy burden. The student will need to expend a lot of effort to continue succeeding and, if the outcome is unsuccessful, and having spent much effort, the student will inevitably attribute failure to low ability. When this situation is coupled with incentives to perform rather than to master a task, early success actually can lead to later avoidance. The cycle is insidious because a successful outcome that follows low effort almost necessarily has to be attributed to luck. Rather than break the maladaptive pattern, success just confirms it, robbing the student of satisfaction that might actually have been earned.

What promotes feelings of satisfaction and pride? Attributions to controllable internal factors, such as effort and astute use of task knowledge, are contributors. These help establish and sustain students' beliefs that competence can be upgraded in increments, as opposed to their believing they are stuck with static aptitude. Social incentives that strike a balance between acceptance by others and individuality are other factors that contribute to feelings of satisfaction. Imbalances exact costs in two arenas that are both important to students.

Interest and Curiosity. These two frames of mind fit snugly with notions about intrinsic motivation. Intrinsically motivated students select tasks without external prompting, show temperament that contributes to reaching self-set goals, and persist. They explore a bit, but not substantially, beyond the boundaries of their current competence.

A motivational pattern that links with a student's interest and curiosity is complicated, but three major features dominate. First, mastery incentives are central to interest. When the incentive value of a task is oriented mainly to performance incentives, interest is usually low. Second, the social incentive of autonomy is closely tied to interest. Logically, students cannot exercise exploratory behavior if there is no latitude for it, nor can they look at actions and their outcomes as intrinsically connected to self without some autonomy. Third, in situations judged interesting, attributions for mistakes or setbacks are not made to stable, uncontrollable factors such as ability or overly difficult tasks. Rather, interest expressed as positive beliefs about efficacy are sustained by generally attributing errors and failures to lack of effort, bad luck, or the need to exercise more strategic competence.

Guilt and shame follow quite directly from attributions to low effort, especially when unsuccessful outcomes are salient. Guilt emerges when students perceive they have ability or could have developed it. Shame ensues when performance incentives overpower mastery incentives.

Self-Confidence and Anxiety. Self-confidence matches, by definition, with mastery incentives. When tasks emphasize performance incentives or, to a lesser degree, social incentives, self-confidence can be in jeopardy. In this situation, anxiety can creep into students' perceptions. Spending effort and making progress, such as by eliminating alternatives, also seems a critical ingredient in building self-confidence. Students do not necessarily need to reach ultimate success in order to build self-confidence and avoid anxiety.

Under certain conditions, anxiety can follow closely on the heels of low efficacy expectations. Thus, anxiety precedes actual outcomes and comes to interfere in the process a student carries while working on a task. When students remember past failure they had attributed to uncontrollable factors, especially when those failures occurred in a context where performance incentives were salient, this is a trigger to interpret high levels of arousal as anxiety. These same high levels of arousal are not always debilitating, however. When remembered efficacy information leads the student to expect to make progress toward achievement, and when attributions that the student recalls highlight controllable factors, these same high levels of arousal can be interpreted as a feeling that boosts involvement and increases chances for success.

Links Between Motivation and Achievement

Previous task knowledge is the most substantial predictor of how well a student can acquire new task knowledge and apply it to solve problems. All the positive motivation in the world will not overcome ignorance. But, by definition, knowledge is not enough. Knowledge that has bearing must be brought to bear, and this entails motivational knowledge.

Efficacy is the motivational knowledge that most strongly predicts achievement. This makes sense—efficacy expectations are grounded directly in previous experience with earlier tasks and what students learned in those experiences. Changes in efficacy are motivational reflections of learners' perceptions about changes in their task knowledge.

Interlude

Routes to students' interest and sensible self-concepts, and bypasses around anxiety and disparagement, are not secret. To get to feelings, go through motivation by following principles about how to design instruction *to teach motivational knowledge*. It is helpful to distinguish two levels of principles. One set applies to individual tasks, though tasks may be small or large. The other set relates to a larger view of classrooms, their climates, and global features of teaching within which individual tasks are situated. These two sets of principles are topics of the next two sections.

Links Between Factors of Tasks and Motivation

The COPES model that I introduced earlier is a useful scheme for organizing a discussion of links between factors of tasks and motivation.

Conditions. Two features about how tasks are presented to students are especially important conditions. First, the medium of the task is important since it influences how information about the task can be made available to students. For instance, orally presented information is transient. If it is not stored mentally or otherwise, it cannot stimulate either task or motivational knowledge that plays a role in performing a task.

Employing common media—using manipulatives or allowing access to some external resources—does not always work to encourage motivational knowledge. This can make a task seem more complicated because students need to keep more information in mind, juggling information in the environment with what is in their mind. A perception that a task is complicated can lower efficacy expectations. On the other hand, if mental effort is not needed because the manipulatives or resources (a book, a peer) carry the load, gains to motivational and task knowledge can be short circuited when the student realizes the utility of using external resources rather than doing the job "the hard way." If performance incentives govern the situation, the choice of how to perform tasks seems simple, but it will not be the choice that develops the most appropriate task and motivational knowledge.

Second, a task's conditions may include or exclude prompts that can guide students' recall and use of motivational and task knowledge in the course of performing the task. For example, explicitly reminding students of parallels between a current task and a previous one grants the teacher who knows students' previous accomplishments stronger control over the efficacy expectations students will have. A powerful intervention is having a "model" student demonstrate how to identify cues for efficacy and then, while performing the task, think out loud about how motivational and task knowledge are applied. The model permits students some autonomy (since the model offers rather than dictates) and refreshes important motivational and task knowledge.

Operations. The mental operations and strategies entailed in carrying out tasks determine how difficult a task is. Students reflect on the demands that these cognitive operations make to form their own judgments about difficulty. Methods that are not or cannot be explained clearly to students (that is, black box procedures) leave students little alternative but to attribute difficulty or failure to low ability. In addition, success cannot have mastery incentives when cognitive operations that produced that accomplishment are opaque—literally, there is "no thing" to learn. Having a vocabulary for talking about mental operations is a useful tool to have in planning teaching. Using this vocabulary while teaching the traditional subjects can help students learn the vocabulary. Knowing how to talk about cognitive strategies, beyond just knowing them, extends students' capacities for autonomy and self-regulation. With this, they can mentally talk themselves through tasks they wrestle with to learn. A vocabulary of cognition and self-talk also gives students conscious access to grounds on which to judge the utility of a cognitive strategy.

Obviously, students cannot select a cognitive strategy that they do not know, and they may hesitate to select one that appears to have low utility because it is new, fragile, or unproven. Volumes of experience and pages of research concur that it is critical to teach students about cognitive strategies directly, explicitly, and with every bit as much tolerance for false starts and mistakes as appears in other subject areas.

The cognitive operations and strategies that students select for working through learning activities are always and intrinsically selected by students. Teachers and factors in instructional tasks can only guide students' thinking. Thus, the motivational knowledge students have about a task determines the nature of cognitive engagement that students have.

The motivational knowledge that levers particular cognitive operations and strategies into action combines two main items. First, tasks that have mastery incentives for students also lead them to select the more complicated (higher-order) cognitive approaches to learning that, in fact, lead to greater accomplishments. Second, when mastery incentives dominate, other factors, including the presence of performance incentives and students' previous levels of achievement in the subject matter, are weak influences on students' selections about how they will cognitively engage with tasks.

Products. Products are the actual outcomes of efforts to work through and complete a task. Not all products are observable, since many exist only in students' minds. A plausible hypothesis is that encouraging students to show *all* the steps and reasons involved in a task at least makes products available for their attention (and the teacher's). These can play the role of self-generated prompts, but students may need to be taught explicitly that they can be used this way. More products means more opportunities to make utility judgments. Plausibly, smaller steps correspond to lessening undesirable consequences of retreating to a previous stage.

A balance is needed between asking for too many products and asking for too few. Excessive detail depletes options for autonomy and probably diminishes attributions to stable internal factors that support positive efficacy and self-concept. "It's not *my* work," says a student. "All I did was follow directions."

Evaluations. After intermediate and final products are created, they are evaluated. Evaluating a product means comparing it to standards (discussed shortly) and then noting discrepancies and assessing worth. It addresses two aspects of students' efforts. One is features of performance, such as how long one worked and how much effort one spent. The second is qualities of products, such as how complete and how elegant a composition is.

Very young students mistake effort spent for competence. Care in distinguishing these features is needed in the verbal evaluations teachers provide. A request to "try harder" may just sustain this mistake.

Information in evaluations that teachers supply should focus on the task knowledge involved in doing the task. When evaluations allow students to perceive options about how they could have performed the task, their thoughts are channelled toward learnable information and away from attributions to low ability, luck, or other uncontrollable factors. Information-giving evaluations can also be instructive rather than merely an assessment. A key in giving evaluations is keeping open options while being informative. If evaluations tightly control a student's next attempts, this immediately lowers his or her feelings of autonomy. Afterwards, it can downgrade mastery incentives because the student cannot attribute success on a future task, if achieved, to something he or she controlled—task knowledge that was personally selected and applied to complete the task. Moreover, evaluations that are too directive can inadvertently encourage a student to become dependent on them. The utility of getting help early or midway in a task greatly surpasses the risk of failing overall relative to less than warming feelings that follow a weak chance for success. Breaking out of this spiral becomes an objective well out of reach for many students.

While a teacher's modeling of feelings associated with specific evaluations during a demonstration can prompt students to make the same links, a student's motivation and feelings very probably will not change when a teacher just tries persuasion after a product is realized. This applies equally to achievements and to failures.

In sum, the best medicine is preventive. Oft-provided informative evaluations about inspectable outcomes help to keep tasks manageable and avail students with means for working through tasks on their own. Mistakes are correctable in small portions, and making corrections fits snugly with incentives for mastery, attributions to one's use of learnable information, and predictions of efficacy about coping with tough tasks, not merely overall success.

Standards. It is important that standards for tasks make it a challenge to succeed, but not an improbability. This reminds students that effort is a key component. Prompts for students to use task and motivational knowledge can be embedded in standards, as when a teacher reminds students about rules to use in performing tasks (e.g., "Use the outline we developed yesterday to check that every important dimension of family behavior is addressed in your story about "The Picnic.""). This added specificity gives students opportunities to judge efficacy more frequently (i.e., goals are proximal) and decreases ambiguity about outcomes. The upshot is usually a reduction in anxiety, and if the task is difficult or poorly performed, the student's attributions can be appropriately steered toward particular needs for task knowledge rather than toward his or her inaptitude.

Having students set their own standards involves them directly in exercising links between motivational and task knowledge. In this, it is important to rein in unreasonable notions about what can or cannot be accomplished. Reaching proximal goals will better contribute to a sense of efficacy, but small steps have to lead somewhere and the student must understand they lead there. In short, clear standards can increase opportunities to make clear judgments about utilities.

Links Between Factors of Instruction and Motivation

Teachers can set up classroom activities in many ways, and differences in these arrangements have important effects on students' motivation and achievements. It now appears that the most important objective toward which teachers should strive is developing students' sense of mastery incentives. Many individual factors in classroom activities can contribute to achieving this, but weaving the fabric well cannot be done by adding just a few "quick stitches" to teaching. As in the world's ecosystem, complex interactions abound in the ecology of a classroom's motivation and achievements. Thus, what is especially important to note in the following sketches is this: Single factors that past research has suggested benefit students' motivation and achievements can fail to contribute to reaching objectives or can even impede reaching them. The weave of multiple factors is critical.

When activities in a classroom are structured so that students almost inevitably are drawn to compare their outcomes with each other, competition among peers naturally leads students to emphasize performance incentives over mastery incentives. It would be foolish to imagine that students' natural tendencies to compete and to compare themselves to peers can be eliminated by subtly designing activities for learning. Rather than attempt the impossible, a long-term coordinated approach is needed that fosters mastery incentives and utility judgments about activities that can sustain mastery incentives.

One factor that influences students' adoption of performance incentives is the stability of memberships in working groups, which teachers establish for reading, science labs, or social studies projects. When groups are constant, a pattern of students' rankings can and almost surely will emerge. This is not necessarily detrimental. When students in a group have approximately equal task knowledge (ability) and motivation, that is, when the variance of factors that determines outcomes is narrow, "friendly" competition can nurture motivation and achievements. And, because talents and flairs are not widely different, accomplishments will vary among students somewhat unpredictably. The upshot is a group in which the emphasis is on learning as well as competition, and both incentives can co-exist in harmony.

The scenario is less promising when variance is broad among students in a group. In heterogeneous groups, students really are differently equipped to approach tasks. In this situation, failures by less prepared students can be attributed to uncontrollable, stable factors such as low competence, and successes seem unstable and uncontrollable, that is, attributable to luck. Mastery incentives really are out of reach for these students in the group, and they end up making realistic judgments about weak efficacy. The high-achieving students find their level of performance the salient feature of their membership. Mastery incentives are submerged beneath performance incentives even for successes on complex tasks.

Grouping students homogeneously by talent and motivation, however, is not a sufficient manipulation to avoid pitfalls in guiding students toward cognitive and motivational accomplishments. Other conditions also contribute to diverting motivation from mastery incentives and judgments about the high utility of challenging cognitive operations for performing tasks. When students' autonomy is removed, because all of them work on identical tasks under the same imposed conditions, differences among students in their outcomes are properly attributable to differences in ability or uncontrollable factors such as mood or luck. When evaluations of those outcomes are individualized, it's sensible to limit attributions for successes and mistakes to internal factors. Making these evaluations public, by announcing them to the group or less explicitly by posting only the best projects on the wall, shows students that the final product is the salient feature of learning tasks. Motivational knowledge taught in this setting emphasizes extrinsic rewards, competitive social and performance incentives, attributions that cannot elevate self-concept, and, ultimately, realistically low efficacy judgments. The student's defense is predictable—disengage or become reliant on constant extra help. Neither of these behaviors breaks the cycle.

Transferring Control to Students

Before the cognitive revolution, motives were unconscious forces that compelled people to act. Now, by translating motives into motivational knowledge, people can hold "motives" in their mind's eyes, examine them, and take steps to change. Students thus are welcomed as integral, conscious, and rational participants in instructional activities.

From this perspective, there is good reason to propose that teachers should teach students the same methods they themselves use in planning to guide students toward productively linking task knowledge, motivational knowledge, and feelings. Then, students themselves can engineer their approaches to tasks so that links they make among cognition, motivation, and affect bestow qualities of effectiveness and enjoyment on learning. Students who learn these skills would be capable of *self-regulated learning*, the pinnacle of actively engaging in learning where they thoughtfully direct their own cognition, affect, and motivational control (or conation). (See Corno and Rohrkemper, 1985.)

In planning teaching of self-regulation, it's important to remember that the objectives of instruction are not limited to one subject, such as mathematics or vocabulary. Intimate connections between motivation and subject matter achievement develop in tandem. High levels of cognitive achievement alone do not guarantee high levels of productive motivational knowledge and positive feelings, as I have discussed. Motivational knowledge needs direct instruction, too.

CAUTION! EXPERIMENTAL TEACHING AT WORK

Why Cognitive Accounts of Motivation Are Attractive

The cognitive view of motivation has two special qualities that make it worthwhile to use it to do the work needed to improve models for teaching and research, and that justify tolerating uncertainty along the way. One quality is that in a way not achieved before, the cognitive view of motivation integrally joins understandings about cognition and feeling rather than keeps learning, motivation, and affect in three separate boxes. While this does complicate instructional design, research is demonstrating that an integrated view is more useful for designing effective teaching.

The second quality is that this integration points toward specific ways to teach feelings and motivation in conjunction with subject matter knowledge. Before, good feelings and constructive motivation were hoped for, but there was not much direction about how to enhance them jointly along with gains in the subject areas. This second quality adds important dimensions to concepts of effective teaching. Because motivations are critical determinants of how students view learning and how well they can be equipped to succeed at it, effective teaching is now expanded in a forceful way to include teaching motivation and teaching feelings.

Experimental Teaching Is Needed

It is important that I remind you that the cognitive view of motivation I have described in this chapter is an area of active research, not a field of firmly established facts. Researchers and teachers are still exploring links between cognition, motivation, and affect. While the models I have described have been demonstrated to be valid on the whole, specifics are still being made clearer and links between variables are yet being stabilized. In short, our understandings are reasonable but tentative.

Teaching in the middle of a theoretical construction zone, where footings for making teaching effective are still being designed and poured, is hazardous enough. When teachers experiment with instructional variables, especially when the outcomes of trials are students' motivation and feelings, special care is needed. The job cannot be sidestepped, but it needs to be undertaken with as much knowledge as possible.

My survey of fundamental ideas and main research findings could not delve deeply enough into the subtleties and nuances of this field. It might even be claimed that because I have glossed some important details, my summaries mislead. I will not debate this claim. Instead, I use it to emphasize a critical point: Teachers will have to help researchers to continue exploring this very promising model. Students cannot wait until theory becomes everyday fact and common procedure. Teachers can use what I have sketched, and that is a challenge. The bigger challenge, however, is to contribute more to what we know now.

REFERENCES

Ames, Russell E., and Ames, Carole, eds. *Research on Motivation in Education: Vol. 1, Student Motivation.* Orlando, Fla.: Academic Press, 1984.

Ames, Carole, and Ames, Russell E., eds. *Research on Motivation in Education: Vol. 2, The Classroom Milieu.* Orlando, Fla.: Academic Press, 1985.

Ames, Carole, and Ames, Russell E., eds. *Research and Motivation in Education: Vol. 3, Goals and Cognitions.* Orlando, Fla.: Academic Press, 1989.

Bandura, Albert. *Social Foundations of Thought and Action*. Englewood Cliffs, N.J.: Prentice-Hall, 1986.

Brophy, Jere. "Teacher Praise: A Functional Analysis," *Review of Educational Research* *51* (1981): 5–32

Corno, Lyn, and Rohrkemper, Mary M. "The Intrinsic Motivation to Learn in Classrooms." In *Research on Motivation in Education: Vol. 2, The Classroom Milieu*, edited by Carole Ames and Russell Ames, pp. 53–90. Orlando, Fla.: Academic Press, 1985.

Winne, Philip H. "Minimizing the Black Box Problem to Enhance the Validity of Theories about Instructional Effects," *Instructional Science* 11 (1982): 13–28.

Winne, Philip H. "Steps toward Promoting Cognitive Achievement," *Elementary School Journal* 85 (1985): 673–693.

Winne, Philip H., and Marx, Ronald W. "A Cognitive-Processing Analysis of Motivation within Classroom Tasks." In *Research on Motivation in Education: Vol. 3, Goals and Cognitions*, edited by Carole Ames and Russell Ames, pp. 223–257. Orlando, Fla.: Academic Press, 1989.